Holiday COOKING VOLUME 5

DIABETIC LIVING® HOLIDAY COOKING IS
PART OF A BOOK SERIES PUBLISHED BY
BETTER HOMES AND GARDENS SPECIAL
INTEREST MEDIA, DES MOINES, IOWA

Ginger-Orange-Glazed
Turkey Breasts
recipe on page 49

Letter from the Editor

The holiday season provides plenty of opportunities to rejoice in fun, festive ways. If you're like me, the celebration always starts in the kitchen. Whether it's a golden roasted bird, yummy yeast bread, or a made-from-scratch gift, fabulous food makes these times memorable.

Along with millions of others, I have dear ones living with diabetes. When hosting a holiday dinner or festive celebration, I want to serve delicious foods everyone can enjoy. That's why this volume of holiday-special recipes will be my new kitchen companion. These lightened-up, flavorful dishes will appeal to everyone around your table.

Our *Diabetic Living®* food professionals and the experts in the Better Homes and Gardens® Test Kitchen have provided the merriest recipes of the season. Perfect for those with diabetes as well as the whole family, all of the recipes have been carb-counted and boosted with nutritious ingredients. From flavor-packed side dishes to decked-out desserts, each offers delicious flavor and helps keep your blood sugar levels on target.

Every family already has treasured favorites. This year, add something new to your list of must-have seasonal foods.

- If roasting a whole bird doesn't fit your time frame, try the Ginger-Orange-Glazed Turkey Breasts on page 49. The skinless, boneless breasts roast in just 45 to 50 minutes.
- Looking for a fresh and flavorful side dish your kids will love? Whip up Veggie Mash on page 85. Low-carb cauliflower is hiding within the potato and carrot combo.
- For a homemade gift, stir together a batch of Sweet Party Mix on page 130. The light coating makes it a great munchable snack.

This season, give yourself and others the gift of satisfying, health-conscious meals. Enjoy!

Martha

Martha Miller Johnson
Editor, *Diabetic Living®* magazine

ON THE COVER:
Lemon Poppy Seed Tea Cake
recipe on page 152

Photographer: Jason Walsmith
Food stylist: Jessica Jones

CONSUMER MARKETING

Vice President, Consumer Marketing	JANET DONNELLY
Consumer Product Marketing Director	HEATHER SORENSEN
Consumer Product Marketing Manager	WENDY MERICAL
Business Director	RON CLINGMAN
Production Manager	AL RODRUCK
Contributing Project Manager	SHELLI McCONNELL, PURPLE PEAR PUBLISHING, INC.
Contributing Photographers	JASON DONNELLY, JASON WALSMITH
Contributing Food Stylist	DIANNA NOLIN, JENNIFER PETERSON
Test Kitchen Director	LYNN BLANCHARD
Test Kitchen Product Supervisor	ELIZABETH ELLIOT, MPH, RD, LD
Editorial Assistant	LORI EGGERS

SPECIAL INTEREST MEDIA

Editorial Director	GREGORY H. KAYKO
Managing Editor	DOUG KOUMA

DIABETIC LIVING® MAGAZINE

Editor	MARTHA MILLER JOHNSON
Art Director, Health	MICHELLE BILYEU
Assistant Art Director	ALEXIS WEST-HUNTOON
Senior Editor, Food & Nutrition	JESSIE SHAFER
Assistant Editor	LORI BROOKHART-SCHERVISH

MEREDITH NATIONAL MEDIA GROUP

President TOM HARTY

Chairman and Chief Executive Officer STEPHEN M. LACY

Vice Chairman MELL MEREDITH FRAZIER

In Memoriam — E.T. MEREDITH III (1933-2003)

Diabetic Living® Holiday Cooking is part of a series published by Meredith Corp., 1716 Locust St., Des Moines, IA 50309-3023.

If you have comments or questions about the editorial material in *Diabetic Living® Holiday Cooking*, write to the editor of *Diabetic Living* magazine, Meredith Corp., 1716 Locust St., Des Moines, IA 50309-3023. Send an e-mail to diabeticlivingmeredith.com or call 800/678-2651. *Diabetic Living* magazine is available by subscription or on the newsstand. To order a subscription to *Diabetic Living* magazine, go to *DiabeticLivingOnline.com*.

contents

Mocha Shortcakes with White
Chocolate Peppermint Mousse
recipe on page 135

comforting breakfasts

Caramelized Onion and
Potato Breakfast Casserole

*a*hhh . . . there's something special about waking to the tempting aroma of a fresh-made breakfast. This holiday, treat everyone in the house to a healthful version of a layered egg casserole, a steamy stack of pancakes, or a caramelly cinnamon roll. They'll savor this delicious start to the day!

Caramelized Onion and Potato Breakfast Casserole

If you own a mandoline slicer, use it to quickly and evenly slice the potatoes.

SERVINGS 8 (¾ cup each)
CARB. PER SERVING 22 g

 4 cups sliced yellow potatoes, such as Yukon gold, cut ⅛ to ¼ inch thick (about 1½ pounds)
 1 tablespoon olive oil
 2 ounces pancetta, chopped
 3 cups thinly sliced sweet onions, such as Vidalia or Maui
    Nonstick cooking spray
 6 eggs, lightly beaten
 ½ cup fat-free milk
 1 cup shredded Gruyère cheese or Swiss cheese (4 ounces)
 1 teaspoon snipped fresh rosemary
 ¾ teaspoon salt
 ½ teaspoon black pepper

1. In a large saucepan cook potatoes, covered, in boiling lightly salted water about 5 minutes or until slightly tender but still firm. Drain; set aside. In a large skillet heat olive oil over medium-high heat. Add pancetta; cook until lightly browned. Using a slotted spoon, remove pancetta, reserving drippings in skillet. Set pancetta aside. Add onions to skillet. Cook and stir over medium-low heat about 20 minutes or until lightly browned and very tender. Remove from heat. Carefully stir potatoes and pancetta into onions in skillet.
2. Preheat oven to 350°F. Coat a 2-quart rectangular baking dish with cooking spray. Spread potato mixture into prepared dish. In a medium bowl whisk together eggs and milk. Add cheese, rosemary, salt, and pepper; stir until well mixed. Pour evenly over potato mixture in baking dish.
3. Bake, uncovered, for 45 to 50 minutes or until golden and a knife inserted in the center comes out clean. Let stand for 15 minutes before serving.
MAKE-AHEAD DIRECTIONS: Prepare as directed through Step 2 but do not preheat oven. Cover and chill potato mixture in baking dish for 4 to 24 hours. Bake as directed.
PER SERVING: 247 cal., 12 g total fat (5 g sat. fat), 160 mg chol., 463 mg sodium, 22 g carb. (3 g fiber, 4 g sugars), 13 g pro. Exchanges: 0.5 vegetable, 1.5 starch, 1 medium-fat meat, 1 fat. Carb choices: 1.5.

Cajun Breakfast Skillet

Andouille sausage, typically made of pork and garlic, is a staple of Cajun cooking. Look for the leaner chicken variety to use in this Southern-style breakfast.

SERVINGS 4 (1½ cups each)
CARB. PER SERVING 11 g

Nonstick cooking spray
1 medium sweet potato, peeled and cut into ½-inch cubes
1 small onion, chopped
¼ cup water
1 medium green sweet pepper, cut into thin bite-size strips
2 3-ounce links chicken andouille sausage or desired flavored chicken sausage, halved lengthwise and cut crosswise into ½-inch-thick slices
¼ cup thinly sliced celery
2 teaspoons canola oil
½ teaspoon Cajun seasoning
4 eggs
4 egg whites
¼ cup fat-free milk

1. Coat an unheated large nonstick skillet with cooking spray. In skillet cook sweet potato, onion, and water, covered, over medium heat for 8 minutes, stirring once or twice. Add the sweet pepper, sausage, celery, and oil. Cook, uncovered, over medium heat about 5 minutes or until vegetables are tender and sausage is lightly browned, stirring occasionally. Stir the Cajun seasoning into the vegetable mixture.
2. Meanwhile, in a medium bowl beat together eggs, egg whites, and milk with a rotary beater or whisk.
3. Pour the egg mixture over the vegetable mixture. Cook over medium heat, without stirring, until mixture begins to set on the bottom and around edges. Using a spatula or large spoon, lift and fold the partially cooked egg mixture so the uncooked portion flows underneath. Continue cooking about 4 minutes more or until egg mixture is cooked through but still slightly moist. Remove from heat and let stand 2 minutes before serving.

PER SERVING: 230 cal., 11 g total fat (3 g sat. fat), 223 mg chol., 411 mg sodium, 11 g carb. (2 g fiber, 4 g sugars), 20 g pro. Exchanges: 0.5 vegetable, 0.5 starch, 2 medium-fat meat. Carb choices: 1.

Baked Eggs with Roasted Vegetables

Roasted veggies nestle the eggs during baking. For easy serving, use a large spoon to lift out some of the veggies along with an egg.

SERVINGS 6 (1 egg and ¾ cup vegetables each)
CARB. PER SERVING 21 g

Nonstick cooking spray
3 cups small broccoli florets (about 1 inch in size)
12 ounces yellow potatoes, such as Yukon gold, cut into ½- to ¾-inch pieces (about 2 cups)
1 large sweet potato, cut into ½- to ¾-inch pieces (about 1 cup)
1 small red onion, cut into thin wedges
2 tablespoons olive oil
¼ teaspoon salt
6 eggs
2 ounces Manchego cheese, shredded (½ cup)
½ teaspoon cracked black pepper

1. Preheat oven to 425°F. Coat a 2-quart rectangular baking dish with cooking spray. In a large bowl combine broccoli, yellow potatoes, sweet potato, onion, olive oil, and salt; toss to coat vegetables.
2. Spread vegetables evenly in the prepared pan. Roast for 10 minutes. Stir vegetables; roast about 5 minutes more or until vegetables are tender and starting to brown. Remove from oven. Spread vegetables evenly in the prepared baking dish; cool. Cover and chill for 8 to 24 hours.
3. Let chilled vegetables stand at room temperature for 30 minutes. Meanwhile, preheat oven to 375°F.
4. Bake vegetables, uncovered, for 5 minutes. Remove from oven; make six wells in the layer of vegetables. Break an egg into each well. Bake for 5 minutes more. Sprinkle with cheese. Bake for 5 to 10 minutes more or until eggs whites are set and yolks start to thicken. Sprinkle with pepper.

PER SERVING: 232 cal., 12 g total fat (4 g sat. fat), 218 mg chol., 332 mg sodium, 21 g carb. (4 g fiber, 4 g sugars), 11 g pro. Exchanges: 1 vegetable, 1 starch, 1 medium-fat meat, 1 fat. Carb choices: 1.5.

Baked Eggs with
Roasted Vegetables

Poblano-Chorizo Strata

Poblano-Chorizo Strata

If you can't find queso fresco at your regular supermarket, look for it at Mexican food stores. Or you can substitute feta cheese in this casserole.

SERVINGS 12 (¾ cup each)
CARB. PER SERVING 17 g

- 8 ounces uncooked chorizo sausage
- 2 medium onions, thinly sliced
- 2 medium fresh poblano chile peppers, seeded and thinly sliced*
- 1 medium red sweet pepper, thinly sliced
- 8 cups 1-inch cubes Mexican bolillo rolls or crusty Italian bread
- 6 eggs, lightly beaten
- 2½ cups fat-free milk
- 1 teaspoon dried Mexican oregano or regular oregano, crushed
- ½ teaspoon paprika
- ½ cup queso fresco, crumbled
  Snipped fresh cilantro (optional)

1. In a large skillet cook chorizo over medium heat until browned. Using a slotted spoon, transfer chorizo to a bowl, reserving 1 tablespoon drippings in skillet. Add onions to drippings in skillet; cook and stir over medium heat about 10 minutes or just until tender. Stir in chile peppers and sweet pepper; cook about 5 minutes or just until peppers are tender. Remove from heat. Stir in chorizo.

2. Lightly grease a 3-quart rectangular or oval baking dish. Spread half of the bread cubes in the prepared dish. Spoon half of the chorizo mixture over bread. Repeat layers.

3. In a large bowl whisk together eggs, milk, oregano, and paprika. Pour egg mixture evenly over layers in baking dish. Cover with foil and chill for at least 2 hours or up to 24 hours.

4. Preheat oven to 325°F. Bake, covered, for 30 minutes. Uncover; bake for 30 to 45 minutes more or until an instant-read thermometer inserted into the center registers 170°F. Sprinkle with cheese the last 5 minutes of baking. Let stand for 10 minutes before serving. If desired, sprinkle with cilantro.

***TEST KTICHEN TIP:** Because chile peppers contain volatile oils that can burn your skin and eyes, avoid direct contact with them as much as possible. When working with chile peppers, wear plastic or rubber gloves. If your bare hands do touch the peppers, wash your hands and nails well with soap and warm water.

PER SERVING: 222 cal., 11 g total fat (4 g sat. fat), 114 mg chol., 364 mg sodium, 17 g carb. (1 g fiber, 4 g sugars), 13 g pro. Exchanges: 0.5 vegetable, 1 starch, 1 medium-fat meat, 1 fat. Carb choices: 1.

quick tip

To quickly thaw the corn, place it in a colander and then under cold running water until thawed. To keep the corn from watering out during baking, drain it thoroughly and pat dry with paper towels.

Southwestern Breakfast Bake

If your meal plan allows, spoon this protein-packed egg bake on a small flour tortilla to serve.

SERVINGS 8 (¾ cup each)
CARB. PER SERVING 16 g

Nonstick cooking spray
1 15-ounce can no-salt-added black beans, rinsed and drained
1 cup frozen whole kernel corn, thawed
½ cup enchilada sauce
2 4-ounce cans diced green chile peppers, undrained
½ cup thinly sliced green onions
2 cloves garlic, minced
Several dashes bottled hot pepper sauce (optional)
1 cup shredded reduced-fat sharp cheddar cheese and/or Monterey Jack cheese with jalapeño peppers (4 ounces)
3 egg whites
3 egg yolks
¼ teaspoon salt
1 tablespoon snipped fresh cilantro
Snipped fresh cilantro (optional)
Reduced-fat sour cream (optional)
Bottled salsa (optional)
Bottled hot pepper sauce (optional)

1. Preheat oven to 350°F. Coat a 2-quart square baking dish with cooking spray. Set aside. In a medium saucepan combine black beans, corn, enchilada sauce, chile peppers, green onions, garlic, and, if desired, several dashes hot pepper sauce. Heat thoroughly over medium heat. Pour into prepared baking dish. Sprinkle with half of the cheese.

2. In a medium bowl beat egg whites with an electric mixer on medium speed until soft peaks form (tips curl); set aside. In a large bowl combine egg yolks and salt. Beat egg yolk mixture with an electric mixer on medium to high speed about 3 minutes or until mixture lightens in color and thickens. Fold beaten egg whites and the 1 tablespoon cilantro into yolk mixture. Carefully pour over bean mixture in dish. Sprinkle with remaining cheese.

Southwestern Breakfast Bake

3. Bake, uncovered, about 20 minutes or until egg mixture is puffed and lightly browned. Let stand for 5 minutes before serving. If desired, serve with additional cilantro, sour cream, salsa, and additional hot pepper sauce.

PER SERVING: 149 cal., 5 g total fat (2 g sat. fat), 77 mg chol., 343 mg sodium, 16 g carb. (4 g fiber, 1 g sugars), 11 g pro. Exchanges: 1 starch, 1 lean meat, 0.5 fat. Carb choices: 1.

Egg White Omelet with Veggies and Avocado Cream

You can forget fretting about what to do with the yolks when you start with a carton of refrigerated egg whites.
SERVINGS 4 (1 omelet and ¼ cup avocado mixture each)
CARB. PER SERVING 12 g

 1 small avocado
 ¼ cup light tub-style cream cheese, softened
 ¼ teaspoon finely shredded lemon peel
 1 tablespoon lemon juice
 ¼ teaspoon salt
 Nonstick cooking spray
 1 cup chopped zucchini
 ¾ cup chopped sweet onion
 1 16-ounce carton refrigerated egg whites
 ¼ cup water
 ¼ teaspoon salt
 ¼ teaspoon black pepper
 2 medium tomatoes, seeded and chopped
 1 cup coarsely chopped fresh spinach
 1 tablespoon snipped fresh chives

1. Halve and seed the avocado. Scoop the avocado from the peel into a medium bowl. Using a potato masher, mash the avocado. Stir in cream cheese, lemon peel, lemon juice, and the ¼ teaspoon salt. Cover the surface of the avocado mixture with plastic wrap and set aside.
2. Coat an unheated medium nonstick skillet with flared sides with cooking spray. Heat skillet over medium heat. Add zucchini and onion. Cook about 5 minutes or until vegetables are just tender, stirring occasionally. Transfer vegetables to a medium bowl.
3. In another medium bowl whisk together egg whites, water, ¼ teaspoon salt, and pepper. Add half of the chopped tomatoes and all of the spinach to the zucchini mixture in the bowl and toss to combine. Wipe out the medium skillet used to cook the vegetables. Coat skillet with cooking spray and heat over medium-high heat.
4. Add one-fourth of the egg white mixture to the hot skillet. Lower heat to medium. Begin to stir egg white mixture gently but continuously with a wooden spoon until mixture resembles small pieces of cooked egg surrounded by liquid egg. Stop stirring. Cook 30 to 60 seconds more or until egg mixture is set but shiny.
5. Spoon one-fourth of the zucchini mixture across one half of the omelet. With a spatula, lift the plain side up over the vegetables. Remove from the heat and transfer the omelet to a serving plate. Repeat with the remaining egg white mixture and zucchini mixture to make three more omelets.
6. Top each omelet evenly with the remaining chopped tomato. Spoon avocado mixture on top of the omelets and sprinkle with chives.
PER SERVING: 160 cal., 6 g total fat (2 g sat. fat), 8 mg chol., 565 mg sodium, 12 g carb. (3 g fiber, 5 g sugars), 16 g pro. Exchanges: 1 vegetable, 0.5 carb., 2 lean meat, 0.5 fat. Carb choices: 1.

Italian Sausage and Zucchini Quiche

If you have plenty of fresh thyme, garnish each crustless quiche with a small sprig or two.
SERVINGS 4 (1 individual dish each)
CARB. PER SERVING 6 g

 Nonstick cooking spray
 4 ounces uncooked turkey Italian sausage links, removed from casing
 1 small red sweet pepper, chopped
 1 cup coarsely shredded, unpeeled zucchini
 ¼ cup finely shredded Parmesan cheese
 1½ cups refrigerated or frozen egg product, thawed, or 6 eggs, lightly beaten
 ¼ cup fat-free milk
 ⅛ teaspoon black pepper
 ⅓ cup shredded part-skim or reduced-fat mozzarella cheese

1. Preheat oven to 325°F. Coat four 8-ounce shallow ramekins or quiche dishes or one 9-inch pie plate with cooking spray. Set aside.
2. In a medium skillet cook turkey sausage, sweet pepper, and zucchini until turkey is cooked through and pepper is just tender, stirring to break up turkey as it cooks. Combine cooked turkey mixture and Parmesan cheese. Divide mixture among prepared dishes or spoon into pie plate. In a medium bowl whisk together egg, milk, and black pepper. Pour egg mixture into the ramekins or pie plate. Sprinkle with mozzarella cheese.
3. Bake individual servings about 25 minutes or pie plate about 35 minutes or until a knife inserted in center(s) comes out clean. Cool on a wire rack for 10 minutes before serving.
PER SERVING: 151 cal., 5 g total fat (3 g sat. fat), 25 mg chol., 588 mg sodium, 6 g carb. (1 g fiber, 4 g sugars), 18 g pro. Exchanges: 0.5 vegetable, 2.5 lean meat, 0.5 fat. Carb choices: 0.5.

Italian Sausage
and Zucchini Quiche

Festive Holiday Strata

Festive Holiday Strata

Green and red sweet peppers fill this lightened-up egg bake with the colors of the season. Convert it to a springtime casserole by using yellow and/or orange sweet peppers.

SERVINGS 8 (1 cup each)

CARB. PER SERVING 17 g

1 to 1¼ pounds uncooked ground turkey breast
1 teaspoon onion powder
½ teaspoon coarsely ground black pepper
½ teaspoon dried sage, crushed
¼ teaspoon ground nutmeg
¼ teaspoon crushed red pepper
⅛ teaspoon dried marjoram, crushed
  Nonstick cooking spray

3 whole grain English muffins, split
1 cup refrigerated or frozen egg product, thawed
4 eggs
2 cups fat-free milk
1 teaspoon dry mustard
¼ teaspoon salt
¼ teaspoon paprika
2 small green sweet peppers, chopped (1 cup)
2 small red sweet peppers, chopped (1 cup)
¼ cup sliced green onions
1 cup shredded reduced-fat cheddar cheese (4 ounces)

1. In a large bowl combine ground turkey breast, onion powder, black pepper, sage, nutmeg, crushed red pepper, and marjoram; use your clean hands to mix well. In a large skillet cook turkey mixture over medium heat until brown.
2. Lightly coat a 3-quart rectangular baking dish with cooking spray. Cut English muffins into quarters; arrange in an even layer in baking dish. Sprinkle cooked turkey mixture evenly over English muffins.
3. In a large bowl whisk together egg product, eggs, milk, dry mustard, salt, and paprika; pour over turkey mixture and English muffins. Sprinkle sweet peppers and green onions over egg mixture. Cover with foil and chill for at least 8 hours or up to 24 hours.
4. Preheat oven to 350°F. Bake, uncovered, for 45 minutes. Sprinkle with cheese. Bake, uncovered, for 5 to 10 minutes more or until a knife inserted near the center comes out clean. Let stand for 5 minutes before serving.

PER SERVING: 235 cal., 6 g total fat (3 g sat. fat), 142 mg chol., 448 mg sodium, 17 g carb. (3 g fiber, 7 g sugars), 28 g pro. Exchanges: 1 starch, 3.5 lean meat. Carb choices: 1.

Goat Cheese Polenta Topped with Kale and Fried Eggs

Some goat cheese is softer than others, so you may need to crumble it with your fingers.
SERVINGS 6 (2 polenta triangles, ⅔ cup kale, and 1 egg each)
CARB. PER SERVING 27 g

---

2 cups water
¾ cup polenta-style cornmeal
½ cup fat-free milk
¼ teaspoon salt
3 green onions
4 ounces soft goat cheese (chèvre), cut up
½ cup water
8 cups coarsely chopped fresh kale (about one 12-ounce bunch)
¼ teaspoon salt
1 tablespoon olive oil
6 eggs
¼ teaspoon salt
2 teaspoons snipped fresh thyme
¼ teaspoon freshly ground black pepper

1. Preheat oven to 300°F. In a medium saucepan combine 2 cups water, the polenta-style cornmeal, milk, and ¼ teaspoon salt. Bring to boiling, stirring constantly. Reduce heat to medium-low. Simmer, uncovered, about 20 minutes, stirring frequently, or until polenta is thick and tender. Reduce heat to low if polenta is bubbling too heavily. Meanwhile, thinly slice the green onions, keeping the green tops separate from the white bottoms. Add the green onion tops and goat cheese to the polenta and stir until cheese is melted and mixture is well combined.
2. Pour hot polenta mixture into a 2-quart rectangular baking dish, spreading to an even layer. Cover with foil and place in the oven until serving time.
3. In a very large nonstick skillet bring ½ cup water to boiling. Add the kale, sliced white parts of green onions, and ¼ teaspoon salt. Cover and reduce heat to medium-low. Steam about 8 minutes or until kale is nearly tender, stirring once or twice. Uncover and continue cooking, stirring, for 1 to 2 minutes more or until water evaporates. Remove kale from skillet and keep warm.
4. For fried eggs, heat olive oil in the same skillet over medium heat. Break eggs into skillet, leaving space between the eggs. Sprinkle eggs with ¼ teaspoon salt. Reduce heat to low; cook eggs for 3 to 4 minutes or until whites are completely set and yolks start to thicken. When the whites are completely set and the yolks start to thicken, turn the eggs over and cook until desired doneness (30 seconds more for over easy or 1 minute more for over hard). Remove eggs from the skillet.
5. To serve, remove polenta from oven. Cut the polenta into six equal squares. Cut each square diagonally in half to make a total of 12 triangles. Place kale on each of six serving plates. Top each with two triangles of polenta. Place one egg on each serving. Sprinkle with thyme and pepper. Serve warm.

PER SERVING: 268 cal., 12 g total fat (5 g sat. fat), 195 mg chol., 483 mg sodium, 27 g carb. (3 g fiber, 4 g sugars), 15 g pro. Exchanges: 2 starch, 1 medium-fat meat, 1 fat. Carb choices: 2.

Eggs Benedict French Toast

*Two classic breakfast menu items combine
to make one great morning meal.*

SERVINGS 4 (1 French toast slice, 1 ounce
ham, 1 onion slice, 1 egg, and
1 tablespoon sauce each)

CARB. PER SERVING 20 g

3 egg whites, lightly beaten
⅓ cup fat-free milk
2 tablespoons light sour cream
½ teaspoon finely shredded lemon peel
  Nonstick cooking spray
4 eggs
4 ½-inch-thick slices whole grain or white country
   Italian bread
4 ounces thinly sliced reduced-sodium deli ham
1 small tomato, cut into 4 slices
¼ cup plain fat-free Greek yogurt
2 teaspoons lime juice
1 teaspoon yellow mustard
¼ teaspoon white or black pepper
⅛ teaspoon salt
1 tablespoon snipped fresh chives

1. Beat together egg whites, milk, sour cream, and
lemon peel. Transfer to a shallow dish; set aside.
2. Coat an unheated large skillet with cooking spray;
half-fill skillet with water. Bring water to boiling; reduce
heat to simmering (bubbles should begin to break surface).
3. Break 1 whole egg into a measuring cup. Carefully
slide egg into simmering water, holding the lip of the
cup as close to the water as possible. Repeat with
remaining eggs, allowing each egg an equal amount of
space. Simmer eggs, uncovered, for 3 to 5 minutes or
until whites are completely set and yolks begin to
thicken but are not hard.
4. Meanwhile, coat an unheated large griddle with
cooking spray; heat over medium heat. Dip bread slices
into egg white mixture, coating both sides (let soak in
egg mixture about 5 seconds on each side). Add the
bread slices to the hot griddle and cook for 2 to
3 minutes on each side or until golden brown. Remove
from griddle and keep warm.
5. Add the ham slices to the hot griddle and cook about
1 minute or until warm, turning once. To serve, place
one French toast slice on each of four serving plates. Top
evenly with ham and tomato slices. Using a slotted
spoon, remove the poached eggs from the water and
place one egg on each serving.

6. In a small bowl stir together yogurt, lime juice,
mustard, and ⅛ teaspoon of the pepper. Spoon over
eggs. Sprinkle with remaining pepper, salt, and chives.
PER SERVING: 233 cal., 8 g total fat (2 g sat. fat), 201 mg chol.,
548 mg sodium, 20 g carb. (4 g fiber, 6 g sugars), 20 g pro.
Exchanges: 1 starch, 2.5 lean meat, 0.5 fat. Carb choices: 1.

Sweet Potato Waffles with Cranberry Syrup

*If you prefer, use 2 lightly beaten eggs instead of
the egg product to make these hearty waffles.*

SERVINGS 10 (2 waffle squares and
2½ tablespoons syrup each)

CARB. PER SERVING 33 g

1 recipe Cranberry Syrup
1¼ cups whole wheat pastry flour
½ cup all-purpose flour
2 tablespoons packed brown sugar*
1 tablespoon baking powder
¼ teaspoon salt
¼ teaspoon ground cinnamon
1½ cups fat-free milk
1 cup pureed, cooked sweet potatoes
½ cup refrigerated or frozen egg product, thawed
2 tablespoons canola oil

1. Prepare Cranberry Syrup; set aside. In a large bowl
combine flours, brown sugar, baking powder, salt, and
cinnamon. In a medium bowl combine milk, sweet
potatoes, eggs, and oil; add all at once to flour mixture.
Stir just until moistened (batter should be lumpy).
2. Pour about ¾ cup batter onto grids of a preheated,
lightly greased waffle baker. Close lid quickly; do not
open until done. Bake according to manufacturer's
directions. When done, use a fork to lift waffle off grids.
Repeat with remaining batter. Serve waffles with syrup.
CRANBERRY SYRUP: In a medium saucepan combine 1½ cups
fresh cranberries, ¾ cup reduced-calorie maple-flavor
syrup, ⅓ cup orange juice, and ½ teaspoon ground
cinnamon. Cook and stir over medium-high heat until
boiling. Reduce heat and simmer, uncovered, for 3 to
5 minutes or until cranberries pop. Mash cranberries
slightly. Remove from heat and set aside.
*SUGAR SUBSTITUTE: We do not recommend using a sugar
substitute for this recipe.
PER SERVING: 172 cal., 3 g total fat (0 g sat. fat), 1 mg chol.,
246 mg sodium, 33 g carb. (3 g fiber, 13 g sugars), 5 g pro.
Exchanges: 2 starch. Carb choices: 2.

quick tip

For crispy golden waffles, resist peeking and wait until the doneness indicator lights or sounds before lifting the lid on the waffle maker.

Sweet Potato Waffles with Cranberry Syrup

Chocolate Chip Pancakes with Cherry-Orange Sauce

This batter may be a little stiff, so slightly spread it as necessary once it's dropped onto the hot griddle.

SERVINGS 6 (2 pancakes and 3 tablespoons cherry sauce each)

CARB. PER SERVING 40 g or 36 g

1	recipe Cherry-Orange Sauce
¾	cup whole wheat flour
¼	cup all-purpose flour
1	tablespoon packed brown sugar*
1½	teaspoons baking powder
⅛	teaspoon salt
1	egg white, lightly beaten
1	cup fat-free milk
2	tablespoons vegetable oil
⅓	cup miniature semisweet chocolate pieces

1. Prepare Cherry-Orange Sauce and set aside. In a medium bowl stir together flours, brown sugar, baking powder, and salt. In another bowl use a fork to combine egg white, milk, and oil. Add milk mixture all at once to flour mixture. Stir just until moistened (batter should be slightly lumpy). Stir in chocolate pieces.

2. For each pancake, pour about 2 tablespoons batter onto a hot, lightly greased griddle or heavy skillet.

3. Cook over medium heat for 1 to 2 minutes on each side or until pancakes are golden brown; turn over when surfaces are bubbly and edges are slightly dry. Serve warm with Cherry-Orange Sauce.

CHERRY-ORANGE SAUCE: In a medium saucepan combine 1 tablespoon granulated sugar* and 1 teaspoon cornstarch. Stir in 1½ cups frozen unsweetened pitted tart red cherries, 1 tablespoon water, and 1 tablespoon butter. Cook and stir for 3 to 4 minutes or until mixture is thickened and bubbly. Cook and stir for 1 minute more. Remove from the heat. Peel, seed, and section 2 medium oranges. Gently stir orange sections into sauce.

*SUGAR SUBSTITUTES: Choose from Sweet'N Low Brown or Sugar Twin Granulated Brown to substitute for the brown sugar. Choose from Splenda Granular or Sweet'N Low bulk or packets to substitute for the granulated sugar. Follow package directions to use amounts equivalent to 1 tablespoon brown sugar and 1 tablespoon granulated sugar.

PER SERVING: 267 cal., 10 g total fat (4 g sat. fat), 6 mg chol., 185 mg sodium, 40 g carb. (4 g fiber, 20 g sugars), 6 g pro. Exchanges: 2 starch, 0.5 fruit, 1.5 fat. Carb choices: 2.

PER SERVING WITH SUBSTITUTES: Same as above, except 251 cal., 36 g carb. (16 g sugars), 184 mg sodium.

Danish Fruit and Cheese Pastries

Danish Fruit and Cheese Pastries

*Take your pick—you can shape these bakery-style
pastries into spirals, turnovers, or envelopes.*

SERVINGS 24 (1 pastry each)

CARB. PER SERVING 25 g or 24 g

- 2 **16-ounce loaves frozen sweet roll dough, thawed**
- ½ **8-ounce package reduced-fat cream cheese (Neufchâtel), softened**
- 1 **egg yolk**
- 2 **tablespoons sugar***
- 1 **tablespoon flour**
- ¼ **teaspoon vanilla**
- ¼ **teaspoon almond extract or finely shredded orange peel**
- ¼ **cup desired flavor low-sugar jam or preserves**
- 1 **recipe Lemon Curd Icing**

1. Line two large baking sheets with parchment paper; set aside.

2. To shape spiral pastries, on a lightly floured surface roll 1 loaf of dough into a 12-inch square. Cut the square into twelve 12×1-inch strips. Coil each strip into a spiral round (3 inches in diameter), tucking the outside end underneath. Repeat with remaining strips, placing 2 inches apart on baking sheets. Repeat with the remaining loaf of sweet roll dough. Cover and let rise in a warm place until nearly double in size (30 to 45 minutes).

3. Preheat oven to 350°F. Make an indentation in center of each spiral. In a small bowl combine cream cheese, egg yolk, sugar, flour, vanilla, and almond extract. Beat with an electric mixer on medium speed until well

mixed and smooth. Fill each indentation with a level teaspoon of the cream cheese mixture.

4. Bake for 15 to 18 minutes or until golden. Cool pastries slightly on a wire rack. Place jam in a small microwave-safe bowl. Microwave on 100 percent power (high) for 20 seconds or until just melted. Spoon ½ teaspoon of the melted jam in the center of each pastry coil. Drizzle with Lemon Curd Icing. Serve warm or at room temperature.

LEMON CURD ICING: In a small bowl combine ¾ cup powdered sugar, 1 tablespoon lemon curd, ¼ teaspoon vanilla, and, if desired, ⅛ teaspoon almond extract. Stir in 1 tablespoon milk. If necessary, add additional milk, 1 teaspoon at a time, to reach drizzling consistency.

TURNOVERS: On a lightly floured surface roll 1 loaf of dough into a 12×9-inch rectangle. Cut rectangle into twelve 3-inch squares. Place a rounded measuring teaspoon of cream cheese mixture into the center of each square. Top each with ½ teaspoon jam. Fold each pastry square diagonally in half. Using the tines of a fork, seal edges. With fork, poke a few holes in the top of each triangle. Place on prepared baking sheets. Cover and let rise in a warm place until nearly double in size (30 to 45 minutes). Repeat with the the remaining loaf of sweet roll dough, remaining cream cheese mixture, and remaining jam. Bake as directed in Step 3. If desired, drizzle with Lemon Curd Icing. Serve warm or at room temperature.

ENVELOPES: On a lightly floured surface roll 1 loaf of dough into a 12×9-inch rectangle. Cut rectangle into twelve 3-inch squares. Place a rounded measuring teaspoon of cream cheese mixture into the center of each square. Top each with ½ teaspoon jam. Fold points to the center, forming an envelope. Pinch points together in the center to seal. (If necessary to seal, lightly moisten points with water.) Cover and let rise in a warm place until nearly double in size (30 to 45 minutes). Repeat with the remaining loaf of sweet roll dough, remaining cream cheese mixture, and remaining jam. Bake as directed in Step 3. If desired, drizzle with Lemon Curd Icing. Serve warm or at room temperature.

*****SUGAR SUBSTITUTES:** Choose from Splenda Granular or Sweet'N Low bulk or packets. Follow package directions to use product amount equivalent to 2 tablespoons sugar.

PER SERVING: 150 cal., 4 g total fat (2 g sat. fat), 33 mg chol., 85 mg sodium, 25 g carb. (1 g fiber, 10 g sugars), 4 g pro. Exchanges: 1.5 starch, 0.5 fat. Carb choices: 1.5.

PER SERVING WITH SUBSTITUTE: Same as above, except 146 cal., 24 g carb. (9 g sugars).

Almond Cinnamon Roll Breakfast Ring

Here's a keeper—one yummy dough recipe that's used to create two great sweet roll options.

SERVINGS 15 (1 frosted piece each)
CARB. PER SERVING 29 g or 23 g

- 1 cup warm water (105°F to 115°F)
- ¼ cup granulated sugar*
- 1 package active dry yeast
- 2 to 2¼ cups all-purpose flour
- 1 cup whole wheat flour
- ¼ cup refrigerated or frozen egg product, thawed
- 2 tablespoons canola oil
- 1 teaspoon salt
  Nonstick cooking spray
- 1½ tablespoons butter, melted
- 1 tablespoon ground cinnamon
- ½ cup sliced almonds, toasted
- 1 recipe Cream Cheese Icing

1. In a large bowl stir together the water, ¼ cup sugar, and the yeast. Let stand for 5 minutes. Stir in 2 cups of the all-purpose flour, the whole wheat flour, egg, oil, and salt.

2. On a lightly floured surface knead in enough of the remaining all-purpose flour to make a moderately soft dough that is smooth and elastic (3 to 5 minutes total). Lightly coat a large bowl with cooking spray. Place dough in bowl; turn to coat surface of dough. Cover; let rise in a warm place until double in size (about 1 hour).

3. Roll the dough into a 17×12-inch rectangle. Brush dough with melted butter. Sprinkle with ¼ cup sugar and the cinnamon. Sprinkle the dough with all but 2 tablespoons of the sliced almonds.

4. Starting with a long side, roll up dough into a spiral; pinch seam to seal. (This will make a spiral that is about 20 inches long.) Lightly coat a baking sheet with cooking spray. Form a ring out of the dough spiral, sealing the ends together. Place the ring, seam side down, on the prepared baking sheet. Using kitchen scissors, cut from the edge toward the center at about 1½-inch intervals, cutting about two-thirds of the way through the dough spiral. Turn each dough section slightly to one side.

5. Cover the ring and chill in the refrigerator for 8 to 24 hours. (If baking right away, cover and let rise in a warm place until double in size, about 45 minutes.)

6. If ring was chilled, let stand at room temperature for 30 to 60 minutes before baking. Meanwhile, preheat oven to 350°F. Bake, uncovered, about 25 minutes or until golden brown. Let cool on baking sheet on a wire rack for 20 minutes. Carefully transfer ring to a serving platter. Drizzle with Cream Cheese Icing. Sprinkle with reserved 2 tablespoons almonds.

CREAM CHEESE ICING: In a medium bowl combine ¼ cup reduced-fat cream cheese (Neufchâtel), ¼ cup powdered sugar, 1 tablespoon fat-free milk, and 1 teaspoon vanilla. Beat with an electric mixer on medium speed until well mixed and smooth. If necessary, beat in enough additional milk, 1 teaspoon at a time, to make icing drizzling consistency.

***SUGAR SUBSTITUTES:** Choose from Splenda Granular or Sweet'N Low bulk or packets. Follow package directions to use product amount equivalent to ½ cup granulated sugar.

PER SERVING: 182 cal., 6 g total fat (2 g sat. fat), 6 mg chol., 187 mg sodium, 29 g carb. (2 g fiber, 9 g sugars) , 5 g pro. Exchanges: 1 starch, 1 carb., 1 fat. Carb choices: 2.

PER SERVING WITH SUBSTITUTE: Same as above, except 159 cal., 23 g carb. (3 g sugars). Exchanges: 0.5 carb. Carb choices: 1.5.

ALMOND CARAMEL CINNAMON ROLLS: Prepare dough through Step 2. Meanwhile, for caramel sauce, in a small bowl stir together ⅓ cup packed brown sugar,* 2 tablespoons melted butter, and 2 tablespoons hot water. Lightly coat a 3-quart rectangular baking dish with cooking spray. Add caramel sauce, spreading evenly in the dish. Prepare dough as in Step 3, brushing with butter, sprinkling with sugar and cinnamon, and sprinkling all of the almonds over the dough rectangle. Starting with a long side, tightly roll up dough into a spiral; pinch seam to seal. Cut spiral crosswise into 15 even slices. Arrange slices over caramel sauce in baking dish. Continue with Step 5. If rolls were chilled, let stand at room temperature for 30 to 60 minutes before baking. Preheat oven to 350°F. Bake, uncovered, about 25 minutes or until golden brown. Let cool in baking dish on wire rack for 5 minutes. Invert onto a serving platter; remove baking dish. Omit the Cream Cheese Icing. Makes 15 rolls.

SUGAR SUBSTITUTES: Choose from Splenda Granular or Sweet'N Low bulk or packets for the granulated sugar. Choose from Sweet'N Low Brown or Sugar Twin Granulated Brown for the brown sugar. Follow package directions to use product amounts equivalent to ½ cup granulated sugar and ⅓ cup brown sugar.

PER ROLL: 196 cal., 6 g total fat (2 g sat. fat), 7 mg chol., 189 mg sodium, 31 g carb. (2 g fiber, 12 g sugars), 4 g pro. Exchanges: 1 starch, 1 carb., 1 fat. Carb choices: 2.

PER ROLL WITH SUBSTITUTES: Same as above, except 154 cal., 21 g carb. (1 g sugars), 188 mg sodium. Exchanges: 0.5 carb. Carb choices: 1.5.

Almond Cinnamon
Roll Breakfast Ring

Spiced Maple-Walnut Pear Scones

Irresistible—a simple cream cheese and maple-flavor syrup drizzle dresses up these fruit-and-nut-loaded pastries.

SERVINGS 12 (1 scone each)
CARB. PER SERVING 33 g or 29 g

2 to 2¼ cups all-purpose flour
¾ cup whole wheat pastry flour or whole wheat flour
¼ cup sugar*
2 teaspoons baking powder
1 teaspoon ground cinnamon
½ teaspoon salt
¼ teaspoon ground cloves
4 tablespoons butter, cut up
½ cup refrigerated or frozen egg product, thawed, or 2 eggs, lightly beaten
½ cup fat-free milk
2 tablespoons light maple-flavor syrup
¼ teaspoon maple-flavor extract
1 cup shredded, unpeeled pear (about 1 large pear)
½ cup chopped walnuts, toasted
¼ cup raisins
1 tablespoon fat-free milk
2 tablespoons light tub-style cream cheese, softened
2 tablespoons light maple-flavor syrup

1. Preheat oven to 400°F. In a large bowl stir together the flours, sugar, baking powder, cinnamon, salt, and cloves. Cut in butter until mixture resembles coarse crumbs. Make a well in center of the flour mixture.
2. In small bowl combine egg, ½ cup milk, 2 tablespoons syrup, and the maple-flavor extract; stir in shredded pear, walnuts, and raisins. Add the milk mixture all at once to the flour mixture. Using a fork, stir just until moistened.
3. Turn dough out onto a floured surface. Knead dough by folding and gently pressing it for 10 to 12 strokes or until nearly smooth. Pat or lightly roll dough into an 8-inch circle. Cut dough circle into 12 wedges.
4. Place dough wedges 2 inches apart on an ungreased baking sheet. Brush the top of the scones with 1 tablespoon milk. Bake for 17 to 20 minutes or until edges are light brown. Meanwhile, in a small bowl place cream cheese; whisk in 2 tablespoons syrup until smooth. Transfer warm scones to a serving platter. Drizzle tops with cream cheese mixture.
***SUGAR SUBSTITUTES:** Choose from Splenda Granular, Equal Spoonful or packets, or Sweet'N Low bulk or packets. Follow package directions to use product amount equivalent to ¼ cup sugar.

PER SERVING: 217 cal., 8 g total fat (3 g sat. fat), 12 mg chol., 246 mg sodium, 33 g carb. (2 g fiber, 10 g sugars), 5 g pro. Exchanges: 2 starch, 1 fat. Carb choices: 2.
PER SERVING WITH SUBSTITUTE: Same as above, except 203 cal., 29 g carb. (7 g sugar).

Curried Squash Muffins

Add a little heat to these spiced muffins by stirring ½ teaspoon cayenne pepper into the flour mixture.

SERVINGS 16 (1 muffin each)
CARB. PER SERVING 20 g or 16 g

1 cup all-purpose flour
½ cup white whole wheat flour
2 teaspoons baking powder
2 teaspoons ground cinnamon
1 teaspoon curry powder
½ teaspoon salt
½ cup butter, softened
½ cup packed brown sugar*
1 cup mashed roasted butternut squash or 1 cup frozen cooked winter squash, thawed
¼ cup finely chopped crystallized ginger
1 egg
1 teaspoon vanilla
⅓ cup light vanilla soymilk

1. Preheat oven to 350°F. Line sixteen 2½-inch muffin cups with paper bake cups; set aside. In a bowl combine flours, baking powder, cinnamon, curry powder, and salt; set aside.
2. In a large bowl beat butter with an electric mixer for 30 seconds. Add brown sugar; beat until combined. Add squash, ginger, egg, and vanilla; beat until combined. Alternately add the flour mixture and soymilk, beating on low speed after each addition just until combined.
3. Spoon batter into prepared muffin cups, filling each about two-thirds full. Bake about 20 minutes or until muffin tops spring back when lightly touched. Cool in cups for 5 minutes. Remove from cups. Serve warm.
***SUGAR SUBSTITUTE:** Choose Splenda Brown Sugar Blend. Follow package directions to use product amount equivalent to ½ cup brown sugar.
PER SERVING: 140 cal., 6 g total fat (4 g sat. fat), 27 mg chol., 179 mg sodium, 20 g carb. (1 g fiber, 7 g sugars), 2 g pro. Exchanges: 1 starch, 1 fat. Carb choices: 1.
PER SERVING WITH SUBSTITUTE: Same as above, except 129 cal., 177 mg sodium, 16 g carb. (3 g sugars).

quick tip

A light coating of nonstick cooking spray in the paper cups prevents the muffins from sticking.

Apricot-Pecan Muffins

Apricot-Pecan Muffins

To keep the dried apricots from sticking to your kitchen scissors, lightly coat the blades with nonstick cooking spray and then snip the fruit.

SERVINGS 12 (1 muffin each)
CARB. PER SERVING 21 g or 17 g

- 1 cup flour
- 1 cup quick-cooking rolled oats
- 3 tablespoons packed brown sugar*
- 1½ teaspoons baking powder
- ½ teaspoon ground allspice
- ¼ teaspoon salt
- ½ cup snipped dried apricots
- ⅔ cup fat-free milk
- ⅓ cup canola oil
- ¼ cup refrigerated or frozen egg product, thawed, or 1 egg, lightly beaten
- ¼ cup chopped pecans

1. Preheat oven to 400°F. Line twelve 2½-inch muffin cups with paper bake cups; lightly coat insides of cups with *nonstick cooking spray*. Set aside.

2. In a large bowl stir together flour, oats, brown sugar, baking powder, allspice, and salt. Stir in the apricots. Make a well in the center of the flour mixture. In a small bowl whisk together the milk, oil, and egg; add all at once to the flour mixture. Using a fork, stir just until moistened.

3. Spoon batter into prepared muffin cups, filling each two-thirds full. Sprinkle pecans evenly over top. Bake about 15 minutes or until a toothpick inserted near the centers comes out clean. Cool in pan on a wire rack for 5 minutes. Remove muffins from muffin cups; serve warm.

*****SUGAR SUBSTITUTES:** Choose from Sweet'N Low Brown or Sugar Twin Granulated Brown. Follow package directions to use product amount equivalent to 3 tablespoons brown sugar.

PER SERVING: 166 cal., 8 g total fat (1 g sat. fat), 0 mg chol., 111 mg sodium, 21 g carb. (2 g fiber, 7 g sugars), 3 g pro. Exchanges: 1 starch, 0.5 carb., 1.5 fat. Carb choices: 1.5.

PER SERVING WITH SUBSTITUTE: Same as above, except 153 cal., 17 g carb. (4 g sugar), 110 mg sodium. Exchanges: 0 carb. Carb choices: 1.

Overnight Blueberry Coffee Cake

Jump-start breakfast—stir together this gingerbreadlike cake the day before and then bake it in the morning.

SERVINGS 12 (1 piece each)
CARB. PER SERVING 25 g or 19 g

Nonstick cooking spray
- 1 cup whole wheat pastry flour
- ¾ cup yellow cornmeal
- ⅓ cup granulated sugar*
- 1½ teaspoons ground cinnamon
- 1 teaspoon baking soda
- ½ teaspoon ground ginger
- ¼ teaspoon salt
- 1 cup plain fat-free Greek yogurt
- ¾ cup refrigerated or frozen egg product, thawed, or 3 eggs, lightly beaten
- ⅓ cup canola oil
- ¼ cup unsweetened applesauce
- 1 tablespoon butter flavoring
- 2 cups frozen blueberries
- 2 tablespoons packed dark brown sugar*
- Frozen light whipped dessert topping, thawed (optional)
- Ground ginger (optional)

1. Lightly coat a 2-quart rectangular baking dish with cooking spray; set aside. In a large bowl stir together pastry flour, cornmeal, granulated sugar, 1 teaspoon of the cinnamon, the baking soda, the ½ teaspoon ginger, and salt.

2. In a medium bowl whisk together yogurt, egg, oil, applesauce, and butter flavoring until well mixed; add to the flour mixture, stirring just until combined. Spread half of the batter into the prepared dish.

3. Sprinkle with 1 cup of the frozen blueberries. Spread the remaining batter evenly over top. Cover and chill for 8 to 24 hours.

4. Allow the coffee cake to stand at room temperature while the oven preheats to 350°F. In a small bowl toss together the remaining 1 cup frozen blueberries, the brown sugar, and the remaining ½ teaspoon cinnamon; sprinkle over the batter.

5. Bake, uncovered, about 35 minutes or until a toothpick inserted near the center comes out clean. Serve warm. If desired, serve with whipped topping and sprinkle with additional ginger.

*SUGAR SUBSTITUTES: Choose from Splenda Granular or Sweet'N Low bulk or packets for the granulated sugar. Choose Splenda Brown Sugar Blend for the brown sugar. Follow package directions to use product amounts equivalent to ⅓ cup granulated sugar and 2 tablespoons brown sugar.

PER SERVING: 175 cal., 7 g total fat (0 g sat. fat), 0 mg chol., 195 mg sodium, 25 g carb. (2 g fiber, 12 g sugars), 5 g pro. Exchanges: 1 starch, 0.5 carb., 1 fat. Carb choices: 1.5.
PER SERVING WITH SUBSTITUTES: Same as above, except 152 cal., 19 g carb. (5 g sugars). Exchanges: 0 carb. Carb choices: 1.

Overnight Blueberry
Coffee Cake

Pumpkin-Apple Quick Oatmeal

Canned pumpkin, dried apples, and warm spices bring seasonal flavors to this old-fashioned favorite.

SERVINGS 4 (¾ cup oatmeal and 2 tablespoons yogurt each)
CARB. PER SERVING 35 g or 32 g

- 1⅓ cups water
- ⅔ cup apple juice or apple cider
- ½ cup canned pumpkin
- ⅓ cup chopped dried apples
- 1¼ cups quick-cooking rolled oats
- 1 tablespoon packed brown sugar*
- 1 teaspoon ground cinnamon
- ¼ teaspoon ground nutmeg
- ½ cup vanilla fat-free yogurt
- Ground cinnamon (optional)

1. In a medium saucepan combine the water, apple juice, pumpkin, and dried apples. Bring to boiling. In a small bowl combine oats, brown sugar, the 1 teaspoon cinnamon, and the nutmeg; stir into boiling water mixture. Cook for 1 minute, stirring occasionally.

2. Divide hot oatmeal among four serving bowls. Top each serving with a spoonful of yogurt and, if desired, garnish with additional cinnamon.

*SUGAR SUBSTITUTES: Choose from Sweet'N Low Brown or Sugar Twin Granulated Brown. Follow package directions to use product amount equivalent to 1 tablespoon brown sugar.

PER SERVING: 168 cal., 2 g total fat (0 g sat. fat), 1 mg chol., 30 mg sodium, 35 g carb. (4 g fiber, 15 g sugars), 5 g pro. Exchanges: 0.5 fruit, 1.5 starch. Carb choices: 2.

PER SERVING WITH SUBSTITUTE: Same as above, except 155 cal., 32 g carb. (12 g sugars), 29 mg sodium.

Cinnamon Toast and Fruit Breakfast Parfaits

If fresh mangoes are not at their peak, substitute chopped refrigerated mango slices.

SERVINGS 4 (1 parfait each [about ¾ cup])

CARB. PER SERVING 43 g

- 1 tablespoon light stick butter (not margarine)
- ½ teaspoon ground cinnamon
- 2 slices light oatmeal bread, cut into cubes
- 2 6-ounce cartons plain fat-free Greek yogurt
- ¼ cup strawberry spreadable fruit
- 1 medium banana, coarsely chopped or thinly sliced (about 1 cup)
- ¾ cup fresh blueberries
- 1 medium mango, peeled, seeded, and cubed
- 4 teaspoons honey

1. In a medium skillet combine butter and cinnamon. Heat over medium heat until melted. Add bread cubes and toss to coat. Continue to cook over medium heat for 3 to 4 minutes or until bread cubes are lightly browned and crisp, stirring occasionally. Remove from heat and set aside to cool.

2. In a small bowl combine yogurt and spreadable fruit. In a large bowl combine banana, blueberries, and mango.

3. To serve, spoon one-third of the fruit evenly into four parfait glasses or 8-ounce clear drinking glasses. Top with half of the bread cubes. Spoon half of the yogurt mixture on top of the bread cubes. Repeat layers once, using half of the remaining fruit, all of the remaining bread cubes, and all of the remaining yogurt mixture.

Cinnamon Toast and
Fruit Breakfast Parfaits

Top evenly with remaining fruit. Drizzle with honey. Serve immediately.

PER SERVING: 217 cal., 2 g total fat (1 g sat. fat), 4 mg chol., 106 mg sodium, 43 g carb. (3 g fiber, 31 g sugars), 10 g pro. Exchanges: 0.5 milk, 1 fruit, 1.5 starch. Carb choices: 3.

Hot Breakfast Nog

Rich and creamy, this fun breakfast drink makes a comforting snack as well.

SERVINGS 6 (½ cup each)

CARB. PER SERVING 16 g or 8 g

    4 egg yolks
   ¼ cup sugar*
   ¼ teaspoon ground cinnamon
   ⅛ teaspoon ground nutmeg
 3¼ cups low-fat milk (1%)
    1 teaspoon vanilla
   ¼ teaspoon rum extract (optional)
       Long, thin strips of orange peel and/or cinnamon sticks (optional)
    1 recipe Frothed Milk (optional)
       Freshly grated nutmeg (optional)

Hot Breakfast Nog

1. In a large heavy saucepan whisk together egg yolks, sugar, cinnamon, and ⅛ teaspoon nutmeg until smooth. (If using sugar substitute, reserve and stir in once the milk has reached the proper temperature.) Gradually whisk in milk. Cook and stir over medium heat until milk mixture is slightly thickened and reaches 160°F. Remove from the heat and stir in vanilla, sugar substitute (if using), and rum extract (if using).

2. Ladle hot nog into mugs. If desired, add a strip of orange peel and/or a cinnamon stick to each mug. If desired, top each serving with a spoonful of frothed milk and sprinkle with freshly grated nutmeg.

FROTHED MILK: Pour ½ cup low-fat milk (1%) into a 2-cup microwave-safe glass measure. Microwave on 70 percent power (medium-high) for 50 to 60 seconds or just until bubbly. Use a milk frothing wand to whip the milk until all of the milk is a foamy consistency. Immediately spoon onto the servings of hot nog.

***SUGAR SUBSTITUTES:** Choose from Splenda Granular, Equal Spoonful or packets, or Sweet'N Low bulk or packets. Follow package directions to use product amount equivalent to ¼ cup sugar.

PER SERVING: 127 cal., 4 g total fat (2 g sat. fat), 130 mg chol., 64 mg sodium, 16 g carb. (0 g fiber, 15 g sugars), 6 g pro. Exchanges: 0.5 milk, 0.5 carb., 0.5 medium-fat meat. Carb choices: 1.

PER SERVING WITH SUBSTITUTE: Same as above, except 98 cal., 8 g carb. (8 g sugars). Exchanges: 0 carb. Carb choices: 0.5.

Sparkling Pomegranate Tea

Pomegranate seeds sparkle like little rubies, but kumquat slices, orange wedges, and/or fresh cranberries make pretty garnishes, too.

SERVINGS 4 (¾ cup each)

CARB. PER SERVING 13 g or 7 g

   ¾ cup water
    2 bags green tea or 2 teaspoons loose-leaf green tea
    2 tablespoons sugar*
   ¾ cup pomegranate juice or light cranberry juice
       Ice cubes
    1 12-ounce bottle sparkling water, chilled
       Pomegranate seeds (optional)

1. In a small saucepan bring water just to boiling. Remove from the heat. Add the tea bags or loose-leaf tea. Cover and let steep for 4 minutes. Remove the tea bags (if using), squeezing out any excess liquid, or strain

out the loose-leaf tea and discard. Stir in the sugar until dissolved. Pour tea into a 2-cup glass measure. Cover and chill about 1 hour or until well chilled.

2. Add the pomegranate juice to the tea and stir to combine. To serve, pour tea mixture into four tall glasses half-filled with ice. Add sparkling water and stir lightly to mix. If desired, garnish drinks with pomegranate seeds.

*SUGAR SUBSTITUTES: Choose from Splenda Granular, Equal Spoonful or packets, or Sweet'N Low bulk or packets. Follow package directions to use product amount equivalent to 2 tablespoons sugar

PER SERVING: 51 cal., 0 g total fat, 0 mg chol., 24 mg sodium, 13 g carb. (0 g fiber, 12 g sugars), 0 g pro. Exchanges: 1 carb. Carb choices: 1.

PER SERVING WITH SUBSTITUTE: Same as above, except 30 cal., 7 g carb. (7 g sugars). Exchanges: 0.5 carb. Carb choices: 0.5.

Sparkling Pomegranate Tea

tasty party bites

Chicken and
Eggplant
Stuffed Shells

$\mathcal{G}$ather family and friends to celebrate all that the season brings—joy, love, friendship, and great food. Share with them these healthful versions of hot dips, sizzling skewers, saucy meatballs, crunchy snack mixes, and more. Each is sure to bring good cheer.

Chicken and Eggplant Stuffed Shells

Set the timer when boiling the pasta shells so they cook just to al dente. If cooked too long, they break easily.

SERVINGS 12 (1 filled shell and 1 tablespoon sauce each)

CARB. PER SERVING 15 g

Olive oil nonstick cooking spray
12 dried jumbo shell macaroni
⅓ cup chopped onion
⅓ cup chopped red sweet pepper
1 tablespoon olive oil
¾ cup chopped eggplant
2 cloves garlic, minced
¼ teaspoon fennel seeds, crushed
½ cup chopped cooked chicken breast
½ cup crumbled reduced-fat feta cheese
¼ cup refrigerated or frozen egg product, thawed, or 1 egg, beaten
⅓ cup seasoned fine dry bread crumbs
⅓ cup fresh basil, thinly sliced
¾ cup marinara sauce, warmed

1. Preheat oven to 375°F. Line a 15×10×1-inch baking pan with foil and coat foil with cooking spray; set aside. Cook macaroni shells according to package directions; drain. Rinse with cold water; drain again. Invert shells, outsides of the shells facing up, on paper towels to dry.

2. Meanwhile, in a medium skillet cook onion and sweet pepper in hot olive oil over medium heat for 3 minutes, stirring occasionally. Add eggplant, garlic, and fennel seeds. Cook for 3 to 4 minutes more or until vegetables are tender, stirring occasionally. Remove from heat and stir in chicken and feta cheese. Set aside.

3. Pour egg into a small bowl. Pour bread crumbs into another small bowl. Dip the outsides of each pasta shell in the egg, allowing excess to drip off. Dip coated shells in bread crumbs, turning to coat the whole outsides with crumbs. Lightly coat outsides of shells with cooking spray. Place coated shells in prepared pan, crumb sides down. Spoon chicken mixture evenly into the shells.

4. Bake the shells for 18 to 20 minutes or until heated through and bread crumbs are lightly browned. Transfer shells to a platter and sprinkle with basil just before serving. Serve warm with marinara sauce for dipping.

PER SERVING: 111 cal., 3 g total fat (1 g sat. fat), 7 mg chol., 240 mg sodium, 15 g carb. (1 g fiber, 2 g sugars), 6 g pro. Exchanges: 1 starch, 1 lean meat. Carb choices: 1.

Spiced Pork Quesadillas

Not the typical cheese quesadilla, this one is loaded with a creamy pork and veggie filling.
SERVINGS 12 (1 wedge each)
CARB. PER SERVING 13 g

- 8 ounces lean ground pork*
- ¾ cup chopped zucchini
- 1 small onion, chopped
- 1 clove garlic, minced
- ½ teaspoon ground coriander
- ¼ teaspoon ground ginger
- ¼ teaspoon ground cumin
- ⅛ teaspoon crushed red pepper
- ¾ cup fresh spinach, chopped
- ¼ cup golden raisins
- ¼ cup light cream cheese spread
- 2 tablespoons snipped fresh mint
- 4 8-inch whole wheat tortillas
  Nonstick cooking spray

1. In a large skillet cook pork, zucchini, onion, and garlic over medium heat until pork is no longer pink and vegetables are tender, stirring to break up meat as it cooks. Drain off fat if needed. Stir in coriander, ginger, cumin, and crushed red pepper. Cook and stir for 1 minute. Remove from the heat and stir in spinach, raisins, cream cheese, and mint.
2. Lightly coat one side of each tortilla with cooking spray. Place tortillas, sprayed sides down, on a cutting board or waxed paper. Divide pork mixture evenly among tortillas, spreading it to an even layer on one half of each tortilla. Fold the other side of the tortilla over filling.
3. Heat an indoor grill pan or large nonstick skillet over medium heat. Add two of the quesadillas to the pan or skillet. Cook quesadillas for 4 to 6 minutes or until lightly browned, turning once. Remove quesadillas from pan or skillet; place on a baking sheet. Keep warm in a 300°F oven. Repeat with remaining quesadillas. To serve, cut each quesadilla into three wedges.
***TEST KITCHEN TIP:** For really lean ground pork, have your butcher grind pork loin.
PER SERVING: 95 cal., 2 g total fat (1 g sat. fat), 14 mg chol., 168 mg sodium, 13 g carb. (1 g fiber, 4 g sugars), 6 g pro. Exchanges: 1 starch, 1 lean meat. Carb choices: 1.

Chorizo and Kale Flatbread Wedges

When paired with nutrient-rich kale, the spicy meat mixture makes a great topper for this pizzalike appetizer.
SERVINGS 8 (2 wedges each)
CARB. PER SERVING 12 g

- 4 ounces lean ground pork*
- 1 ounce uncooked chorizo sausage or lean ground turkey sausage
- 1 medium onion, halved and thinly sliced
- 2 cloves garlic, thinly sliced
- 6 ounces fresh kale, trimmed and coarsely chopped (about 4 cups)
- 2 10-inch whole wheat low-carb flour tortillas
  Nonstick cooking spray
- 2 ounces Manchego cheese or Parmesan cheese, shredded (½ cup)

1. Preheat broiler. In a large skillet cook pork, chorizo, and onion over medium heat until onion is very tender and lightly browned, stirring to break up pork and chorizo as it cooks. Add garlic and cook for 30 seconds. Add kale. Cook for 3 to 5 minutes or until kale is just tender, tossing with tongs so kale cooks evenly.
2. Lightly coat both sides of tortillas with cooking spray. Place tortillas on a large baking sheet. Broil 5 to 6 inches from the heat for 1 to 2 minutes or until lightly browned and beginning to crisp (watch carefully so that tortillas don't burn). Remove from broiler and turn tortillas over.
3. Divide kale mixture evenly between the tortillas and spread mixture evenly over the tortillas to within 1 inch of the edge. Sprinkle evenly with the cheese. Broil about 2 minutes more or until cheese is melted. To serve, cut each tortilla into eight wedges.
***TEST KITCHEN TIP:** For really lean ground pork, have your butcher grind pork loin.
PER SERVING: 147 cal., 7 g total fat (3 g sat. fat), 16 mg chol., 296 mg sodium, 12 g carb. (6 g fiber, 1 g sugars), 10 g pro. Exchanges: 1 starch, 1 lean meat. Carb choices: 1.

Chorizo and Kale
Flatbread Wedges

Saucy Spiced
Apricot Meatballs

SPICED APRICOT SAUCE: In a small saucepan combine 1 cup apricot nectar, 2 teaspoons cornstarch, ½ teaspoon ground ancho chile pepper or chili powder, ¼ teaspoon salt, and ¼ teaspoon ground nutmeg. Cook and stir over medium heat until thickened and bubbly. Cook and stir for 1 minute more. .

MAKE-AHEAD DIRECTIONS: Prepare meatballs as directed through Step 2; cool meatballs for 30 minutes. Store meatballs in an airtight container in the refrigerator for up to 24 hours. Store Spiced Apricot Sauce in an airtight container in the refrigerator for up to 2 days. Place chilled meatballs in a 1½-quart slow cooker. Add chilled sauce; toss gently to coat. Cover and cook on low-heat setting for 2½ to 3 hours or until heated through. Turn to warm setting if available. Keep warm for up to 2 hours.

PER SERVING: 76 cal., 2 g total fat (1 g sat. fat), 16 mg chol., 180 mg sodium, 7 g carb. (0 g fiber, 5 g sugars), 7 g pro. Exchanges: 0.5 carb., 1 lean meat. Carb choices: 0.5.

Saucy Spiced Apricot Meatballs

*Made with a combination of lean pork and turkey,
these meatballs are lower in fat than most.*
SERVINGS 12 (2 meatballs each)
CARB. PER SERVING 7 g

- ½ cup soft bread crumbs
- 2 tablespoons fat-free milk
- 1 egg white
- ¼ cup finely chopped onion
- ¼ cup finely snipped dried apricots
- ½ teaspoon salt
- 1 clove garlic, minced
- ¼ teaspoon ground ancho chile pepper or chili powder
- 6 ounces lean ground pork (see tip, page 31)
- 6 ounces uncooked ground turkey breast
- 1 recipe Spiced Apricot Sauce

1. Preheat oven to 350°F. Line a 15×10×1-inch baking pan with foil; lightly grease foil. Set aside. In a bowl combine bread crumbs and milk. Let stand for 5 minutes. Stir in egg white, onion, apricots, salt, garlic, and ground chile pepper. Add pork and turkey; mix well.

2. Shape meat mixture into 24 meatballs. Place meatballs in the prepared baking pan. Bake for 15 to 20 minutes or until meatballs are cooked through (165°F). If necessary, drain meatballs on paper towels.

3. Place meatballs in a 1½-quart slow cooker. Add Spiced Apricot Sauce; toss gently to coat. Turn cooker to warm setting or low-heat setting; keep warm for up to 2 hours.

Blue Cheese Meatballs with Apple-Dijon Sauce

*A slightly sweet and salty flavor combo comes through
in this version of cheesy beef meatballs.*
SERVINGS 12 (1 meatball, 1 piece apple, and
2 teaspoons sauce each)
CARB. PER SERVING 5 g

- Butter-flavor nonstick cooking spray
- ⅓ cup finely chopped celery
- ⅓ cup finely chopped onion
- 1 clove garlic, minced
- ⅓ cup soft whole wheat bread crumbs
- 2 tablespoons refrigerated or frozen egg product, thawed
- 2 teaspoons snipped fresh thyme
- ½ cup crumbled reduced-fat blue cheese
- 8 ounces 90 percent lean ground beef
- ¼ cup apple juice or pear nectar
- 2 tablespoons Dijon-style mustard
- 1 tablespoon honey
- 12 thin wedges apple or pear

1. Preheat oven to 350°F. Line a 9×9×2-inch baking pan with foil. Coat foil with cooking spray; set aside. Coat an unheated large nonstick skillet with cooking spray; heat skillet over medium heat. Add celery and onion. Cook about 5 minutes or until vegetables are tender, stirring frequently. Stir in garlic and remove from the heat.

2. In a large bowl combine bread crumbs, egg, thyme, ⅛ teaspoon *salt*, and ⅛ teaspoon *black pepper*. Stir in celery mixture. Add blue cheese and beef and mix well. Shape meat mixture into twelve 1½-inch-diameter meatballs. Place meatballs in the prepared baking pan. Bake for 18 to 20 minutes or until done (160°F).

3. Meanwhile, in a small bowl whisk together apple juice, mustard, and honey. Thread a wedge of apple onto a cocktail pick, pushing it about 2 inches from the bottom of the pick. Drain meatballs on paper towels. Push one of the cocktail picks into each meatball so the apple wedge rests on top of the meatball. Place meatballs on a platter. Spoon about 1 teaspoon of the sauce over each appetizer. Serve remaining sauce with appetizers.

PER SERVING: 68 cal., 3 g total fat (1 g sat. fat), 15 mg chol., 176 mg sodium, 5 g carb. (1 g fiber, 3 g sugars), 6 g pro. Exchanges: 1 medium-fat meat. Carb choices: 0.

Grilled Shrimp with Ginger Wasabi Soup Shooters

Grilled and chilled, each shrimp is served in a "shot" of a thick and creamy, loaded with good-for-you-ingredients soup.

SERVINGS 12 (¼ cup soup and 1 shrimp each)
CARB. PER SERVING 4 g

- ½ cup chopped sweet onion
- 2 teaspoons canola oil
- 1 tablespoon grated fresh ginger
- 2 cloves garlic, minced
- 2 cups water
- 1 cup frozen shelled sweet soybeans (edamame)
- ¼ cup instant brown rice
- 2 cups fresh baby spinach leaves
- 2 tablespoons rice vinegar
- 1 tablespoon reduced-sodium soy sauce
- 1½ teaspoons wasabi paste
- ¼ teaspoon salt
- 12 large fresh or frozen shrimp, peeled and deveined (6 to 8 ounces total)
- ¼ teaspoon salt
- ¼ teaspoon black pepper
- 1 tablespoon sesame seeds, toasted

1. In a large saucepan cook onion in hot oil over medium-low heat for 5 minutes, stirring occasionally. Stir in ginger and garlic; cook for 30 seconds more. Add water, edamame, and rice. Bring to boiling; reduce heat. Simmer, covered, for 10 minutes or until edamame and rice are very tender. Remove from the heat and stir in spinach, vinegar, soy sauce, wasabi paste, and ¼ teaspoon salt. Cool slightly.

2. Transfer soup to a blender or food processor. Cover and blend or process until very smooth. Transfer soup to a bowl; cover and chill for 4 to 24 hours.

3. Meanwhile, thaw shrimp, if frozen. Rinse shrimp and pat dry with paper towels. Sprinkle shrimp with ¼ teaspoon salt and pepper. Coat an unheated nonstick grill pan with *nonstick cooking spray.* Heat over medium-high heat. Add shrimp. Cook for 2 to 3 minutes or until shrimp are opaque, turning once halfway through cooking. Transfer shrimp to an airtight container. Cover and chill for 4 to 24 hours.

4. To serve, stir soup. Ladle chilled soup into twelve 3- to 5-ounce decorative glasses or tea cups. Top each serving of soup with a grilled shrimp and sprinkle with sesame seeds.

PER SERVING: 51 cal., 2 g total fat (0 g sat. fat), 18 mg chol., 232 mg sodium, 4 g carb. (1 g fiber, 1 g sugars), 4 g pro. Exchanges: 0.5 medium-fat meat. Carb choices: 0.

Grilled Shrimp with Ginger Wasabi Soup Shooters

Coconut-Crusted Tuna Bites with Mango-Lime Sauce

Use kitchen scissors to snip the mango in the chutney into small pieces.

SERVINGS 8 (2 skewers and 1 tablespoon sauce each)

CARB. PER SERVING 17 g

- 2 5- to 6-ounce fresh or frozen tuna steaks, cut 1 to 1½ inches thick
- ¼ cup reduced-fat unsweetened coconut milk
- ½ teaspoon ground ginger
- ¼ teaspoon salt
- ¼ teaspoon cayenne pepper (optional)
- ½ cup whole wheat or white panko (Japanese-style bread crumbs)
- ⅓ cup flaked coconut
- ¼ cup very finely chopped almonds
- ⅓ cup mango chutney, finely snipped
- 2 tablespoons mango nectar
- 1 tablespoon lime juice
- ½ teaspoon grated fresh ginger or ⅛ teaspoon ground ginger
- 2 tablespoons snipped fresh mint or cilantro

1. Thaw fish, if frozen. Rinse fish; pat dry. Cut each fish steak into eight equal cubes. Place fish cubes in a resealable plastic bag set in a medium bowl. Set aside.

2. In a small bowl combine coconut milk, ½ teaspoon ground ginger, salt, and, if desired, cayenne pepper. Pour over fish in bag; seal bag and turn to coat fish. Marinate in the refrigerator for 30 to 60 minutes, turning bag occasionally.

3. Preheat oven to 450°F. Meanwhile, in a shallow dish combine panko, coconut, and almonds. Drain fish, discarding marinade. Dip fish cubes into panko mixture, turning to coat well. Thread one fish cube onto each of sixteen 6- to 8-inch metal or wooden skewers. Place skewers on a lightly greased baking pan. Lightly coat fish cubes with *nonstick cooking spray*; turn and lightly coat the other sides.

4. Bake for 6 to 8 minutes or until panko mixture is browned and fish is slightly pink in the centers.

5. Meanwhile, in a small saucepan combine the mango chutney, mango nectar, lime juice, and ginger. Heat and stir over medium-low heat until heated through. Remove from heat; stir in mint. Serve sauce with tuna skewers.

PER SERVING: 157 cal., 5 g total fat (2 g sat. fat), 13 mg chol., 221 mg sodium, 17 g carb. (1 g fiber, 8 g sugars), 10 g pro. Exchanges: 1 starch, 1 lean meat, 0.5 fat. Carb choices: 1.

Mini Gruyère Puffs

Baking at two different temperatures creates puffs that are hollow on the inside and slightly crispy on the outside.

SERVINGS 20 (1 puff each)

CARB. PER SERVING 2 g

- ½ cup water
- ¼ cup butter
- ½ teaspoon dried basil, crushed
- ¼ teaspoon garlic salt
  Dash cayenne pepper
- ½ cup flour
- 2 eggs
- 2 ounces Gruyère cheese or Swiss cheese, shredded (½ cup)
- 2 tablespoons grated Parmesan cheese

1. Preheat oven to 450°F. Grease a baking sheet; set aside. In a small saucepan combine the water, butter, basil, garlic salt, and cayenne pepper. Bring to boiling over medium heat, stirring to melt butter. Immediately add flour all at once, stirring vigorously. Cook and stir until mixture forms a ball that doesn't separate. Remove from heat. Cool for 5 minutes.

2. Add eggs, one at a time, to mixture in saucepan, beating with a spoon after each addition until smooth. Stir in shredded Gruyère cheese.

3. Drop dough by rounded teaspoons about 2 inches apart onto the prepared baking sheet. Or pipe the dough using a pastry bag fitted with a ½-inch open-star tip; spoon dough into bag and pipe small mounds of dough about 2 inches apart onto the prepared baking sheet. Sprinkle with Parmesan cheese.

4. Bake for 10 minutes. Reduce oven temperature to 375°F. Bake for 10 to 12 minutes more or until puffed and golden. Serve warm.

MAKE-AHEAD DIRECTIONS: Transfer baked puffs to a wire rack to cool completely. Place puffs in an airtight container; cover. Freeze for up to 1 month. Thaw overnight in the refrigerator. Preheat oven to 325°F. Arrange puffs on a baking sheet. Bake for 8 to 10 minutes or until warm.

PER SERVING: 53 cal., 4 g total fat (2 g sat. fat), 28 mg chol., 57 mg sodium, 2 g carb. (0 g fiber, 0 g sugars), 2 g pro. Exchanges: 0.5 fat. Carb choices: 0.

Mini Gruyère Puffs

Eggplant Bruschetta

When roasted, eggplant acquires a subtly sweet flavor and silky-smooth texture that tastes amazing in this easy-to-make mixture to serve on baguette slices.

SERVINGS 20 (3 tablespoons dip and 2 slices French bread each)

CARB. PER SERVING 11 g

2 eggplants or 2 pounds baby eggplants (about 6)
2 garlic bulbs
½ cup olive oil
1 teaspoon salt
1½ cups coarsely chopped red sweet peppers (4 medium)
3 tablespoons lemon juice
¼ cup snipped fresh Italian (flat-leaf) parsley
2 tablespoons snipped fresh oregano
   Fresh oregano leaves (optional)
8 ounces baguette-style French bread,
   thinly sliced and toasted (about 40 slices)

1. Preheat oven to 400°F. Wash eggplants; trim ends and cut into ½- to 1-inch pieces. Transfer eggplant to two 15×10×1-inch baking pans* or shallow roasting pans. Using a sharp knife, cut off the top ½ inch from garlic bulbs to expose individual cloves. Leaving garlic bulbs whole, remove any of the loose, papery outer layers. Place garlic bulbs on a 12-inch square of heavy foil; drizzle with 1 tablespoon of the olive oil. Wrap foil up around the garlic bulbs to completely enclose.

2. Drizzle ¼ cup of the remaining olive oil over eggplant

Eggplant Bruschetta

in each pan and sprinkle half of the salt over eggplant in each pan; toss to coat. Place eggplant and garlic packet in oven, placing pans on separate oven racks. Roast for 20 minutes, stirring once. Add half of the sweet peppers to each pan with eggplant; stir to combine. Roast about 20 minutes more or until vegetables are tender, stirring once. Remove pans and garlic from oven and cool.

3. Transfer eggplant and peppers to a large glass or nonreactive bowl. Squeeze garlic pulp from individual cloves into a small bowl; using the back of a spoon, mash garlic pulp. Add the remaining 3 tablespoons olive oil and the lemon juice to garlic; whisk to combine. Add garlic mixture, parsley, and snipped oregano to eggplant mixture; toss to combine.

4. If desired, garnish with oregano leaves. Serve with French bread.

*TEST KITCHEN TIP: If you do not have two 15×10×1-inch baking pans, use one 15×10×1-inch baking pan and one 13×9×2-inch baking pan.

MAKE-AHEAD DIRECTIONS: You can toast the baguette slices a day ahead, cool, and place in a resealable plastic bag. When ready to serve, preheat oven to 400°F. Place baguette slices on a baking sheet and crisp in the oven for 5 minutes. After combining the dip in Step 3, cover with plastic wrap; chill for up to 3 days. Let stand at room temperature for 30 minutes before serving. (Or transfer mixture to a freezer container. Cover and freeze for up to 3 months. Thaw overnight in the refrigerator. Let stand at room temperature for 30 minutes before serving.)

PER SERVING: 99 cal., 6 g total fat (1 g sat. fat), 0 mg chol., 177 mg sodium, 11 g carb. (2 g fiber, 2 g sugars), 2 g pro. Exchanges: 1 starch, 1 fat. Carb choices: 1.

Toasted Pumpkin Seeds

Toasted Pumpkin Seeds

Keep some of these crunchy seeds on hand to use as a topper for salads.

SERVINGS 24 (2 tablespoons each)
CARB. PER SERVING 3 g or 2 g

Nonstick cooking spray
1 egg white
2 tablespoons sugar*
1 tablespoon canola oil
1 teaspoon finely shredded lemon peel
¼ teaspoon kosher salt
¼ teaspoon ground cinnamon
¼ teaspoon ground nutmeg
¼ teaspoon ground allspice
¼ teaspoon chili powder
¼ teaspoon cayenne pepper
¼ teaspoon black pepper
2 cups unsalted pumpkin seeds (pepitas)

1. Preheat oven to 325°F. Line a baking sheet with parchment paper or foil; lightly coat paper or foil with cooking spray. Set aside.

2. In a medium bowl combine egg white, sugar, oil, lemon peel, salt, cinnamon, nutmeg, allspice, chili powder, cayenne pepper, and black pepper; whisk until egg white is frothy and sugar is nearly dissolved. Add pumpkin seeds; toss gently to coat.

3. Spread pumpkin seeds evenly on the prepared baking sheet. Bake for 20 to 25 minutes or until pumpkin seeds are dry and crisp. Cool completely; break into pieces.

*SUGAR SUBSTITUTES: Choose from Splenda Granular or Sweet'N Low bulk or packets. Follow package directions to use product amount equivalent to 2 tablespoons sugar.

PER SERVING: 72 cal., 6 g total fat (1 g sat. fat), 0 mg chol., 25 mg sodium, 3 g carb. (0 g fiber, 1 g sugars), 3 g pro. Exchanges: 1 fat. Carb choices: 0.
PER SERVING WITH SUBSTITUTE: Same as above, except 69 cal., 2 g carb. (0 g sugars).

quick tip

Serve these fresh and tasty veggies
with a spoon or let your guests pluck out what they
want using decorative wooden or plastic picks.

Pumpkin Pesto

*Pop the extra canned pumpkin puree in an airtight
freezer container and freeze it for another use.*

SERVINGS 14 (2 tablespoons pesto and
2 baguette slices each)
CARB. PER SERVING 19 g

1	cup packed fresh basil leaves
1	cup packed fresh parsley leaves
1	cup canned pumpkin
⅓	cup chopped walnuts, toasted
¼	cup finely shredded Parmesan cheese (1 ounce)
2	tablespoons honey
3	cloves garlic, minced
1	teaspoon lemon juice
¼	teaspoon salt
¼	teaspoon black pepper
2	tablespoons olive oil
	Finely shredded Parmesan cheese (optional)
14	ounces toasted baguette slices (about 28 thin slices), assorted crackers, and/or pita wedges

1. In a food processor combine basil, parsley, pumpkin, walnuts, the ¼ cup Parmesan cheese, honey, garlic, lemon juice, salt, and pepper. Cover and process with several on/off pulses until coarsely chopped. With processor running, add oil in a thin, steady stream. Stop processor and scrape down sides of bowl as needed.
2. Transfer pesto to a serving bowl. If desired, sprinkle with additional Parmesan cheese. Serve with toasted baguette slices, crackers, and/or pita wedges.
MAKE-AHEAD DIRECTIONS: Prepare as directed through Step 1. Transfer to a serving bowl. Cover and chill for up to 24 hours. If desired, sprinkle with additional Parmesan cheese. Serve as above.
PER SERVING: 136 cal., 5 g total fat (1 g sat. fat), 1 mg chol., 235 mg sodium, 19 g carb. (2 g fiber, 3 g sugars), 4 g pro. Exchanges: 1 starch, 1 fat. Carb choices: 1.

Herbed Dijon-Marinated Veggies

*Cremini mushrooms, also known as brown mushrooms,
have a slightly woodsy flavor. If they are not available,
substitute the traditional white button mushrooms.*

SERVINGS 8 (½ cup each)
CARB. PER SERVING 3 g

3	tablespoons dry white wine or reduced-sodium chicken broth
2	tablespoons snipped fresh basil
1	tablespoon snipped fresh parsley
1	tablespoon olive oil
2	teaspoons snipped fresh thyme or oregano or ½ teaspoon dried thyme or oregano, crushed
2	teaspoons Dijon-style mustard
1	clove garlic, minced
¼	teaspoon salt
1½	cups fresh small cremini mushrooms
1	cup grape tomatoes or cherry tomatoes
1	cup yellow and/or orange sweet pepper strips
1	small zucchini, quartered lengthwise and cut into 1-inch pieces (about 1 cup)

1. In a large bowl whisk together wine, basil, parsley, oil, thyme, mustard, garlic, and salt. Add mushrooms, tomatoes, sweet pepper, and zucchini; toss gently to coat.
2. Cover and marinate vegetables at room temperature for 30 to 60 minutes, stirring occasionally.
3. To serve, use a slotted spoon to transfer vegetables to a serving bowl.
MAKE-AHEAD DIRECTIONS: Prepare vegetables as directed in Step 1. Cover and marinate in the refrigerator for 4 to 24 hours, stirring once or twice. Let stand at room temperature for 30 to 60 minutes before serving.
PER SERVING: 38 cal., 2 g total fat (0 g sat. fat), 0 mg chol., 107 mg sodium, 3 g carb. (1 g fiber, 2 g sugars), 1 g pro. Exchanges: 0.5 vegetable, 0.5 fat. Carb choices: 0.

Herbed Dijon-Marinated Veggies

Avocado
Cream
Cheese

Party Pointers

Choosing a menu for an appetizer party can seem a bit daunting. Follow these tips to put a palate-pleasing spread on the table next time you are the host.

1. **Start** by selecting a couple recipes to serve cold and a recipe or two to serve warm.

2. **Think** about the flavor, color, and texture of foods and pick those that complement each other.

3. **Fill** in the food spread with an array of colorful vegetable crudités and fruits.

4. **Plan** at least one serving of each recipe per person if the appetizers are the only course being served.

5. **Select** a beverage recipe that offers an alcoholic and nonalcoholic versions. Or purchase an assortment of beverages.

Honey-Sesame
Snack Mix

Mushroom-
Stuffed Tomatoes
with Balsamic

Citrus Martini

Skewered Scallops
with Honey-
Grapefruit Drizzle

*Recipes on
pages 42–43*

Avocado Cream Cheese Dip

An avocado is ripe and ready when it feels slightly soft when squeezed. Pictured on page 40.
SERVINGS 6 (2½ tablespoons dip and 1 cup vegetable dippers each)
CARB. PER SERVING 9 g

  1 ripe medium avocado, halved, seeded, and peeled
  ¼ cup low-fat buttermilk
  3 tablespoons reduced-fat whipped cream cheese spread
  1 tablespoon lime juice
  2 cloves garlic
  ½ teaspoon salt
  ⅛ teaspoon cayenne pepper
     Dash cayenne pepper
  6 cups fresh vegetable dippers, such as red sweet pepper strips, cucumber slices, celery sticks, Belgian endive leaves, and/or fresh cauliflower florets

1. Set aside one-fourth of the avocado. In a blender or food processor combine the remaining three-fourths of the avocado, the buttermilk, cream cheese, lime juice, garlic, salt, and the ⅛ teaspoon cayenne pepper. Cover and blend or process until smooth. Coarsely chop the reserved avocado; stir into pureed mixture. Cover and chill for 30 minutes to 24 hours.
2. Spoon into a serving bowl; sprinkle with the dash cayenne pepper. Serve with fresh vegetable dippers.
PER SERVING: 85 cal., 5 g total fat (1 g sat. fat), 4 mg chol., 254 mg sodium, 9 g carb. (4 g fiber, 4 g sugars), 2 g pro. Exchanges: 1 vegetable, 1 fat. Carb choices: 0.5.

Skewered Scallops with Honey-Grapefruit Drizzle

No skewers? Place the scallops directly onto the rack of a broiler pan and use a metal spatula to turn them halfway through cooking. Pictured on page 40.
SERVINGS 8 (1 scallop, ¼ cup arugula, 2 tablespoons grapefruit, and about 2 teaspoons grapefruit drizzle each)
CARB. PER SERVING 8 g

  8 fresh or frozen sea scallops (about 12 ounces total)
  ⅛ teaspoon salt
  ⅛ teaspoon black pepper
  ¼ cup fresh grapefruit juice
  1 to 2 tablespoons honey
  1 tablespoon snipped fresh mint
  ½ teaspoon grated fresh ginger
     Nonstick cooking spray
  2 cups fresh baby arugula or sliced fresh baby spinach
  1 cup fresh grapefruit sections, coarsely chopped

1. Thaw scallops, if frozen. Rinse scallops and pat dry with paper towels. Thread 1 scallop on the end of each of eight 6- to 8-inch skewers. Sprinkle scallops with the salt and pepper. Set aside.
2. In a small bowl combine grapefruit juice, honey, mint, and ginger. Set aside. Coat an unheated nonstick indoor grill pan with cooking spray. Heat pan over medium-high heat. Add skewered scallops. Reduce heat to medium. Cook for 4 to 6 minutes or until scallops are opaque, turning once halfway through cooking. (Or to broil the scallops, coat the unheated rack of a broiler pan with cooking spray. Place skewered scallops on the rack. Broil 3 to 4 inches from the heat for 4 to 6 minutes or until scallops are opaque, turning once halfway through cooking.)
3. To serve, arrange arugula on a platter. Top with coarsely chopped grapefruit and scallops. Stir the grapefruit juice mixture to make sure honey is mixed in and drizzle evenly over the scallops.
PER SERVING: 54 cal., 0 g total fat, 10 mg chol., 205 mg sodium, 8 g carb. (1 g fiber, 5 g sugars), 6 g pro. Exchanges: 0.5 carb., 1 lean meat. Carb choices: 0.5.

Honey-Sesame Snack Mix

For a mix that packs a little punch, use the wasabi-flavored dried peas and the horseradish. Pictured on page 41.
SERVINGS 16 (½ cup each)
CARB. PER SERVING 13 g

  2 cups rice square cereal
  2 cups puffed wheat cereal
  1½ cups lightly salted brown rice crisps or chips*
  1½ cups sea-salt flavored thin almond crackers or sea salt-flavored baked almond chips*
  ½ cup pumpkin seeds (pepitas) or wasabi-flavored dried peas
  ½ cup unsalted soy nuts
  2 tablespoons toasted sesame oil
  2 tablespoons honey
  2 tablespoons lemon juice
  2 tablespoons reduced-sodium soy sauce
  1 tablespoon sesame seeds
  2 teaspoons prepared horseradish (optional)

1. Preheat oven to 300°F. In a shallow baking pan combine rice cereal, wheat cereal, rice crackers, almond crackers, pumpkin seeds, and soy nuts. In a small saucepan stir together oil, honey, lemon juice, soy sauce, sesame seeds, and, if desired, horseradish. Cook and stir just until boiling. Remove from heat. Pour over cereal mixture, tossing just until coated. Spread cereal mixture in an even layer.

2. Bake, uncovered, for 20 to 25 minutes or until mixture is lightly toasted and crisp, stirring twice. Remove from oven. Immediately turn out onto a large piece of foil; cool completely. Store in an airtight container at room temperature for up to 2 days or freeze for up to 2 weeks.

*TEST KITCHEN TIP: We used Riceworks Gourmet Brown Rice Crisps and Blue Diamond Almond Nut-Thins or Blue Diamond Baked Nut Chips.

PER SERVING: 117 cal., 6 g total fat (1 g sat. fat), 0 mg chol., 109 mg sodium, 13 g carb. (1 g fiber, 3 g sugars), 4 g pro. Exchanges: 1 starch, 1 fat. Carb choices: 1.

Citrus Martini

Party-perfect! These fruity cocktails taste merry and bright with or without the alcohol. Pictured on page 41.
SERVINGS 4 (4 ounces each [without vodka])
CARB. PER SERVING 22 g

- ¾ cup reduced-calorie orange juice
- ¾ cup lime juice
- ½ cup vodka (optional)
- ¼ cup agave nectar or honey
  Ice cubes
- 4 ¼-inch-thick slices lime

1. In a cocktail shaker combine 6 tablespoons of the orange juice, 6 tablespoons of the lime juice, ¼ cup of the vodka (if using), and 2 tablespoons of the agave nectar. Add ¾ cup ice cubes. Cover and shake very well. Strain liquid into two chilled martini glasses. Discard ice cubes from the cocktail shaker. Repeat with remaining orange juice, lime juice, vodka (if using), agave, and ¾ cup fresh ice cubes. Garnish each martini with a lime slice.

PER SERVING: 81 cal., 0 g total fat, 0 mg chol., 3 mg sodium, 22 g carb. (1 g fiber, 18 g sugars), 0 g pro. Exchanges: 1.5 carb. Carb choices: 1.5.

Mushroom-Stuffed Tomatoes with Balsamic

Use a small saucepan to heat the balsamic vinegar and reduce it to 2 tablespoons. If the pan is larger, it may reduce too quickly and burn. Pictured on page 41.
SERVINGS 8 (2 stuffed tomato halves and about 1 teaspoon balsamic vinegar each)
CARB. PER SERVING 10 g

- 8 large roma tomatoes
  Nonstick cooking spray
- ½ cup good-quality balsamic vinegar
- 2 cups fresh mushrooms, chopped, such as cremini, button, or stemmed shiitake
- 2 medium shallots, chopped (¼ cup)
- 1 tablespoon olive oil
- 2 cloves garlic, minced
- 2 teaspoons snipped fresh thyme or ½ teaspoon dried thyme, crushed
- ¼ teaspoon salt
- ⅛ teaspoon black pepper
- ¼ cup fine dry whole wheat or white bread crumbs
- ¼ cup finely shredded Parmesan cheese (1 ounce)

1. Cut tomatoes in half crosswise. Cut a thin slice from the uncut ends of each tomato half so the halves will stand upright. Using a melon baller or small spoon, scoop out the core, seeds, and pulp, leaving about a ¼-inch-thick shell. Discard core, seeds, and pulp. Place tomatoes, hollowed-out sides down, on paper towels to drain.

2. Preheat oven to 375°F. Line a 15×10×1-inch baking pan with foil; coat foil with cooking spray; set aside. In a small saucepan bring vinegar to boiling. Boil gently, uncovered, for 10 to 15 minutes or until vinegar is slightly thickened and reduced to 2 tablespoons total (vinegar will continue to thicken as it cools).

3. Meanwhile, in a large skillet cook mushrooms and shallots in hot oil over medium heat for 5 to 8 minutes or until tender and lightly browned, stirring occasionally. Stir in garlic, thyme, salt, and pepper; cook for 30 seconds more. Remove from heat.

4. Place tomato halves, ends down, in prepared baking pan. Spoon mushroom mixture evenly into tomato shells. In a small bowl combine bread crumbs and cheese. Sprinkle evenly on top of stuffed tomatoes.

5. Bake tomatoes about 10 minutes or until just heated and crumb mixture is lightly browned. Transfer tomatoes to a platter and serve with reduced balsamic vinegar.

PER SERVING: 79 cal., 3 g total fat (1 g sat. fat), 2 mg chol., 159 mg sodium, 10 g carb. (2 g fiber, 6 g sugars), 3 g pro. Exchanges: 1 vegetable, 0.5 starch, 0.5 fat. Carb choices: 0.5.

Apple-Pancetta
Stuffed Belgian Endive

Mini Grilled Mozzarella Sandwiches

When hungry appetites await, pull these toasty finger sandwiches off the press for a fast feast.

SERVINGS 8 (1 mini sandwich each)
CARB. PER SERVING 11 g

- 16 slices whole grain party bread
- 8 2-inch squares or circles ¼-inch-thick fresh mozzarella cheese* (about 4 ounces)
- 1 teaspoon snipped fresh rosemary
- 8 2-inch squares drained and patted dry bottled roasted red sweet peppers
  Olive oil nonstick cooking spray

1. To assemble sandwiches, place half of the bread slices on a tray. Top with the mozzarella cheese pieces. Sprinkle evenly with the rosemary. Top with pepper pieces. Top with remaining bread slices. Coat the tops and bottoms of the sandwiches with cooking spray.
2. Heat a panini press according to manufacturer's directions or heat an indoor grill pan over medium heat. Place assembled sandwiches in panini press if using. Close the lid and cook for 3 minutes or until bread is toasted and cheese is just melted. (If using grill pan, place assembled sandwiches on the preheated grill. Weight sandwiches down with a large skillet. Cook for 2 minutes or until bottoms are browned. Carefully remove the top skillet and turn the sandwiches. Weight down with the skillet and cook for 2 minutes more or until bottoms are browned and cheese is just melted.) Serve sandwiches immediately.
*TEST KITCHEN TIP: For a simple way to cut the squares of mozzarella cheese, purchase a package of unwrap-and-roll-style fresh mozzarella cheese. Unwrap the cheese onto a cutting board and use a sharp knife or pizza cutter to cut 2-inch squares of cheese.
PER SERVING: 98 cal., 4 g total fat (2 g sat. fat), 10 mg chol., 163 mg sodium, 11 g carb. (2 g fiber, 1 g sugars), 5 g pro. Exchanges: 1 starch, 0.5 medium-fat meat. Carb choices: 1.

Apple-Pancetta-Stuffed Belgian Endive

Cut the root end from the endive and then peel apart each of the canoe-shape leaves.

SERVINGS 6 (2 filled leaves each)
CARB. PER SERVING 3 g

- 2 ounces pancetta, chopped
- 3 tablespoons chopped celery
- 3 tablespoons chopped shallot
- ⅓ cup chopped cooking apple, such as Gala, Jonathan, or Cortland
- 12 Belgian endive leaves (about 1 large head)
- 1 ounce semisoft goat cheese (chèvre), crumbled
  Snipped fresh chives

1. In a medium skillet cook pancetta, celery, and shallot over medium heat for 5 minutes, stirring occasionally. Add chopped apple. Cook for 3 to 4 minutes more or until apple is just tender and pancetta is browned and just crisp. Remove from heat and cool for 5 minutes.
2. Spoon about 2 teaspoons of the apple mixture into the cup of each Belgian endive leaf. Top apple mixture evenly with goat cheese and garnish with chives.
PER SERVING: 62 cal., 4 g total fat (2 g sat. fat), 10 mg chol., 202 mg sodium, 3 g carb. (0 g fiber, 2 g sugars), 3 g pro. Exchanges: 1 fat. Carb choices: 0.

Fruit Chutney with Spiced Chips

If you wish, make and bake the crispy sugared chips the day ahead and store them in an airtight container.

SERVINGS 24 (2½ tablespoons chutney, 3 chips, and 1 teaspoon cheese each)

CARB. PER SERVING 21 g or 18 g

- 2 large apples, such as Braeburn, cored and cut into 1-inch pieces
- 2 large pears, such as Anjou, cored and cut into 1-inch pieces
- 1 small sweet onion, chopped
- 1 cup fresh or frozen whole cranberries, thawed
- ⅓ cup packed brown sugar*
- ¼ cup balsamic vinegar
- 1 teaspoon ground cinnamon
- 1 teaspoon ground ginger
- ⅛ teaspoon salt
- 1 tablespoon cornstarch
- 2 tablespoons cold water
- 1 recipe Spiced Chips
- 4 ounces goat cheese (chèvre), crumbled

1. For fruit chutney, in a 3½- or 4-quart slow cooker combine apples, pears, onion, cranberries. brown sugar, vinegar, cinnamon, ginger, and salt.

2. Cover and cook on high-heat setting for 1 hour. In a small bowl combine cornstarch and the cold water; stir into cooker. Cover and cook on high-heat setting for 1 hour more.

3. Serve chutney warm or at room temperature with Spiced Chips. Top each serving with crumbled goat cheese.

SPICED CHIPS: Preheat oven to 400°F. Using a pizza wheel, cut 9 whole wheat tortillas into eight equal wedges each. Place tortilla wedges in a single layer on baking sheets. Lightly coat wedges with nonstick cooking spray. Mix together ½ teaspoon granulated sugar and ¼ teaspoon ground coriander. Sprinkle evenly over tortilla wedges. Bake for 10 minutes, turning once halfway through baking.

*SUGAR SUBSTITUTES: Choose from Sweet'N Low Brown or Sugar Twin Granulated Brown. Follow package directions to use product amount equivalent to ⅓ cup brown sugar.

PER SERVING: 114 cal., 2 g total fat (1 g sat. fat), 4 mg chol., 182 mg sodium, 21 g carb. (2 g fiber, 9 g sugars), 3 g pro. Exchanges: 1 starch, 0.5 carb., 0.5 fat. Carb choices: 1.5.

Fruit Chutney with Spiced Chips

PER SERVING WITH SUBSTITUTE: Same as above, except 102 cal., 181 mg sodium, 18 g carb. (7 g sugars). Exchanges: 0 carb. Carb choices: 1.

Hot Wing Dip

quick tip
Keep an assortment of
vegetables on hand to create
dippers for an impromptu
party or informal gathering.

Spicy Tomato Dip

Hot Wing Dip

Leave this creamy dip in the cooker or transfer it to a warm bowl to serve.

SERVINGS 10 (2 tablespoons dip and 4 celery pieces each)

CARB. PER SERVING 3 g

8 ounces reduced-fat cream cheese (Neufchâtel), cut up
¼ to ½ cup bottled Buffalo wing sauce
1½ tablespoons bottled reduced-calorie blue cheese salad dressing
1 cup chopped cooked chicken breast
1 stalk celery, finely chopped (½ cup)
1 fresh jalapeño chile pepper, seeded and minced*
20 stalks celery, halved crosswise
Fresh jalapeño chile pepper, seeded and sliced* (optional)

1. In a 1½-quart slow cooker combine cream cheese, wing sauce, dressing, chicken, finely chopped celery, and minced jalapeño pepper.

2. Cover and cook on low-heat setting for 3 to 4 hours. If no heat setting is available, cook for 3 hours. Serve with celery pieces. If desired, garnish dip with a few slices of jalapeño chile pepper.

***TEST KITCHEN TIP:** Because chile peppers contain volatile oils that can burn your skin and eyes, avoid direct contact with them as much as possible. When working with chile peppers, wear plastic or rubber gloves. If your bare hands do touch the peppers, wash your hands and nails well with soap and warm water.

PER SERVING: 99 cal., 7 g total fat (3 g sat. fat), 29 mg chol., 168 mg sodium, 3 g carb. (1 g fiber, 2 g sugars), 7 g pro. Exchanges: 1 vegetable, 1 high-fat meat. Carb choices: 0.

Spicy Tomato Dip

If you have any of this pizza fondue-style dip left over, toss it with hot cooked whole grain pasta for a quick lunch.

SERVINGS 10 (¼ cup dip and ½ cup vegetables each)

CARB. PER SERVING 15 g

1 15-ounce can no-salt-added tomato sauce
1 14.5-ounce can no-salt-added diced tomatoes, drained
1 medium onion, finely chopped (½ cup)
½ 6-ounce can no-salt-added tomato paste (⅓ cup)
1½ teaspoons dried oregano, crushed
1½ teaspoons dried basil, crushed
2 cloves garlic, minced

1 teaspoon sugar*
⅛ teaspoon cayenne pepper
3 tablespoons chopped pitted ripe olives
5 cups assorted vegetable dippers, such as baby carrots, red sweet pepper slices, zucchini slices, and/or fresh mushrooms

1. In a 1½- or 2-quart slow cooker stir together tomato sauce, tomatoes, onion, tomato paste, oregano, basil, garlic, sugar, and cayenne pepper.

2. Cover and cook on low-heat setting for 5 to 6 hours. If no heat setting is available, cook for 5 to 6 hours.

3. Stir in olives. Serve warm with vegetable dippers.

***SUGAR SUBSTITUTES:** Choose from Splenda Granular or Sweet'N Low bulk or packets. Follow package directions to use product amount equivalent to 1 teaspoon sugar

PER SERVING: 68 cal., 1 g total fat (0 g sat. fat), 0 mg chol., 94 mg sodium, 15 g carb. (4 g fiber, 8 g sugars), 2 g pro. Exchanges: 2 vegetable. Carb choices: 1.

PER SERVING WITH SUBSTITUTE: Same as above, except 66 cal.

Avocado and Pumpkin Salsa

Canned pumpkin puree creates a salsa that is similar in texture to a chunky guacamole.

SERVINGS 8 (¼ cup salsa and 1 ounce tortilla chips each)

CARB. PER SERVING 27 g

1 cup canned pumpkin
1 large tomato, seeded and chopped
1 avocado, halved, seeded, peeled, and chopped
½ small onion, chopped
1 tablespoon snipped fresh cilantro
1 tablespoon lime juice or lemon juice
1 clove garlic, minced
Bottled hot pepper sauce
Dash salt
Fresh cilantro leaves (optional)
8 ounces baked tortilla chips

1. In a medium bowl combine pumpkin, tomato, avocado, onion, snipped cilantro, lime juice, garlic, hot pepper sauce, and salt. If desired, garnish with cilantro leaves. Serve salsa with baked tortilla chips.

PER SERVING: 165 cal., 6 g total fat (1 g sat. fat), 0 mg chol., 148 mg sodium, 27 g carb. (4 g fiber, 2 g sugars), 3 g pro. Exchanges: 0.5 vegetable, 1.5 starch, 1 fat. Carb choices: 2.

main-dish masterpieces

Ginger-Orange-Glazed
Turkey Breasts

Selecting the
Scenterpiece food

is a first step for

planning the holiday

meal. A golden roasted

bird, juicy beef roast,

and flaky fish dish

make perfect fancy

fare. And a pot of soup,

bubbly casserole, and

sizzling fondue are just

right casual eats. Make

one of these new, light

and tasty dishes your

holiday star.

Ginger-Orange-Glazed Turkey Breasts

With slivers of garlic and chile pepper tucked into each turkey breast, plus a sweet, gingery glaze, this holiday entrée is bursting with fantastic flavors from all angles.

SERVINGS 8 (5 ounces cooked turkey each)
CARB. PER SERVING 17 g

- 2 1½-pound skinless, boneless turkey breasts
- 2 cloves garlic, cut into 12 slivers total
- 1 to 2 small fresh red chile peppers, cut into 12 pieces (see tip, page 75)
- ¼ cup orange juice
- ¼ cup olive oil
- 1 cup low-sugar orange marmalade
- ½ cup finely chopped green onions (4)
- ½ cup orange juice
- 1 tablespoon grated fresh ginger
- 1 clove garlic, minced
- 1 tablespoon orange liqueur or orange juice
- 1 teaspoon black pepper
- ½ teaspoon salt
  Sliced green onion, chopped chile peppers (see tip, page 75), and/or finely shredded orange peel (optional)

1. Using a sharp paring knife, cut 12 slits into the top of each turkey breast. Tuck a garlic sliver or a chile pepper piece into each slit, alternating garlic and chile pepper. Place turkey breasts side by side in a shallow glass baking dish.

2. In a small bowl combine the ¼ cup orange juice and the olive oil; pour over turkey. Cover; marinate in the refrigerator for 12 to 24 hours, turning occasionally.

3. For glaze, in a small saucepan combine marmalade, green onions, the ½ cup orange juice, the ginger, and minced garlic. Bring to boiling; reduce heat. Simmer, uncovered, 5 minutes. Remove from heat; stir in liqueur.

4. Preheat oven to 350°F. Remove turkey breasts from marinade; discard marinade. Arrange turkey breasts on a rack in a large roasting pan. Spoon some of the glaze over turkey breasts, being careful not to let the spoon touch the uncooked turkey. Sprinkle with the black pepper and salt.

5. Roast for 45 to 50 minutes or until an instant-read thermometer inserted into the thickest part of each turkey breast registers 160°F, spooning some of the remaining glaze over breasts every 15 minutes of roasting, each time being careful not to let the spoon touch the uncooked turkey. Let turkey stand for 5 minutes before slicing. If desired, garnish with additional sliced green onion, chopped chile peppers, and/or finely shredded orange peel.

PER SERVING: 320 cal., 8 g total fat (1 g sat. fat), 105 mg chol., 231 mg sodium, 17 g carb. (0 g fiber, 12 g sugars), 42 g pro. Exchanges: 1 carb., 6 lean meat. Carb choices: 1.

Turkey and Sweet Potato Shepherd's Pies

Turkey and sweet potatoes make this casserole more nutritious than the classic shepherd's pie.

SERVINGS 4 (1 individual pie each)
CARB. PER SERVING 44 g

- 1½ pounds sweet potatoes, peeled and cut into 2-inch pieces
- 2 cloves garlic, halved
- ¼ cup fat-free milk
- 12 ounces uncooked ground turkey breast
- 1 medium onion, chopped (½ cup)
- 1 medium zucchini, coarsely chopped (1¼ cups)
- 2 medium carrots, chopped (1 cup)
- ½ cup frozen whole kernel corn
- ¼ cup water
- 1 8-ounce can no-salt-added tomato sauce
- 2 tablespoons Worcestershire sauce
- 2 teaspoons snipped fresh sage

1. Preheat oven to 375°F. In a medium saucepan cook sweet potatoes and garlic, covered, in enough boiling water to cover for 15 to 20 minutes or until tender; drain. Mash with a potato masher or beat with an electric mixer on low speed. Gradually add milk and ¼ teaspoon *salt*, mashing or beating to make potato mixture light and fluffy. Cover and keep warm.

2. Meanwhile, in a large skillet cook turkey and onion over medium heat until meat is browned, stirring to break up turkey as it cooks. Stir in zucchini, carrots, corn, and the water. Bring to boiling; reduce heat. Simmer, covered, 5 to 10 minutes or until vegetables are tender.

3. Add tomato sauce, Worcestershire sauce, sage, and ⅛ teaspoon *black pepper* to turkey mixture; heat through. Divide turkey mixture among four ungreased 10-ounce ramekins, spreading evenly. Spoon mashed sweet potato mixture in mounds onto turkey mixture.

4. Bake, uncovered, for 20 to 25 minutes or until heated through. If desired, garnish with *fresh sage leaves.*
PER SERVING: 283 cal., 1 g total fat (0 g sat. fat), 42 mg chol., 389 mg sodium, 44 g carb. (7 g fiber, 14 g sugars), 25 g pro. Exchanges: 1 vegetable, 2.5 starch, 2 lean meat. Carb choices: 2.5.

Roast Turkey with Arugula-Pesto Rub

Use your fingers to spread this tasty, saucelike rub onto the meat and over the skin.

SERVINGS 30 (4 ounces each)
CARB. PER SERVING 0 g

- 1 12- to 14-pound turkey
- ½ cup packed fresh arugula leaves
- 2 tablespoons snipped fresh basil
- 1 to 2 tablespoons grated Romano cheese
- 1 tablespoon finely chopped, toasted walnuts
- 1 tablespoon olive oil
- 1 clove garlic

1. Preheat oven to 325°F. Remove neck and giblets from turkey; discard. Rinse cavity of turkey; pat dry.

2. To prepare rub, in a blender or food processor combine arugula, basil, cheese, walnuts, olive oil, garlic, ½ teaspoon *salt*, and ¼ teaspoon *black pepper*. Cover and blend or process with several on/off turns until a paste forms, stopping several times to scrape the side.

3. To apply rub, slip your fingers between the skin and meat on the breast to loosen skin. Lift skin and spread the rub from front to back. If desired, rub any remaining mixture on the outside skin of the turkey or rub with vegetable oil. Skewer neck skin to back. Tie drumsticks together or to the tail with clean 100-percent-cotton kitchen string. Twist wing tips under back. Place turkey, breast side up, on a rack in a shallow roasting pan.

4. Insert an oven-going meat thermometer, not touching bone, into the center of an inside thigh muscle. Cover turkey loosely with foil. Roast for 2½ hours. Remove foil; cut band of skin or kitchen string between drumsticks. Continue roasting for 30 to 75 minutes more or until the meat thermometer registers 180°F and turkey is no longer pink (the juices should run clear and drumsticks should move easily in their sockets). Remove from oven. Cover; let stand for 15 to 20 minutes before carving. Transfer to a cutting board and carve.
PER SERVING: 186 cal., 6 g total fat (2 g sat. fat), 110 mg chol., 100 mg sodium, 0 g carb. (0 g fiber, 0 g sugars), 31 g pro. Exchanges: 4 lean meat. Carb choices: 0.

Turkey and Sweet Potato Shepherd's Pies

Roast Turkey with
Arugula-Pesto Rub

Thai Noodle Bowl

Thai Noodle Bowl

Look for rice noodles in the Asian food or organic or special diet section of the supermarket. They are gluten-free!

SERVINGS 4 (2 cups each)
CARB. PER SERVING 36 g

4	cups no-salt-added chicken broth
1½	tablespoons reduced-sodium soy sauce
2	cups small broccoli florets
2	cups thinly sliced carrots
1	cup bean sprouts
4	ounces banh pho (Vietnamese wide rice noodles)
12	ounces chopped cooked turkey or chicken breast
¼	cup sliced green onions (2)

1. In a 4-quart Dutch oven bring broth and soy sauce to boiling. Stir in broccoli, carrots, bean sprouts, noodles, and turkey. Return to boiling; reduce heat. Simmer, covered, 10 minutes or until vegetables and noodles are tender. Ladle into bowls; sprinkle with green onions.
PER SERVING: 295 cal., 1 g total fat (0 g sat. fat), 71 mg chol., 513 mg sodium, 36 g carb. (4 g fiber, 5 g sugars), 33 g pro. Exchanges: 1 vegetable, 2 starch, 3.5 lean meat. Carb choices: 2.5.

Goat Cheese Pizza

Cut the tomato and then place the slices on paper towels to absorb some of the juices.

SERVINGS 2 (½ pizza each)
CARB. PER SERVING 38 g

1	8-inch whole wheat Italian bread shell (such as Boboli)
1	teaspoon olive oil
1	cup fresh baby spinach leaves
1	medium roma tomato, sliced
2	ounces shredded cooked turkey or chicken breast
2	tablespoons thinly sliced red onion
¼	cup crumbled goat cheese (chèvre) (1 ounce)
2	tablespoons fresh basil leaves

1. Preheat oven to 450°F. Brush top of bread shell with olive oil. Top with spinach, tomato slices, turkey, red onion, and cheese. Place bread shell directly on a center oven rack. Bake for 8 to 10 minutes or until heated through. Garnish with basil leaves.
PER SERVING: 307 cal., 9 g total fat (4 g sat. fat), 35 mg chol., 452 mg sodium, 38 g carb. (7 g fiber, 5 g sugars), 21 g pro. Exchanges: 1 vegetable, 2 starch, 2 lean meat, 1 fat. Carb choices: 2.5.

quick tip

Pull any leftover turkey from the bone and use it in one of the easy-to-make recipes on pages 52–55. Each is full-flavored and family-friendly.

Sweet Potato Hash

*Evenly chop the sweet potato and the apple
so they take the same amount of time to cook.*

SERVINGS 2 (1½ cups each)

CARB. PER SERVING 33 g

- 2 teaspoons olive oil
- 1 cup peeled, chopped sweet potato (5 ounces)
- 1 medium apple, chopped (1⅓ cups)
- 6 ounces shredded cooked turkey or chicken breast
- ¼ cup reduced-sodium chicken broth
- 2 tablespoons dried cranberries
- Dash ground cinnamon
- 2 tablespoons chopped, toasted pecans

1. In a large nonstick skillet heat oil over medium-high heat. Add sweet potato. Cook, stirring frequently, for 3 minutes. Reduce heat to medium. Add apple, turkey, broth, cranberries, and cinnamon. Cook and stir about 7 minutes or until sweet potato and apple are tender and turkey is hot.

2. Divide between serving bowls; sprinkle with pecans.

PER SERVING: 332 cal., 10 g total fat (1 g sat. fat), 71 mg chol., 151 mg sodium, 33 g carb. (5 g fiber, 17 g sugars), 28 g pro. Exchanges: 1 fruit, 1 starch, 3 lean meat, 1 fat. Carb choices: 2.

Sweet Potato Hash

Goat
Cheese
Pizza

Quick Chili Bowl

Turkey Taco Salad

quick tip

If you don't have any leftover bird, roast or grill a turkey breast during the weekend, then use the meat to make quick weekday meals. Or divide the meat into portions and freeze some of it to use later.

Turkey-Cranberry Wrap

Chilled Rotini Salad

Quick Chili Bowl

In just 30 minutes you can have a pot of fresh-made chili ready to serve.

SERVINGS 4 (1⅓ cups each)
CARB. PER SERVING 28 g

2 14.5-ounce cans no-salt-added diced tomatoes, undrained
1 15-ounce can no-salt-added red kidney beans, drained and rinsed
8 ounces chopped cooked turkey or chicken breast
½ cup chopped green sweet pepper
½ cup chopped red onion
1½ teaspoons chili powder
¾ teaspoons ground cumin
½ teaspoon salt
¼ teaspoon black pepper

1. In a large saucepan combine tomatoes, beans, turkey, sweet pepper, red onion, chili powder, cumin, salt, and black pepper.
2. Bring mixture to boiling, stirring occasionally. Reduce heat and simmer, uncovered, for 20 to 30 minutes or until desired consistency. Ladle into bowls.
PER SERVING: 213 cal., 1 g total fat (0 g sat. fat), 47 mg chol., 432 mg sodium, 28 g carb. (12 g fiber, 8 g sugars), 26 g pro. Exchanges: 1.5 vegetable, 1 starch, 3 lean meat. Carb choices: 1.5.

Turkey Taco Salad

Feeding a family? Assemble as many of these single-serving salads as you need.

SERVINGS 1 (3 cups)
CARB. PER SERVING 32 g

1 ounce small round tortilla chips (about 24 chips)
2 cups torn romaine lettuce
¼ cup frozen whole kernel corn, thawed
3 ounces shredded cooked turkey or chicken breast
3 tablespoons shredded reduced-fat Mexican-style cheese blend
2 tablespoons bottled salsa

1. Place tortilla chips on a serving plate. Top with romaine, corn, turkey, cheese, and salsa.
PER SERVING: 376 cal., 12 g total fat (4 g sat. fat), 82 mg chol., 545 mg sodium, 32 g carb. (5 g fiber, 3 g sugars), 36 g pro. Exchanges: 1 vegetable, 1.5 starch, 4 lean meat, 1 fat. Carb choices: 2.

Chilled Rotini Salad

Divide this Italian-style pasta salad among airtight containers the night before. In the morning, pack with an ice pack for an easy take-along lunch.

SERVINGS 4 (1½ cups each)
CARB. PER SERVING 29 g

4 ounces dried whole grain or whole wheat rotini pasta (about 1½ cups)
12 ounces cubed cooked turkey or chicken breast
2 medium tomatoes, chopped (1 cup)
1 cup chopped green sweet pepper
½ cup light vinaigrette salad dressing
4 tablespoons shredded Parmesan cheese

1. Cook pasta according to package directions. Drain. In a large bowl toss together cooked pasta, turkey, tomato, sweet pepper, and vinaigrette. Cover and chill for 1 to 24 hours.
2. Divide salad among serving bowls. Top with Parmesan cheese.
PER SERVING: 284 cal., 4 g total fat (1 g sat. fat), 74 mg chol., 423 mg sodium, 29 g carb. (3 g fiber, 7 g sugars), 32 g pro. Exchanges: 1 vegetable, 1.5 starch, 3.5 lean meat. Carb choices: 2.

Turkey-Cranberry Wrap

If you have a whole wheat tortilla around, use it in place of the wrap.

SERVINGS 1 (1 wrap)
CARB. PER SERVING 34 g

1 oval light multigrain wrap
1½ tablespoons whipped reduced-fat cream cheese spread
1 cup torn romaine lettuce
3 ounces sliced cooked turkey or chicken breast meat
2 tablespoons whole cranberry sauce

1. Spread cream cheese over one side of wrap. Top with romaine, sliced turkey, and cranberry sauce. Roll wrap to enclose filling. If desired, cut in half to serve.
PER SERVING: 310 cal., 7 g total fat (3 g sat. fat), 82 mg chol., 431 mg sodium, 34 g carb. (11 g fiber, 14 g sugars), 36 g pro. Exchanges: 0.5 vegetable, 2 starch, 4 lean meat. Carb choices: 2.

Chicken and Duck Hunter Stew

You can make this stew with all chicken pieces. Substitute 12 skinned chicken thighs for the duck and add the browned thighs with the drumsticks in Step 2.

SERVINGS 12 (1 chicken drumstick, ⅔ cup stew, and ½ cup couscous each)

CARB. PER SERVING 31 g

12	chicken drumsticks (about 3 pounds), skinned
3	boneless duck breast halves, skinned and quartered
2	tablespoons olive oil
3	cups assorted sliced fresh mushrooms, such as cremini, shiitake, oyster, and/or button
2	medium onions, sliced
3	cloves garlic, minced
6	medium tomatoes, seeded and chopped
3	medium green sweet peppers, cut into 1-inch pieces
1½	cups dry Marsala wine or lower-sodium beef broth
1	6-ounce can no-salt-added tomato paste

¾ cup pitted Kalamata olives and/or green olives
2 tablespoons balsamic vinegar
½ teaspoon salt
¼ teaspoon black pepper
¼ cup snipped fresh oregano or marjoram
2 tablespoons snipped fresh rosemary
6 cups hot cooked Israeli couscous or couscous

1. In a 6-quart Dutch oven cook chicken drumsticks and duck, half at a time, in hot oil about 15 minutes or until lightly browned, turning to brown evenly. Remove poultry from Dutch oven, reserving drippings in the Dutch oven; set drumsticks aside. Cover and chill the duck portions while cooking vegetables and chicken.
2. Add mushrooms, onions, and garlic to drippings in Dutch oven. Cook and stir about 5 minutes or just until vegetables are tender. Return drumsticks to Dutch oven.
3. Meanwhile, in a large bowl combine tomatoes, sweet peppers, Marsala, tomato paste, olives, vinegar, salt, and black pepper. Pour over drumsticks in Dutch oven. Bring to boiling; reduce heat. Simmer, covered, for 20 minutes. Add duck. Return to boiling; reduce heat. Simmer, covered, for 25 to 30 minutes more or until poultry is tender.
4. Just before serving, stir in oregano and rosemary. Serve stew with couscous.
MAKE-AHEAD DIRECTIONS: Chill the stew quickly by placing the Dutch oven in a sink of ice water. Transfer stew to airtight containers and chill for up to 2 days. (Or transfer to freezer containers and freeze for up to 1 month.) To serve, return chilled stew to Dutch oven. Cook over medium heat for 35 to 40 minutes or just until bubbly (do not overcook or the duck may toughen). Or thaw frozen stew in refrigerator overnight. Return partially thawed stew to Dutch oven. Cook over medium-low heat until stew is completely thawed. Cook over medium heat for 35 to 40 minutes or just until bubbly.
PER SERVING: 390 cal., 12 g total fat (3 g sat. fat), 138 mg chol., 323 mg sodium, 31 g carb. (4 g fiber, 6 g sugars), 32 g pro. Exchanges: 2 starch, 1 vegetable, 3.5 lean meat, 1 fat. Carb choices: 2.

Apple-Glazed Chicken with Braised Spinach and Leeks

Lemon-accented apple jelly serves as a baste for the chicken during broiling and as a dressing for the warm spinach salad. You'll need a Dutch oven or large kettle to hold the fresh spinach while it cooks.
SERVINGS 4 (1 cup greens mixture and 1 chicken breast half each)
CARB. PER SERVING 39 g

⅓ cup apple jelly
2 tablespoons reduced-sodium soy sauce
1 tablespoon snipped fresh thyme or 1 teaspoon dried thyme, crushed
1 teaspoon finely shredded lemon peel
1 teaspoon grated fresh ginger
4 small skinless, boneless chicken breast halves (about 1 pound total)
Nonstick cooking spray
2 medium apples, peeled, cored, and coarsely chopped (1⅓ cups)
1 medium leek, trimmed, cleaned thoroughly, and sliced (white part only) or ⅓ cup chopped onion
2 cloves garlic, minced
1 10-ounce package prewashed spinach, stems removed (about 10 cups)
¼ teaspoon black pepper
⅛ teaspoon salt

1. For glaze, in a small saucepan heat apple jelly, soy sauce, thyme, lemon peel, and ginger just until jelly melts. Remove from heat. Reserve ¼ cup glaze.
2. Preheat broiler. Place chicken on the unheated rack of a broiler pan. Broil chicken 4 to 5 inches from the heat for 12 to 15 minutes or until chicken is tender and no longer pink, turning once and brushing with remaining glaze halfway through broiling.
3. Meanwhile, lightly coat an unheated 4-quart Dutch oven with cooking spray. Heat over medium heat. Add apples, leek, and garlic; cook for 3 minutes, stirring occasionally. Add the reserved ¼ cup glaze; heat to boiling. Add spinach; toss just until wilted. Sprinkle with pepper and salt.
4. To serve, slice each chicken breast half crosswise into six to eight pieces. Divide greens mixture among four dinner plates. Top with sliced chicken.
PER SERVING: 290 cal., 3 g total fat (1 g sat. fat), 73 mg chol., 559 mg sodium, 39 g carb. (5 g fiber, 25 g sugars), 27 g pro. Exchanges: 1 vegetable, 0.5 fruit, 1.5 carb., 3.5 lean meat. Carb choices: 2.5.

Quick Chicken Potpie

Hand over the cookie cutters and let the kids create their own toppers from purchased piecrust.

SERVINGS 6 (1 individual potpie each)
CARB. PER SERVING 29 g

½ of a 15-ounce package rolled refrigerated unbaked piecrust (1 crust)
1 pound chicken breast strips for stir-frying
1 tablespoon canola oil
⅓ cup flour
½ teaspoon snipped fresh thyme or oregano
¼ teaspoon black pepper
2½ cups reduced-sodium chicken broth
1½ cups packed coarsely shredded carrots
1½ cups frozen peas
Milk (optional)
Coarse salt (optional)

1. Preheat oven to 400°F. Let piecrust stand according to package directions. Meanwhile, cut up any large chicken pieces. In a large skillet cook chicken in hot oil over medium heat for 5 to 6 minutes or until chicken is lightly browned and no longer pink, stirring frequently. Stir in flour, thyme, and pepper. Add broth all at once. Stir in carrots. Cook and stir over medium heat until thickened and bubbly. Stir in peas; heat through. Cover and keep warm while preparing piecrust cutouts.
2. For topper, unroll piecrust on a lightly floured surface. Cut rounds from pastry to fit on top of six ungreased 10-ounce custard cups or individual casseroles (4- to 4½-inch), rerolling scraps if needed. Using 1- to 2-inch desired-shape cutters, cut shapes from centers of each pastry round. Spoon chicken mixture into custard cups. Arrange piecrust rounds and shapes on casseroles. If desired, brush piecrust rounds and shapes with milk and sprinkle with coarse salt.
3. Place casseroles in a 15×10×1-inch baking pan. Bake, uncovered, about 20 minutes or until topper is golden brown and mixture is bubbly. Let stand for 10 minutes before serving.
PER SERVING: 321 cal., 12 g total fat (4 g sat. fat), 52 mg chol., 567 mg sodium, 29 g carb. (3 g fiber, 4 g sugars), 20 g pro. Exchanges: 0.5 vegetable, 2 starch, 2 lean meat, 1.5 fat. Carb choices: 2.

Chicken Romano

Set up an assembly line so you can dunk, dip, and cook the chicken pieces with ease.

SERVINGS 4 (1 chicken breast half, ⅓ cup spaghetti, and ⅓ cup sauce each)
CARB. PER SERVING 34 g

Nonstick cooking spray
4 skinless, boneless chicken breast halves (1¼ to 1½ pounds total)
1 egg white
1 tablespoon water
1¼ cups cornflakes, crushed (about ½ cup crushed)
2 tablespoons grated Romano cheese
½ teaspoon dried Italian seasoning, basil, or oregano, crushed
⅛ teaspoon black pepper
4 ounces dried multigrain spaghetti
1⅓ cups low-sodium tomato-base pasta sauce
Shaved or grated Romano cheese (optional)
Snipped fresh Italian (flat-leaf) parsley (optional)

1. Preheat oven to 400°F. Lightly coat a 15×10×1-inch baking pan with cooking spray; set aside. Place each piece of chicken between two pieces of plastic wrap. Using the flat side of a meat mallet, pound chicken lightly until about ½ inch thick. Remove plastic wrap. Set chicken aside.
2. In a shallow dish use a fork to beat together egg white and the water. In another shallow dish combine crushed cornflakes, the 2 tablespoons grated cheese, the Italian seasoning, and pepper. Dip chicken pieces, one at a time, into egg mixture, letting excess drip off. Next dip chicken into cornflake mixture, turning to coat. Place coated chicken in the prepared baking pan.
3. Bake about 18 minutes or until chicken is tender and no longer pink. Meanwhile, cook spaghetti according to package directions; drain. In a small saucepan cook pasta sauce until heated through, stirring occasionally.
4. To serve, divide cooked spaghetti among four serving plates. Top with chicken and pasta sauce. If desired, sprinkle with additional cheese and/or parsley.
PER SERVING: 362 cal., 6 g total fat (1 g sat. fat), 85 mg chol., 405 mg sodium, 34 g carb. (4 g fiber, 5 g sugars), 41 g pro. Exchanges: 2 starch, 5 lean meat. Carb choices: 2.

Quick Chicken Potpie

Chicken Romano

Use 'em Up!

Along with the holidays comes extra cooking, which often means leftover ingredients. Rather than tossing them out, use these ideas for using them up.

1. **Toss** crunchy vegetables such as broccoli, carrots, cauliflower, celery, and fennel into salads. Or cut them up and serve them as dippers along with a creamy dip.

2. **Chop** and sauté fresh mushrooms in a little olive oil and serve over roasted or grilled chicken breasts.

3. **Crumble** or shred reduced-fat cheese and sprinkle over cooked green beans, asparagus, broccoli, and other veggies.

4. **Mix** a few fresh herb leaves such as basil, parsley, and cilantro in with salad greens.

5. **Cut up** fresh fruit such as pears, apples, and oranges and serve with fat-free Greek yogurt.

6. **Use** reduced-sodium chicken broth as part of the liquid for cooking rice or couscous.

7. **Spoon** salsa or other savory sauces over scrambled eggs to add zesty flavor.

8. **Add** lean protein such as roasted pork to a side salad to make it a main dish.

Cashew Chicken

Cashew Chicken

When they're in season, substitute fresh snow pea pods for the frozen variety.

SERVINGS 4 (1¼ cups each)

CARB. PER SERVING 23 g

- 2 tablespoons reduced-sodium soy sauce
- 1 tablespoon cornstarch
- 2 teaspoons grated fresh ginger or ½ teaspoon ground ginger
- 2 teaspoons toasted sesame oil
- 12 ounces skinless, boneless chicken breast halves, cut into ½-inch pieces
- 2 tablespoons water
- 2 tablespoons oyster sauce
- 1 6-ounce package frozen snow pea pods
- ⅓ cup unsalted dry-roasted cashews, coarsely chopped
- 3 teaspoons canola oil
- 1 medium red onion, cut into thin wedges
- 1 medium red sweet pepper, cut into bite-size pieces
- 3 cloves garlic, minced
- 1 8-ounce can sliced water chestnuts, drained

1. In a medium bowl stir together soy sauce, cornstarch, ginger, and sesame oil; add chicken and toss to coat. Cover and marinate at room temperature for 20 minutes. Meanwhile, for sauce, in a small bowl stir together the water and oyster sauce; set aside. Rinse pea pods under cold running water to thaw; set aside to drain well.

2. Heat a large nonstick skillet or wok over medium-high heat. Add cashews to hot skillet; cook about 3 minutes or until nuts start to brown, stirring frequently. Remove cashews from skillet; set aside. Add 1 teaspoon of the canola oil to skillet; add onion and stir-fry for 1 minute. Add sweet pepper, pea pods, and garlic; stir-fry for 1 minute. Stir in water chestnuts.

3. Remove vegetables from skillet. Add the remaining 2 teaspoons canola oil to skillet; add chicken mixture and stir-fry for 2 to 3 minutes or until chicken is cooked through. Return vegetables to skillet. Add the sauce; heat through, scraping up any browned bits from bottom of skillet. Transfer to a serving dish or plates. Sprinkle with the cashews.

PER SERVING: 299 cal., 13 g total fat (2 g sat. fat), 49 mg chol., 551 mg sodium, 23 g carb. (6 g fiber, 5 g sugars), 25 g pro. Exchanges: 1 vegetable, 1 starch, 3 lean meat, 1.5 fat. Carb choices: 1.5.

Fruit-Filled Pork Tenderloin

Soaking the dried fruit in port wine before making the filling gives an extra punch of flavor and moisture.

SERVINGS 8 (3 ounces cooked pork plus filling each)

CARB. PER SERVING 31 g

- ½ cup ruby port wine or pomegranate juice
- ¾ cup golden raisins
- ¾ cup dried cranberries
- ⅔ cup dried apricots, quartered
- ¼ teaspoon apple pie spice
- 2 14- to 18-ounce pork tenderloins
- ½ teaspoon salt
- ¼ teaspoon black pepper
  Cooked carrot slices and green onions (optional)

1. For filling, in a small saucepan bring port just to boiling. Remove from heat. Stir in raisins, dried cranberries, dried apricots, and apple pie spice. Cover and let stand for 15 minutes. Transfer mixture to a food processor. Cover and process for 10 to 15 seconds or until coarsely ground.

2. Make a lengthwise cut down the center of each tenderloin, cutting almost to but not through the other side. Spread open. Place each tenderloin between two pieces of plastic wrap. Using the flat side of a meat mallet, pound meat lightly from center to edges until slightly less than ½ inch thick. Remove plastic wrap.

3. Preheat oven to 425°F. Divide fruit filling between meat portions, spreading to within ½ inch of edges. Starting from a long side, roll up each portion into a spiral. Tie at 2-inch intervals with 100-percent-cotton kitchen string. Sprinkle tenderloin rolls with the salt and pepper.

4. Place tenderloins on a rack in a shallow roasting pan. Roast for 25 to 35 minutes or until juices run clear and an instant-read thermometer inserted into meat registers 155°F. Remove from oven. Cover loosely with foil; let stand for 10 minutes before slicing. (The temperature of the meat after standing should be 160°F.)

5. Remove and discard string. Cut tenderloins into ½-inch-thick slices. Serve warm. If desired, serve with carrots and green onions.

MAKE-AHEAD DIRECTIONS: Prepare tenderloin rolls as directed through Step 3. Wrap each stuffed tenderloin tightly in plastic wrap. Chill for up to 24 hours. To prepare, preheat oven to 425°F. Remove plastic wrap. Place tenderloins on a rack in a shallow roasting pan; let stand at room temperature for 15 minutes. Roast as directed.

PER SERVING: 240 cal., 2 g total fat (1 g sat. fat), 64 mg chol., 202 mg sodium, 31 g carb. (2 g fiber, 22 g sugars), 22 g pro. Exchanges: 2 fruit, 3 lean meat. Carb choices: 2.

Fruit-Filled
Pork Tenderloin

Pork Medallions with Cherry Sauce

Pork is often prepared with fruit such as prunes or apples. These quick-seared medallions cloaked in a sweet cherry sauce provide a whole new reason to pair pork with fruit.

SERVINGS 4 (3 ounces cooked pork and ¼ cup sauce each)

CARB. PER SERVING 13 g

- 1 **pound pork tenderloin**
- ¼ **teaspoon salt**
- ¼ **teaspoon black pepper**
- **Nonstick cooking spray**
- ¾ **cup cranberry juice, cherry juice, or apple juice**
- 2 **teaspoons spicy brown mustard**
- 1 **teaspoon cornstarch**
- 1 **cup fresh sweet cherries (such as Rainier or Bing), halved and pitted, or 1 cup frozen unsweetened pitted dark sweet cherries, thawed**
- **Snipped fresh parsley (optional)**

1. Cut pork crosswise into 1-inch slices. Place each slice between two pieces of plastic wrap. Using the flat side of a meat mallet, lightly pound each slice into a ½-inch-thick medallion. Discard plastic wrap. Sprinkle pork with the salt and pepper.

2. Coat an unheated large nonstick skillet with cooking spray. Heat skillet over medium-high heat. Add pork medallions and cook about 6 minutes or until pork is slightly pink in center and juices run clear, turning once. Transfer to a serving platter; cover with foil to keep warm.

3. For cherry sauce, in a small bowl stir together cranberry juice, mustard, and cornstarch; add to skillet. Cook and stir until thickened and bubbly. Cook and stir for 2 minutes more. Stir in cherries. Serve cherry sauce over pork. If desired, garnish with fresh parsley.

PER SERVING: 178 cal., 2 g total fat (1 g sat. fat), 74 mg chol., 247 mg sodium, 13 g carb. (1 g fiber, 11 g sugars), 24 g pro. Exchanges: 0.5 fruit, 0.5 carb., 3 lean meat. Carb choices: 1.

Pork with Pan-Fried Apples and Celery Root

Celery root, also known as celeriac, is brown and lumpy and should be washed and peeled before used for cooking or eating raw.

SERVINGS 6 (3 ounces cooked pork and ¾ cup apple mixture each)

CARB. PER SERVING 25 g

- 3 tablespoons coarse-ground mustard
- 2 tablespoons sugar-free maple-flavor syrup
- 2 teaspoons prepared horseradish
- ½ teaspoon dried dill weed
- 1 1½-pound boneless pork top loin roast (single loin)
- 1 large celery root (about 1 pound), trimmed, peeled, halved, and cut into ¼-inch-thick wedges, or 1 large fennel bulb, trimmed, cored, and cut into ¼-inch-thick wedges
- 1 tablespoon butter
- 3 large red-skin cooking apples (such as Rome, Jonathon, or Braeburn), cored, halved, and cut into ½-inch-thick wedges
- 2 tablespoons snipped fresh Italian (flat-leaf) parsley

1. Preheat oven to 425°F. In a small bowl combine mustard, syrup, horseradish, and dill weed. Spoon half of the mixture into another small bowl. Cover and set one bowl aside.

2. Trim fat from the roast. Place roast on a rack in a shallow roasting pan. Brush pork with half of the mustard mixture. Roast, uncovered, for 45 minutes. Brush pork with the remaining half of the mustard mixture. Roast about 15 minutes more or until an instant-read thermometer inserted into the center of the roast registers 145°F. Remove from oven; cover with foil. Let stand for 3 minutes before slicing.

3. Meanwhile, in a large skillet cook celery root, covered, in hot butter over medium heat for 3 minutes. Add the apple wedges. Cover and cook for 2 minutes. Uncover and cook for 3 to 4 minutes more or until apples and celery root are just tender, stirring occasionally. Stir in the parsley.

4. Place pork loin on a platter and surround with the apple mixture. Thinly slice the pork to serve.

PER SERVING: 268 cal., 7 g total fat (3 g sat. fat), 83 mg chol., 354 mg sodium, 25 g carb. (4 g fiber, 14 g sugars), 26 g pro. Exchanges: 0.5 fruit, 1 starch, 3 lean meat, 0.5 fat. Carb choices: 1.5.

Scalloped Potatoes and Ham

Not your ordinary creamy potato bake, this version uses round red and sweet potatoes along with turnip.

SERVINGS 4 (1¼ cups each)

CARB. PER SERVING 25 g

- 1 medium onion, chopped (½ cup)
- 1½ cups fat-free milk
- 3 tablespoons flour
- ⅛ teaspoon black pepper
- 1 teaspoon snipped fresh rosemary or ½ teaspoon dried rosemary, crushed
- 1 medium round red potato, cut into ¼-inch-thick slices
- 1 medium sweet potato, peeled and cut into ¼-inch-thick slices
- 1 medium turnip, peeled and cut into ¼-inch-thick slices
- ¼ cup water
- 8 ounces low-fat, reduced-sodium cooked boneless ham, cut into thin strips
  Paprika
  Fresh rosemary sprigs (optional)

1. Preheat oven to 350°F. For sauce, in a medium saucepan cook onion in a small amount of boiling water over medium heat for 3 to 5 minutes or until tender. Drain; return onion to pan. In a screw-top jar combine milk, flour, and pepper; cover and shake until well mixed. Add milk mixture to onion in saucepan. Cook and stir over medium heat until thickened and bubbly. Stir in snipped rosemary.

2. Meanwhile, in a 2-quart microwave-safe baking dish combine potatoes, turnip, and the ¼ cup water. Cover with vented plastic wrap. Microwave on 100 percent power (high) about 8 minutes or just until vegetables are tender. Carefully drain in a colander.

3. In the same ungreased 2-quart baking dish layer half of the ham, half of the potato mixture, and half of the sauce. Top with the remaining potatoes and the remaining ham. Spoon the remaining sauce over all. Sprinkle with paprika.

4. Bake, uncovered, about 30 minutes or until heated through. Let stand for 10 minutes before serving. If desired, garnish with rosemary sprigs.

PER SERVING: 214 cal., 5 g total fat (2 g sat. fat), 34 mg chol., 630 mg sodium, 25 g carb. (3 g fiber, 8 g sugars), 18 g pro. Exchanges: 0.5 vegetable, 1.5 starch, 1.5 lean meat, 0.5 fat. Carb choices: 1.5.

Choucroute Garni

1. In a large saucepan cook pork, onion, and garlic in hot oil over medium heat about 5 minutes or until pork is browned and onion is tender. Remove from pan and set aside. Add ale to the pan, scraping up any browned bits from the bottom of the pan. In a medium bowl stir together apple juice, cornstarch, mustard, caraway seeds, rosemary, and pepper; stir into onion-ale mixture. Cook and stir until thickened and bubbly. Set aside to cool for 10 minutes.

2. Meanwhile, in a large saucepan cook potatoes and carrots, covered, in a large amount of boiling lightly salted water about 10 minutes or until slightly tender but still firm. Drain; set aside.

3. Preheat oven to 350°F. In a 3-quart rectangular baking dish layer browned pork mixture, kielbasa, potato-carrot mixture, apples, and sauerkraut. Spoon apple juice mixture evenly over sauerkraut. Cover with foil.

4. Bake, covered, for 45 to 60 minutes or until potatoes are tender and center is hot.

MAKE-AHEAD DIRECTIONS: Prepare as directed through Step 3. Cover with plastic wrap and chill for up to 24 hours. Let stand at room temperature for 10 minutes before baking. Preheat oven to 350°F. Remove plastic wrap. Bake, covered, for 65 to 70 minutes or until potatoes are tender and center is hot.

PER SERVING: 237 cal., 9 g total fat (3 g sat. fat), 46 mg chol., 642 mg sodium, 22 g carb. (3 g fiber, 8 g sugars), 16 g pro. Exchanges: 1.5 starch, 2 lean meat, 1 fat. Carb choices: 1.5.

Choucroute Garni

If you're a fan of sauerkraut, you'll love this chunky casserole that also features apples, potatoes, pork, and kielbasa.

SERVINGS 12 (¾ cup each)
CARB. PER SERVING 22 g

- 1 1-pound boneless pork loin roast (single loin), trimmed of fat and cut into ¾-inch pieces
- 1 medium red onion, cut into very thin wedges
- 4 cloves garlic, minced
- 1 tablespoon olive oil or vegetable oil
- 1 12-ounce bottle ale or beer or 1½ cups lower-sodium beef broth
- 1½ cups apple juice or apple cider
- 3 tablespoons cornstarch
- 2 tablespoons coarse-ground brown mustard
- 1 tablespoon caraway seeds
- 1 tablespooon snipped fresh rosemary
- ½ teaspoon cracked black pepper
- 12 fingerling potatoes or tiny new potatoes, quartered
- 3 medium carrots, sliced (1½ cups)
- 1 pound cooked smoked light kielbasa, halved lengthwise and bias-sliced into 1-inch pieces
- 2 medium cooking apples (such as Granny Smith or Jonagold), cored and cut into chunks
- 1 14-ounce can sauerkraut, drained, rinsed, and squeezed dry

Sherried Pea Soup with Ham

A spoonful of plain Greek yogurt adds creaminess, and homemade croutons add crunch to each bowl.

SERVINGS 6 (1⅓ cups each)
CARB. PER SERVING 29 g

- 1 tablespoon olive oil
- 1 large onion, chopped (1 cup)
- 2 stalks celery, sliced (1 cup)
- 2 medium carrots, sliced (1 cup)
- 1 tablespoon minced garlic
- 1 tablespoon snipped fresh thyme
- 2 14.5-ounce cans reduced-sodium chicken broth
- 2½ cups water
- 1 cup dry green split peas
- 3 ounces reduced-sodium ham, diced
- ½ teaspoon crushed red pepper
- ½ teaspoon black pepper
- ¼ teaspoon ground mace or nutmeg
- 1 cup frozen green peas

¼ cup snipped fresh parsley
1 to 2 tablespoons dry sherry or reduced-sodium chicken broth
Whole wheat croutons* (optional)
Plain fat-free Greek yogurt (optional)

1. In a Dutch oven heat oil over medium-high heat. Add onion, celery, carrots, garlic, and thyme. Reduce heat to medium; cook about 5 minutes or until tender, stirring frequently.

2. Stir in broth, the water, split peas, ham, crushed red pepper, black pepper, and mace. Bring to boiling; reduce heat. Simmer, covered, for 1 to 1¼ hours or until split peas are soft.

3. Stir in frozen peas and parsley; cook about 5 minutes more or until peas are heated through. Stir in sherry. If desired, serve with croutons and/or yogurt.

*TEST KITCHEN TIP: Use purchased whole wheat croutons or make them at home. For homemade croutons, preheat oven to 350°F. Coat a baking sheet with nonstick cooking spray; set aside. Cut up whole wheat bread slices into ¾- to 1-inch pieces; place on prepared baking sheet. Bake for 8 to 10 minutes or until edges are golden, turning or stirring once halfway through baking time.

PER SERVING: 198 cal., 3 g total fat (1 g sat. fat), 7 mg chol., 519 mg sodium, 29 g carb. (11 g fiber, 7 g sugars), 14 g pro. Exchanges: 1 vegetable, 1.5 starch, 1 lean meat. Carb choices: 2.

Sherried Pea Soup with Ham

Sweet Peppers Stuffed with Bacon Risotto

3. Bake peppers, covered, for 30 to 45 minutes or until heated through. If desired, sprinkle with basil.

MAKE-AHEAD DIRECTIONS: Prepare peppers as directed through Step 2 but do not preheat oven. Chill for up to 12 hours or freeze for up to 6 months. To bake, preheat oven to 375°F. Bake chilled peppers, covered, for 50 to 55 minutes or until heated through. Or bake frozen peppers, covered, about 1 hour or until heated through. If desired, sprinkle with basil.

PER SERVING: 235 cal., 7 g total fat (3 g sat. fat), 13 mg chol., 499 mg sodium, 28 g carb. (3 g fiber, 6 g sugars), 9 g pro. Exchanges: 1 vegetable, 1.5 starch, 0.5 medium-fat meat, 0.5 fat. Carb choices: 2.

Sweet Peppers Stuffed with Bacon Risotto

Use various colors of sweet peppers to give this dish the most attractive look.

SERVINGS 6 (1 stuffed pepper each)
CARB. PER SERVING 28 g

- 6 slices applewood bacon, coarsely chopped
- 1 medium onion, chopped (½ cup)
- ¾ cup Arborio rice
- 1 14.5-ounce can reduced-sodium chicken broth
- ¾ cup dry white wine or reduced-sodium chicken broth
- 1 cup frozen peas, thawed
- ⅓ cup finely shredded Parmigiano-Reggiano cheese or Parmesan cheese
- ¼ teaspoon salt
- ¼ teaspoon black pepper
- 6 small or 3 large red, yellow, or green sweet peppers
- 1 tablespoons snipped fresh basil or Italian (flat-leaf) parsley (optional)

1. In a large saucepan cook bacon over medium heat until crisp. Drain, reserving 1 tablespoon of the bacon drippings in saucepan. Set bacon aside. Cook onion in reserved drippings until tender. Add rice; cook and stir for 2 minutes more. Carefully stir in broth and wine. Bring to boiling; reduce heat. Simmer, covered, about 20 minutes or until liquid is absorbed. Remove saucepan from heat. Stir in bacon and peas. Let stand, covered, for 5 minutes. Stir in cheese, salt, and black pepper.

2. Preheat oven to 375°F. Meanwhile, cut tops off small peppers or halve large peppers lengthwise. Remove membranes and seeds. Spoon risotto mixture into peppers. Place in a shallow baking dish. Cover with foil.

Penne with Broccoli Rabe

Other shapes of multigrain pasta can be fun, too —try rotini or bow ties.

SERVINGS 4 (1¼ cups each)
CARB. PER SERVING 39 g

- 12 ounces broccoli rabe or 2 cups broccoli florets
- 6 ounces dried multigrain penne pasta
- 1 medium onion, chopped (½ cup)
- 1 slice bacon, coarsely chopped
- 2 cloves garlic, minced
- 4 medium roma tomatoes, seeded and chopped
- ⅓ cup dry white wine or reduced-sodium chicken broth
- ¼ teaspoon salt
- ¼ cup shaved Asiago cheese (1 ounce)

1. Wash broccoli rabe, if using; remove and discard woody stems. Coarsely chop leafy greens; set aside.

2. In a large saucepan cook pasta in a large amount of boiling water for 8 minutes. Add broccoli rabe or broccoli florets. Cook about 3 minutes more or just until pasta is tender; drain well. Return mixture to hot saucepan; cover and keep warm.

3. Meanwhile, in a medium saucepan cook onion, bacon, and garlic over medium heat about 5 minutes or until onion is tender, stirring occasionally. Reduce heat to low. Add tomatoes, wine, and salt; cook for 2 minutes more, stirring frequently.

4. Add tomato mixture to pasta mixture; toss gently to combine. Garnish with cheese.

PER SERVING: 296 cal., 7 g total fat (3 g sat. fat), 14 mg chol., 365 mg sodium, 39 g carb. (7 g fiber, 5 g sugars), 14 g pro. Exchanges: 1.5 vegetable, 2 starch, 1 medium-fat meat. Carb choices: 2.5.

quick tip

If a chunk of Parmesan or Romano cheese
is hiding in your refrigerator drawer, use it instead
of the Asiago cheese. Use a vegetable peeler to
create the shavings of varying sizes.

Penne with
Broccoli Rabe

French Beef
Stew au Pistou

Moroccan Beef
and Pumpkin Ba[ke]

French Beef Stew au Pistou

Pistou is the French version of Italian basil pesto. A spoonful of this cold sauce adds a burst of freshness to each bite.

SERVINGS 6 (2 cups stew and 1½ tablespoons pistou each)

CARB. PER SERVING 35 g

- 2 cups fresh basil leaves
- ½ cup grated Parmesan cheese
- 3 tablespoons olive oil
- 2 tablespoons minced garlic
- 1 pound lean beef stew meat, trimmed of fat and cut into ½-inch pieces
- 2 large onions, chopped (1 cups)
- 1 pound roma tomatoes, chopped (about 3 cups)
- 2 cups diced red potatoes (about 12 ounces)
- 2 medium carrots, diced (1 cup)
- 4 cups lower-sodium beef broth
- 2 cups water
- 2 cups chopped zucchini
- 8 ounces green beans, trimmed and halved (2 cups)
- 4 cups chopped fresh spinach
- 1 15-ounce can no-salt-added red kidney beans, rinsed and drained
- ½ teaspoon crushed red pepper

1. For pistou, in a food processor combine basil, Parmesan cheese, 2 tablespoons of the oil, and the garlic. Cover and process until a paste forms; set aside.

2. In a 5- to 6-quart Dutch oven heat the remaining 1 tablespoon oil over medium-high heat. Brown stew meat, half at a time, in hot oil, stirring frequently. Remove meat from Dutch oven; set aside. Add onions to Dutch oven; cook over medium heat about 5 minutes or until tender. Return meat to Dutch oven.

3. Add tomatoes, potatoes, and carrots; cook and stir for 4 minutes more. Stir in broth, the water, zucchini, and green beans. Bring to boiling; reduce heat. Simmer, covered, about 15 minutes or until meat and vegetables are tender.

4. Stir in spinach, kidney beans, and crushed red pepper. Cook about 2 minutes more or just until spinach is wilted. Serve with the pistou.

PER SERVING: 374 cal., 14 g total fat (4 g sat. fat), 49 mg chol., 506 mg sodium, 35 g carb. (11 g fiber, 7 g sugars), 29 g pro. Exchanges: 2 vegetable, 1.5 starch, 3 lean meat, 1.5 fat. Carb choices: 2.

Moroccan Beef and Pumpkin Bake

A cornmeal batter bakes into a crustlike topper over a hearty meat and vegetable base.

SERVINGS 8 (1 cup each) servings

CARB. PER SERVING 32 g or 30 g

Nonstick cooking spray
- 1 pound 95 percent lean ground beef
- 2 cups ½-inch pieces peeled pumpkin or winter squash
- 1 medium red sweet pepper, coarsely chopped (¾ cup)
- 1 medium onion, coarsely chopped (½ cup)
- 2 cloves garlic, minced

1 cup frozen whole kernel corn
½ cup couscous
1 recipe Moroccan Spice Blend
1 cup lower-sodium beef broth
½ of an 8-ounce package reduced-fat cream cheese (Neufchâtel), cut up
½ cup yellow cornmeal
⅓ cup flour
1 tablespoon sugar*
1¼ teaspoons baking powder
¼ teaspoon salt
½ cup fat-free milk
1 egg, beaten
2 tablespoons olive oil
Snipped fresh mint (optional)
Toasted pumpkin seeds (optional)

1. Preheat oven to 400°F. Coat an unheated large nonstick skillet or a skillet with cooking spray. In skillet cook ground beef, pumpkin, sweet pepper, onion, and garlic over medium heat until meat is browned and onion is tender, using a wooden spoon to break up meat as it cooks. Drain off fat. Stir corn, couscous, and spice blend into meat mixture in skillet. Heat through. Add broth and cream cheese, stirring until well mixed. Spoon mixture into a 2-quart baking dish.

2. In a medium bowl combine cornmeal, flour, sugar, baking powder, and salt. In a small bowl whisk together milk, egg, and oil; add to cornmeal mixture all at once. Stir just until moistened. Pour batter over beef mixture in dish.

3. Bake about 20 minutes or until a toothpick inserted into topper comes out clean. If desired, garnish with mint and pumpkin seeds

MOROCCAN SPICE BLEND: In a small bowl stir together 1 teaspoon ground cumin, ½ teaspoon ground coriander, ½ teaspoon ground ginger, ¼ teaspoon salt, and ⅛ teaspoon ground cinnamon.

*SUGAR SUBSTITUTES: Choose from Splenda Granular or Sweet'N Low bulk or packets. Follow package directions to use product amount equivalent to 1 tablespoon sugar.

PER SERVING: 298 cal., 11 g total fat (4 g sat. fat), 72 mg chol., 362 mg sodium, 32 g carb. (2 g fiber, 5 g sugars), 19 g pro. Exchanges: 0.5 vegetable, 2 starch, 2 lean meat, 1 fat. Carb choices: 2.

PER SERVING WITH SUBSTITUTE: Same as above, except 293 cal., 30 g carb. (4 g sugars).

Meat Fondue

Delectably different, these sauces make choosing just one hard. The ginger-wasabi combo offers a touch of hotness, while the lemon-pepper combo is creamy and cool.
SERVINGS 10 (4 ounces cooked meat and 1 to 2 tablespoons desired sauce each)
CARB. PER SERVING 7 g

1 pound fresh or frozen large shrimp in shells
1 pound skinless, boneless chicken breast halves
12 ounces boneless beef sirloin steak
4 cups reduced-sodium chicken broth
½ cup thinly sliced green onions (4)
1 clove garlic, peeled and halved
½ teaspoon whole black peppercorns
¼ teaspoon crushed red pepper (optional)
1 recipe Ginger-Wasabi Sauce and/or Lemon-Pepper Aïoli

1. Thaw shrimp, if frozen. Partially freeze chicken and beef for easier slicing. Peel and devein shrimp; rinse shrimp and pat dry with paper towels. Thinly slice chicken crosswise into bite-size strips. Thinly slice beef across the grain into bite-size strips. Arrange shrimp, chicken, and beef on a platter, keeping meats separate.

2. In a large saucepan combine broth, ½ cup green onions, garlic, peppercorns, and, if desired, crushed red pepper. Bring broth mixture to boiling. Pour into a fondue pot. Return to boiling.

3. To serve, give each person a fondue fork. Dip beef, chicken, and shrimp into broth; cook shrimp until opaque, chicken until no longer pink, and beef until desired doneness. (Allow 1 to 3 minutes for each piece.) Serve with Ginger-Wasabi Sauce and/or Lemon-Pepper Aïoli.

GINGER-WASABI SAUCE: In a small bowl combine ½ cup thinly sliced green onions, ¼ cup rice vinegar, ¼ cup water, 2 tablespoons honey, 1 tablespoon wasabi paste, 2 teaspoons grated fresh ginger, and ¼ teaspoon salt.

LEMON-PEPPER AÏOLI: Place ½ cup well-drained bottled roasted red sweet peppers in a blender or food processor; cover and blend or process until smooth. Transfer to a small bowl. Add ½ cup light mayonnaise; 1 teaspoon finely shredded lemon peel; 2 teaspoons lemon juice; 2 cloves garlic, minced; and ⅛ teaspoon black pepper. Stir until well combined.

PER SERVING: 215 cal., 7 g total fat (2 g sat. fat), 118 mg chol., 501 mg sodium, 7 g carb. (1 g fiber, 5 g sugars), 29 g pro. Exchanges: 0.5 carb., 4 lean meat. Carb choices: 0.5.

quick tip

Let this elegant roast stand for 15 minutes before carving it. This will help to set the juices and lock in the flavors.

Marinated Prime Rib

Marinated Prime Rib

*This special-day meat couldn't be easier.
Marinating a day ahead gives it the best flavor.*

SERVINGS 12 (3 ounces each)

CARB. PER SERVING 0 g

¾ cup dry red wine
1 medium onion, chopped (½ cup)
¼ cup water
¼ cup lemon juice
1 tablespoon Worcestershire sauce
1½ teaspoons snipped fresh rosemary or ½ teaspoon dried rosemary, crushed
½ teaspoon dried marjoram, crushed
¼ teaspoon garlic salt
1 4-pound beef rib roast, trimmed of fat
   Oven-roasted vegetables (optional)

1. For marinade, in a small bowl stir together wine, onion, the water, lemon juice, Worcestershire sauce, rosemary, marjoram, and garlic salt. Place roast in a resealable plastic bag set in a shallow dish. Pour marinade over meat; seal bag. Marinate in the refrigerator for 6 to 24 hours, turning bag occasionally.
2. Preheat oven to 325°F. Drain meat, discarding marinade. Place meat, fat side up, in a large roasting pan. Insert an oven-going meat thermometer into center of roast, making sure thermometer does not touch bone. Roast until desired doneness. Allow 1¾ to 2¼ hours for medium rare (135°F) or 2¼ to 2¾ hours for medium (150°F). Transfer meat to a cutting board. Cover meat with foil and let stand for 15 minutes before slicing. Temperature of the meat after standing should be 145°F for medium rare or 160°F for medium. Slice meat. If desired, serve with roasted vegetables.
PER SERVING: 172 cal., 11 g total fat (4 g sat. fat), 49 mg chol., 56 mg sodium, 0 g carb. (0 g fiber, 0 g sugars), 17 g pro. Exchanges: 2.5 medium-fat meat. Carb choices: 0.

Roast Beef with Mushroom-Fig Sauce

*Unlike those of other mushrooms, shiitake stems are too
tough to eat. Use a sharp knife to trim the stems and discard.*

SERVINGS 8 (3 ounces cooked beef and ¼ cup sauce each)

CARB. PER SERVING 8 g

1 2- to 2½- pound beef eye round roast
½ teaspoon cracked black pepper
¼ teaspoon salt
1 tablespoon olive oil
8 ounces fresh cremini, stemmed shiitake, or button mushrooms, sliced
2 tablespoons finely chopped shallot or sweet onion
½ cup dry red wine or lower-sodium beef broth
1 tablespoon Dijon-style mustard
1 teaspoon snipped fresh rosemary or ½ teaspoon dried rosemary, crushed
¾ cup lower-sodium beef broth
½ cup chopped, stemmed dried figs
   Fresh rosemary sprigs

1. Preheat oven to 325°F. Trim fat from meat. Sprinkle meat with the pepper and salt, rubbing in with your fingers.
2. Place meat on a rack in a shallow roasting pan. Insert an oven-going meat thermometer into center of roast. Roast, uncovered, for 1½ to 1¾ hours or until thermometer registers 135°F (roasting an eye round roast past medium rare is not recommended). Cover meat with foil and let stand for 15 minutes before slicing. Temperature of the meat after standing should be 145°F.
3. Meanwhile, in a large skillet heat oil over medium heat. Add mushrooms and shallot to skillet. Cook over medium heat for 5 to 8 minutes or until mushrooms are just tender and lightly browned, stirring occasionally. Remove from heat and add wine to skillet. Return to the heat and bring to boiling; boil gently, uncovered, about 3 minutes or until wine is reduced by about half. Whisk in mustard and the 1 teaspoon rosemary. Add broth and figs. Bring to boiling; boil gently, uncovered, about 10 minutes or until liquid is slightly thickened and reduced by about one-third.
4. Thinly slice meat and serve with mushroom-fig sauce. Garnish with rosemary sprigs.
PER SERVING: 243 cal., 10 g total fat (4 g sat. fat), 46 mg chol., 226 mg sodium, 8 g carb. (1 g fiber, 5 g sugars), 26 g pro. Exchanges: 0.5 fruit, 3.5 lean meat, 1 fat. Carb choices: 0.5.

Rosemary-Lemon
Lamb Chops with Potato
and Fennel Latkes

quick tip

Brighten the plate
presentation of these
brown-crusted chops and
latkes with a handful of
mixed salad greens.

Rosemary-Lemon Lamb Chops with Potato and Fennel Latkes

Precooking the potato, fennel, and onion in the microwave trims time when pan-frying the tasty latkes.

SERVINGS 4 (2 lamb chops and 2 latkes each)
CARB. PER SERVING 19 g

2	medium russet potatoes (about 10 ounces total)
1	medium fennel bulb
¼	cup finely chopped onion
1	tablespoon snipped fresh rosemary
4	cloves garlic, minced
1	teaspoon finely shredded lemon peel
¼	teaspoon salt
⅛	teaspoon black pepper
8	lamb rib chops, cut about 1 inch thick (2 to 2½ pounds total)
1	egg white, lightly beaten
¼	teaspoon salt
⅛	teaspoon black pepper
1	tablespoon canola oil

1. Peel and coarsely shred the potatoes. Trim the fennel bulb and cut out the core; coarsely shred the fennel bulb.* You should 1½ cups each of potato and fennel. In a medium microwave-safe bowl combine potato, fennel, and onion. Cover with vented plastic wrap.
2. Microwave on 100 percent power (high) for 4 to 5 minutes or until vegetables are just tender, stirring once or twice. Drain off any liquid and set potato mixture aside to cool to room temperature.
3. In a small bowl combine rosemary, garlic, lemon peel, ¼ teaspoon salt, and ⅛ teaspoon pepper. Trim fat from lamb chops and sprinkle chops evenly with the rosemary mixture, rubbing in with your fingers.
4. Coat an unheated indoor grill pan with *nonstick cooking spray*. Heat over medium heat. Add the lamb chops. Cook to desired doneness, turning once halfway through cooking. Allow 12 to 14 minutes for medium rare (145°F) or 15 to 17 minutes for medium (160°F).
5. Meanwhile, add the egg white, ¼ teaspoon salt, and ⅛ teaspoon pepper to the potato mixture. Stir until well combined. Divide mixture into eight equal portions. Coat an unheated large nonstick skillet with cooking spray. Add the oil. Heat skillet over medium-high heat. Add potato portions to the hot skillet and flatten each portion into a circle about ½ inch thick.
6. Cook the potato latkes for 5 minutes or until golden brown, turning once halfway through cooking. Serve the latkes with the lamb chops.

To make quick work of shredding the potatoes and fennel, use a food processor fitted with a shredding blade.

PER SERVING: 276 cal., 12 g total fat (3 g sat. fat), 64 mg chol., 400 mg sodium, 19 g carb. (4 g fiber, 1 g sugars), 23 g pro. Exchanges: 1 starch, 3 lean meat, 1.5 fat. Carb choices: 1.

Cajun Shrimp and Corn Bread Casserole

*Tender corn bread puffs crown this
Southern-style one-dish stunner.*

SERVINGS 6 (1 cup shrimp mixture and 1 dumpling each)

CARB. PER SERVING 36 g

- 1 pound fresh or frozen large shrimp in shells
- 1 teaspoon salt-free Cajun seasoning
- 2 medium green and/or red sweet peppers, coarsely chopped (1½ cups)
- 2 stalks celery, sliced (1 cup)
- 1 medium onion, chopped (½ cup)
- 1 tablespoon canola oil
- 2 cloves garlic, minced
- 1 15-ounce can no-salt-added black-eyed peas, rinsed and drained
- 1 14.5-ounce can no-salt-added stewed tomatoes, undrained and cut up
- 1 recipe Corn Bread Dumplings
- Snipped fresh parsley (optional)

1. Thaw shrimp, if frozen. Preheat oven to 400°F. Peel and devein shrimp, leaving tails intact if desired. Rinse shrimp; pat dry with paper towels. In a large bowl combine shrimp and ½ teaspoon of the Cajun seasoning; toss gently to coat. Set aside.

2. In a large cast-iron skillet or large oven-going skillet cook sweet peppers, celery, and onion in hot oil over medium-high heat for 5 to 7 minutes or until vegetables are tender, stirring frequently. Add shrimp and garlic. Cook and stir for 2 minutes.

3. Stir in black-eyed peas, tomatoes, and the remaining ½ teaspoon Cajun seasoning. Bring to boiling. Drop Corn Bread Dumplings into six mounds on top of shrimp mixture.

4. Bake, uncovered, for 12 to 15 minutes or until a toothpick inserted in centers of dumplings comes out clean. Let stand for 5 minutes before serving. If desired, sprinkle with parsley.

CORN BREAD DUMPLINGS: In a medium bowl stir together ¾ cup all-purpose flour, ⅓ cup yellow cornmeal, 1 tablespoon sugar, 1¼ teaspoons baking powder, and ¼ teaspoon salt. In a small bowl combine 1 lightly beaten egg, ¼ cup fat-free milk, and 2 tablespoons canola oil. Add egg mixture all at once to flour mixture; stir just until moistened.

PER SERVING: 302 cal., 9 g total fat (1 g sat. fat), 127 mg chol., 574 mg sodium, 36 g carb. (5 g fiber, 6 g sugars), 18 g pro. Exchanges: 1 vegetable, 2 starch, 1.5 lean meat, 1 fat. Carb choices: 2.

Cajun Shrimp and
Corn Bread Casserole

Red Cumin-Lime Shrimp
on Jicama Rice

Red Cumin-Lime Shrimp on Jicama Rice

Jicama can be quite large. Cut the extra to toss into salads or use as a dipper for creamy dips.

SERVINGS 4 (¾ cup shrimp mixture and ⅔ cup rice mixture each)

CARB. PER SERVING 26 g

- 12 ounces fresh or frozen peeled and deveined medium shrimp
- 3 teaspoons olive oil
- 3 medium yellow onions, chopped (1½ cups)
- 1 medium fresh Anaheim chile pepper, seeded and sliced*
- 1½ tablespoons chili powder
- 1½ teaspoons ground cumin
- 1 cup hot cooked brown rice
- 1½ cups peeled jicama cut into thin bite-size strips
- 2 tablespoons lime juice
- 2 tablespoons tub-style vegetable oil spread
- ¼ teaspoon salt
- ⅓ cup snipped fresh cilantro

1. Thaw shrimp, if frozen; set aside. In a large nonstick skillet heat 1 teaspoon of the oil over medium-high heat. Tilt skillet to coat bottom lightly. Add onion and chile pepper; cook about 3 minutes or until tender, stirring frequently. Stir in shrimp, chili powder, and cumin; cook for 3 to 4 minutes or until shrimp are opaque.

2. Meanwhile, spoon hot rice into a serving bowl. Stir jicama into rice. Cover and let stand until ready to serve.

3. Remove skillet from heat; stir in the remaining 2 teaspoons oil, the lime juice, vegetable oil spread, and salt. Cover and let stand for 5 minutes to allow flavors to absorb and vegetable oil spread to melt.

4. To serve, add cilantro to rice mixture, tossing to mix well. Serve shrimp mixture over rice mixture.

*TEST KITCHEN TIP: Because chile peppers contain volatile oils that can burn your skin and eyes, avoid direct contact with them as much as possible. When working with chile peppers, wear plastic or rubber gloves. If your bare hands do touch the peppers, wash your hands and nails well with soap and warm water.

PER SERVING: 284 cal., 11 g total fat (2 g sat. fat), 129 mg chol., 350 mg sodium, 26 g carb. (6 g fiber, 4 g sugars), 21 g pro. Exchanges: 1 vegetable, 1.5 starch, 2 lean meat, 1.5 fat. Carb choices: 2.

San Francisco Seafood Stew

Look for bottled clam juice in the canned or packaged fish and seafood section of the supermarket.

SERVINGS 6 (2 cups each)
CARB. PER SERVING 17 g

8 ounces fresh or frozen cod or other white fish
8 ounces fresh or frozen shrimp
1 cup finely chopped leeks
1 medium fennel bulb, trimmed, cored, and chopped (1 cup)
1 stalk celery, chopped (½ cup)
1 medium carrot, chopped (½ cup)
2 tablespoons minced garlic
1 tablespoon olive oil
1 tablespoon tomato paste
2 teaspoons dried Italian seasoning, crushed
¼ cup dry white wine or reduced-sodium chicken broth
1 28-ounce can no-salt-added diced tomatoes, undrained
1 14.5-ounce can reduced-sodium chicken broth
1½ cups water
½ cup clam juice

1 pound mussels, soaked, scrubbed, and beards removed*
½ cup snipped fresh Italian (flat-leaf) parsley

1. Thaw fish and shrimp, if frozen. Rinse fish and shrimp; pat dry with paper towels. Cut fish into 1-inch pieces. Peel and devein shrimp; halve shrimp lengthwise. Set fish and shrimp aside.

2. In an 8-quart Dutch oven cook leeks, fennel, celery, carrot, and garlic in hot oil about 5 minutes or until vegetables are tender. Stir in tomato paste and Italian seasoning; cook for 1 minute. Carefully add wine. Cook and stir until wine is nearly evaporated.

3. Stir in tomatoes, broth, the water, and clam juice. Bring to boiling; reduce heat to medium-low. Simmer, uncovered, for 10 minutes. Add mussels and fish. Cover; cook about 5 minutes or until mussels open. Discard any unopened mussels. Add shrimp; cook for 1 to 2 minutes or until shrimp are opaque. Stir in half of the parsley. Ladle into bowls. Sprinkle with remaining parsley.

*TEST KITCHEN TIP: Scrub mussels in shells under cold running water. Remove beards. In an 8-quart Dutch oven combine 4 quarts cold water and ⅓ cup salt; add mussels. Soak for 15 minutes; drain and rinse. Discard water. Repeat soaking, draining, and rinsing twice.

PER SERVING: 214 cal., 5 g total fat (1 g sat. fat), 90 mg chol., 588 mg sodium, 17 g carb. (4 g fiber, 6 g sugars), 26 g pro. Exchanges: 1.5 vegetable, 0.5 starch, 3 lean meat. Carb choices: 1.

San Francisco
Seafood Stew

Salmon wirh
Pomegranate-
Orange Relish

PER SERVING: 333 cal., 18 g total fat (5 g sat. fat), 70 mg chol., 405 mg sodium, 18 g carb. (3 g fiber, 14 g sugars), 24 g pro. Exchanges: 1 carb., 3.5 medium-fat meat. Carb choices: 1.

Salmon with Pomegranate-Orange Relish

A whole pomegranate contains hundreds of ruby red, sweet-tart seeds. Remove all of the seeds from the flesh and freeze the extras for another use.

SERVINGS 4 (1 salmon fillet and ⅓ cup relish each)
CARB. PER SERVING 18 g

- 2 medium carrots, coarsely chopped (1 cup)
- 4 fresh or frozen skinless salmon fillets, about 1 inch thick (1 to 1¼ pounds total)
- ½ teaspoon salt
- ¼ teaspoon black pepper
- ⅛ teaspoon cayenne pepper
- 1 medium shallot, peeled and thinly sliced
- 1 tablespoon butter
- 2 medium oranges, peeled and sectioned
- 1 tablespoon honey
- ¼ cup pomegranate seeds
- 1 tablespoon snipped fresh chives (optional)

1. In a small saucepan cook carrots in a small amount of boiling water about 4 minutes or until crisp-tender. Drain; set aside.

2. Thaw salmon, if frozen. Rinse salmon with cold water and pat dry with paper towels. Place salmon on the unheated rack of a broiler pan. In a small bowl combine salt, black pepper, and cayenne pepper. Sprinkle evenly over salmon fillets. Measure thickness of fish. Broil salmon 4 to 5 inches from the heat for 4 to 6 minutes per ½-inch thickness of fish or until fish flakes easily when tested with a fork.

3. Meanwhile, for relish, in a large skillet cook carrots and shallot in hot butter over medium heat about 6 minutes or until shallots are tender, stirring occasionally. Add orange sections. Cook for 1 minute more. Drizzle with honey and toss to coat.

4. To serve, spoon relish onto each of four serving plates. Place a salmon fillet on top of relish. Sprinkle with pomegranate seeds and, if desired, chives.

Steamed Asparagus and Lobster Salad

The trio of lemon, dill, and garlic is delightful on this elegant chilled salad. It's perfect to serve for a brunch or lunch.

SERVINGS 4 (¾ cup lobster mixture, 1½ tablespoons dressing, 1 tablespoon cheese, and ½ of a bacon slice each)
CARB. PER SERVING 8 g

- 2 8-ounce fresh or frozen lobster tails
- 1 pound fresh asparagus spears
- ½ teaspoon finely shredded lemon peel
- 2 tablespoons lemon juice
- 2 tablespoons olive oil
- 1 tablespoon minced shallot
- 2 teaspoons snipped fresh dill weed
- 2 teaspoons honey
- ⅛ teaspoon black pepper
- 4 cups torn butterhead (Boston or Bibb) lettuce
- ¼ cup shaved or finely shredded Parmesan cheese
- 2 slices turkey bacon, cooked according to package directions and chopped

1. Thaw lobster tails, if frozen. Butterfly lobster tails by using kitchen shears to cut lengthwise through centers of hard top shells and meat, cutting to but not through bottoms of shells. Spread halves of tails apart. Place a steamer basket in a saucepan. Add water to just below the bottom of the basket. Bring water to boiling. Add lobster tails to steamer basket. Cover and reduce heat. Steam for 8 minutes. Add asparagus; cover and steam for 3 to 5 minutes more or until lobster is opaque and asparagus is tender. When cool enough to handle, remove lobster from shells and coarsely chop. Bias-slice asparagus into 1½-inch pieces.

2. For vinaigrette, in a screw-top jar combine lemon peel, lemon juice, olive oil, shallot, dill weed, honey, and pepper. Cover and shake well to combine.

3. Line a serving platter with lettuce. Arrange asparagus and lobster on lettuce. Drizzle with vinaigrette; sprinkle with cheese and bacon.

PER SERVING: 234 cal., 11 g total fat (3 g sat. fat), 120 mg chol., 507 mg sodium, 8 g carb. (2 g fiber, 5 g sugars), 26 g pro. Exchanges: 1.5 vegetable, 3.5 lean meat, 1 fat. Carb choices: 0.5.

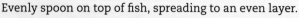

Pine Nut-Crusted Cod with Mediterranean Relish

When individually plated, this golden-topped fish resembles bistro-style food. Divide the onion mixture among eight plates and place a piece of fish on each.

SERVINGS 8 (1 piece fish and ⅓ cup onion mixture each)

CARB. PER SERVING 9 g

8 4-ounce fresh or frozen skinless cod fillets, ½ to 1 inch thick
1 large red onion, thinly sliced
2 tablespoons olive oil
8 medium roma tomatoes, coarsely chopped
½ cup sliced, pitted Kalamata olives
6 cloves garlic, minced
½ cup snipped fresh Italian (flat-leaf) parsley
1 finely shredded lemon peel (set aside)
¼ cup lemon juice
   Nonstick cooking spray
½ teaspoon salt
¼ teaspoon black pepper
⅓ cup whole wheat panko (Japanese-style bread crumbs)
¼ cup chopped pine nuts
   Lemon wedges (optional)
   Snipped fresh Italian (flat-leaf) parsley (optional)

1. Thaw fish, if frozen. Preheat oven to 425°F. In a very large skillet cook onion, covered, in hot oil over medium-low heat for 15 minutes, stirring occasionally. Uncover onion. Cook for 5 to 8 minutes more or until onion is lightly browned and very tender, stirring occasionally. Add tomatoes, olives, and garlic; cook and stir for 3 to 5 minutes more or until tomatoes are just softened and mixture is heated through. Stir in parsley and lemon juice.

2. Meanwhile, line a 15×10×1-inch baking pan with foil; coat foil with cooking spray. Set aside. Rinse fish; pat dry with paper towels. Place fish in prepared pan; measure thickness of fish. Sprinkle fish with salt and pepper. In a small bowl combine panko, pine nuts, and lemon peel.

Evenly spoon on top of fish, spreading to an even layer.

3. Bake fish for 4 to 6 minutes per ½-inch thickness or until fish flakes easily when tested with a fork and crumb mixture is golden brown.

4. To serve, arrange onion mixture on a serving platter. Top with fish. If desired, sprinkle with additional parsley and serve with lemon wedges.

PER SERVING: 201 cal., 8 g total fat (1 g sat. fat), 49 mg chol., 310 mg sodium, 9 g carb. (2 g fiber, 3 g sugars), 22 g pro. Exchanges: 0.5 vegetable, 0.5 starch, 3 lean meat, 0.5 fat. Carb choices: 0.5.

Potato Soup with Cheese Crisps

Make a second batch of the lacy cheese rounds. They freeze well and are also delicious served with leafy salad.

SERVINGS 6 (1½ cups and 2 crisps each)
CARB. PER SERVING 30 g

⅓ cup chopped red onion
1 medium green sweet pepper, chopped (¾ cup)
1 tablespoon canola oil
2 cloves garlic, minced
2¼ cups reduced-sodium chicken broth
3 medium round red potatoes (1 pound), scrubbed and cut into ½-inch pieces (about 3 cups)
3 medium carrots, peeled and thinly sliced (1½ cups)
1½ teaspoons dried thyme, crushed
¼ teaspoon salt
¼ teaspoon black pepper
4 cups fat-free milk
¼ cup all-purpose flour
Fresh thyme sprigs (optional)
1 recipe Cheese Crisps

1. In a large saucepan cook onion and sweet pepper in hot oil over medium heat for 5 minutes, stirring occasionally.

2. Add garlic; cook and stir for 1 minute more. Add broth, potatoes, carrots, dried thyme, salt, and black pepper. Bring to boiling; reduce heat. Simmer, covered, for 12 to 15 minutes or until vegetables are tender, stirring occasionally.

3. In a medium bowl whisk together 2 cups of the milk and the flour until smooth. Add all at once to potato mixture along with remaining milk. Cook and stir until slightly thickened and bubbly. Cook and stir for 1 minute more. If desired, garnish with fresh thyme. Serve with Cheese Crisps.

CHEESE CRISPS: Preheat oven to 400°F. Finely shred 3 ounces of reduced-fat white cheddar cheese. Line a baking sheet with parchment paper. Place cheese in twelve 1-tablespoon mounds about 2 inches apart on the parchment; flatten mounds slightly. Bake for 10 to 12 minutes or until bubbly and lightly browned. Let cool on parchment paper on baking sheet. Peel crisps off parchment.

PER SERVING: 215 cal., 5 g total fat (2 g sat. fat), 11 mg chol., 509 mg sodium, 30 g carb. (3 g fiber, 12 g sugars), 13 g pro. Exchanges: 0.5 milk, 1 vegetable, 1 starch, 1 fat. Carb choices: 2.

Creamy Cheese Fondue

The more the merrier—serve this rich and creamy fondue with several kinds of veggie dippers.

SERVINGS 5 (½ cup fondue and 2 cups vegetables each)
CARB. PER SERVING 23 g

1 6.5-ounce package light semisoft cheese with garlic and herb
1½ cups fat-free milk
1 tablespoon flour
2 ounces thinly sliced reduced-fat smoked provolone cheese or provolone cheese, torn
1 ounce Parmesan cheese, shredded (¼ cup)
Fat-free milk
10 cups assorted vegetable dippers, such as broccoli florets,* cauliflower florets,* sweet pepper strips, carrot sticks, and/or asparagus spears

1. In a medium saucepan heat and stir semisoft cheese over low heat until melted and smooth. In a medium bowl whisk together 1½ cups milk and the flour until smooth; gradually stir into cheese in saucepan. Cook and stir over medium heat until thickened and bubbly. Reduce heat to low. Cook and stir for 1 minute more. Gradually add provolone cheese and Parmesan cheese, whisking until cheeses are melted before adding more.

2. Transfer cheese mixture to a fondue pot; keep warm over fondue burner. (Fondue will thicken as it stands. If necessary, stir in additional milk, 1 to 2 tablespoons at a time, to reach desired consistency.) Whisk well before serving. Serve with vegetable dippers.

***TEST KITCHEN TIP:** If using broccoli and/or cauliflower florets, cook in a small amount of boiling water for 3 minutes or just until crisp-tender. Drain.

PER SERVING: 255 cal., 12 g total fat (8 g sat. fat), 38 mg chol., 527 mg sodium, 23 g carb. (5 g fiber, 13 g sugars), 15 g pro. Exchanges: 2 vegetable, 1 starch, 1 medium-fat meat, 1 fat. Carb choices: 1.5.

seasonal sides and salads

Pumpkin Mashed Potatoes

a new ingredient combo, a flavor twist, or a showy presentation can make a simple side dish seem special enough for the holidays. Make this your go-to collection when planning the trimmings—each intriguing hot or cold dish offers great flavor and is more healthful for you.

Pumpkin Mashed Potatoes

For a hassle-free serving idea, spoon the potato mixture into small ramekins instead of the mini pumpkins.

SERVINGS 4 (¾ cup each)
CARB. PER SERVING 26 g

1 pound medium baking potatoes, peeled and quartered
2 cloves garlic, peeled
1 cup canned pumpkin
2 tablespoons reduced-fat cream cheese (Neufchâtel)
1 tablespoon butter or tub-style vegetable oil spread
¼ teaspoon salt
¼ teaspoon black pepper
⅛ teaspoon ground sage
¼ cup fat-free milk
1 recipe Miniature Pumpkin Bowls (optional)
Fresh sage leaves (optional)

1. In a covered large saucepan cook potatoes and garlic in enough boiling water to cover for 20 to 25 minutes or until potatoes are tender; drain. Mash with a potato masher or beat with an electric mixer on low speed until nearly smooth. Beat in canned pumpkin, cream cheese, butter, salt, pepper, and sage. Slowly add milk, beating until light and fluffy. Return to saucepan; heat through.

2. If desired, spoon mashed potatoes into Miniature Pumpkin Bowls and garnish with sage leaves.

MINIATURE PUMPKIN BOWLS: Preheat oven to 325°F. Cut off ½ inch from the tops of 4 miniature pumpkins (6 to 8 ounces each); discard tops. Using a spoon, scoop out seeds and membranes and discard. Place pumpkins, cut sides down, on a baking sheet. Bake for 20 to 25 minutes or just until pumpkins are easily pierced with a fork.

PER SERVING: 159 cal., 5 g total fat (3 g sat. fat), 13 mg chol., 206 mg sodium, 26 g carb. (4 g fiber, 4 g sugars), 4 g pro. Exchanges: 0.5 vegetable, 1.5 starch, 1 fat. Carb choices: 2.

Green Onion-Potato Pancakes

Whether served as an appetizer or a side dish,
these crispy double-potato pancakes will win raves.

SERVINGS 12 (1 pancake and ½ tablespoon sour cream each)

CARB. PER SERVING 11 g

5	green onions
1	medium sweet potato, peeled (8 ounces)*
1	large potato, peeled (12 ounces)
2	eggs, lightly beaten
3	tablespoons flour
1	tablespoon lemon juice
1	teaspoon snipped fresh tarragon
½	teaspoon salt
¼	teaspoon black pepper
2	tablespoons canola oil
6	tablespoons light sour cream

1. Cut off root ends and 2 inches from tops of green onions. Cut onions into 3-inch pieces. Cut the onion pieces lengthwise into thin julienne strips. Finely shred sweet potato and potato into a large bowl.* Add green onions, eggs, flour, lemon juice, tarragon, salt, and pepper. Mix well.

2. In a very large nonstick skillet heat 1 tablespoon of the oil over medium-high heat. Using a scant ¼ cup for each pancake, drop potato mixture into hot oil; using a spatula, flatten each into a 4-inch pancake. Cook for 6 to 8 minutes or until golden and cooked through, turning once halfway through cooking. Adjust heat to prevent burning. Stir potato mixture between each batch. When half of the pancakes (six) are cooked, add the remaining tablespoon of oil to the skillet and continue cooking the remaining six pancakes. Drain pancakes on paper towels. Serve warm with sour cream.

*TEST KITCHEN TIP: Shred the sweet potato first; the white potato will darken if it is allowed to stand for too long.

PER SERVING: 88 cal., 4 g total fat (1 g sat. fat), 33 mg chol., 126 mg sodium, 11 g carb. (1 g fiber, 1 g sugars), 2 g pro. Exchanges: 1 starch, 0.5 fat. Carb choices: 1.

Curried Butternut Squash Bisque

If you have an immersion blender, use it to blend
this creamy golden soup right in the pot.

SERVINGS 12 (¾ cup and about 3 tablespoons onion mixture each)

CARB. PER SERVING 21 g

	Nonstick cooking spray
3	pounds butternut squash, halved lengthwise and seeds and pulp removed
3	cups reduced-sodium chicken broth
2½	cups water
2	medium apples, such as Cortland, peeled, cored, and coarsely chopped
1	medium carrot, chopped (½ cup)
2	teaspoons grated fresh ginger
1	teaspoon curry powder
½	teaspoon ground cumin
4	slices turkey bacon
1	tablespoon canola oil
¼	cup chopped onion
2	tablespoons sugar* (optional)
1	cup croutons

1. Preheat oven to 400°F. Coat a large shallow baking pan or a 15×10×1-inch baking pan with cooking spray. Place squash, cut sides down, in the prepared pan. Roast, uncovered, for 45 to 60 minutes or until tender. Scoop out flesh from squash into a bowl (discard skin). You should have about 3 cups.

2. In a 4- to 5-quart pot combine the squash, broth, water, apples, carrot, ginger, curry powder, and cumin. Bring to boiling; reduce heat. Simmer, covered, for 10 to 12 minutes or until vegetables are tender. Let soup cool slightly. In a food processor or blender process or blend mixture, one-third at a time, until smooth. Return soup to pot; heat through.

3. Meanwhile, in a large skillet cook bacon according to package directions until crisp. Remove bacon and set aside. Add oil to skillet. Cook onion and sugar (if using) over medium heat until onion is tender. Chop bacon. Stir bacon and croutons into skillet. Sprinkle bacon mixture over individual servings of soup.

*SUGAR SUBSTITUTE: We do not recommend using a sugar substitute for this recipe.

PER SERVING: 109 cal., 3 g total fat (0 g sat. fat), 4 mg chol., 254 mg sodium, 21 g carb. (3 g fiber, 6 g sugars), 3 g pro. Exchanges: 1.5 starch, 0.5 fat. Carb choices: 1.5.

Spiced Cauliflower

Spiced Cauliflower

A nonstick skillet or wok helps keep cooking oil
to a minimum when stir-frying vegetables—
plus it makes cleanup a snap.
SERVINGS 4 (1 cup each)
CARB. PER SERVING 8 g

½ teaspoon dry mustard
¼ teaspoon salt
¼ teaspoon ground turmeric
¼ teaspoon ground cumin
⅛ teaspoon ground coriander
⅛ teaspoon cayenne pepper
1 tablespoon vegetable oil
4 cups cauliflower florets
1 medium red or green sweet pepper,
  cut into 1-inch pieces
4 green onions, bias-sliced into 1-inch pieces
¼ cup reduced-sodium chicken broth

1. In a small bowl combine mustard, salt, turmeric, cumin, coriander, and cayenne pepper. Set aside.
2. In a wok or large skillet heat oil over medium-high heat. (Add more oil if necessary during cooking.) Add cauliflower; cook and stir for 6 minutes. Add sweet pepper and green onions; cook and stir for 1 minute. Reduce heat to medium. Add mustard mixture. Cook and stir for 30 seconds. Carefully stir in broth. Cook and stir about 1 minute more or until vegetables are heated through. Serve immediately.
PER SERVING: 72 cal., 4 g total fat (0 g sat. fat), 0 mg chol., 215 mg sodium, 8 g carb. (3 g fiber, 4 g sugars), 3 g pro. Exchanges: 1 vegetable, 1 fat. Carb choices: 0.5.

Veggie Mash

Roasted
Acorn Squash
with Rosemary

Creamy Coconut
and Snap Pea
Risotto

Season's Eatings

The holiday season need not set off snowballing weight gain or roller-coaster sugar levels. Gift yourself with these strategies.

1. **Manage calories and carbs** by enjoying one must-have per category—such as one appetizer, one main dish, one dessert, and one beverage.

2. **Use a small plate.** It helps you right-size portions so you can enjoy a sensible amount without veering off track.

3. **Drink two glasses** of water before a meal. Hydration is important during the dry, cooler months, and sometimes what feels like hunger may actually be thirst.

4. **Choose water-rich foods when possible.** Fruits and vegetables are about 90 percent water by weight, so they keep you hydrated and feeling full.

5. **Keep moving.** Daily exercise helps you stick with a routine.

Roasted Acorn Squash with Rosemary

SERVINGS 4 (4 slices squash and 2 tablespoons wine mixture each)
CARB. PER SERVING 25 g

- 2 medium acorn squash (about 2 pounds total)
- ¾ cup dry white wine or reduced-sodium vegetable broth
- 2 cloves garlic, very thinly sliced
- ¼ teaspoon salt
- ⅛ teaspoon black pepper
- 2 tablespoons light stick butter (not margarine)
- 1 teaspoon snipped fresh rosemary

1. Preheat oven to 350°F. Cut a squash in half lengthwise; remove and discard seeds. Place squash halves, cut sides down, on a cutting board. Cut the squash halves crosswise into 1-inch slices. Repeat with remaining squash. Pour the wine into a 2-quart rectangular baking dish. Add garlic slices to the wine. Arrange the squash slices in the dish, overlapping slices as needed. Sprinkle squash with salt and pepper.
2. Bake, covered, for 40 minutes. Uncover; bake for 10 to 15 minutes more or until squash is tender. Transfer squash slices to a platter, reserving liquid in dish.
3. Add butter and rosemary to the liquid in the baking dish. Stir until butter is melted. Spoon over squash on the platter and serve warm.

PER SERVING: 155 cal., 3 g total fat (2 g sat. fat), 8 mg chol., 205 mg sodium, 25 g carb. (3 g fiber, 0 g sugars), 2 g pro. Exchanges: 1.5 starch, 0.5 fat. Carb choices: 1.5.

Veggie Mash

SERVINGS 6 (½ cup each)
CARB. PER SERVING 15 g

- 3 medium baking potatoes (1 pound), peeled and cubed
- 1 cup coarsely chopped cauliflower
- ½ cup sliced carrot or coarsely chopped cauliflower
- ¼ cup light sour cream
- ¼ teaspoon salt
- ⅛ teaspoon black pepper
- 2 tablespoons finely shredded Parmesan cheese

1. In a covered medium saucepan cook potatoes, cauliflower, and carrot in enough boiling water to cover for 15 to 20 minutes or until tender; drain. Mash with a potato masher or beat with an electric mixer on low speed. Add sour cream, salt, and pepper. Mash or beat until combined. Top individual servings with Parmesan cheese.

PER SERVING: 81 cal., 1 g total fat (1 g sat. fat), 4 mg chol., 146 mg sodium, 15 g carb. (2 g fiber, 2 g sugars), 2 g pro. Exchanges: 1 starch. Carb choices: 1.

Creamy Coconut and Snap Pea Risotto

SERVINGS 6 (⅔ cup each)
CARB. PER SERVING 24 g

- 1 medium onion, chopped (½ cup)
- 2 teaspoons canola oil
- 1 cup arborio rice
- 2 cups reduced-sodium vegetable broth
- 1½ cups water
- 1 cup fresh sugar snap peas, trimmed
- ½ cup reduced-fat unsweetened coconut milk
- ½ teaspoon ground coriander
- ¼ teaspoon ground cardamom
- 1 cup coarsely chopped fresh spinach
- ¼ cup slivered almonds, toasted

1. In a large saucepan cook onion in hot oil about 5 minutes or until onion is just tender, stirring occasionally. Add rice. Cook and stir over medium heat for 2 to 3 minutes or until rice begins to brown.
2. Meanwhile, in another large saucepan bring broth and water to boiling. Add peas; return to boiling and cook for 1 minute. Remove peas with a slotted spoon; set aside on a cutting board. Reduce heat so broth is simmering.
3. Slowly add 1 cup of the broth to rice mixture, stirring constantly. Continue to cook, stirring frequently, over medium heat until liquid is absorbed. Add another ½ cup of the broth to the rice mixture, stirring constantly. Continue to cook, stirring frequently, until the liquid is absorbed. Add remaining broth, ½ cup at a time, stirring frequently, until the broth has been absorbed. (This should take 15 to 20 minutes.)
4. Meanwhile, cut the peas lengthwise into thin slices. When all of the broth has been added to the rice, stir in the coconut milk, coriander, cardamom, ⅛ teaspoon *salt*, and ⅛ teaspoon *black pepper*. Cook for 1 to 2 minutes more or until rice is just tender but still creamy. Stir in the peas and spinach. Transfer to a serving bowl. Sprinkle with almonds and serve immediately.

PER SERVING: 149 cal., 5 g total fat (1 g sat. fat), 0 mg chol., 243 mg sodium, 24 g carb. (1 g fiber, 2 g sugars), 3 g pro. Exchanges: 0.5 vegetable, 1.5 starch, 0.5 fat. Carb choices: 1.5.

Polenta-Corn Casserole

This double-corn dish is studded with green onions, zucchini, and red sweet pepper.

SERVINGS 6 (½ cup each)
CARB. PER SERVING 21 g

    3   green onions
    ¾   chopped zucchini
    ¾   chopped red sweet pepper
    1   tablespoon butter
    3   cloves garlic, minced
 1⅓   tablespoons reduced-sodium chicken broth
 1⅓   cups water
    ⅔   cup yellow cornmeal
    1   cup frozen whole kernel corn
    ⅓   cup finely shredded Parmesan cheese
    ½   cup quartered cherry tomatoes
    ¼   cup coarsely chopped fresh basil

1. Thinly slice green onions, keeping the white bottoms separate from the green tops. Set green tops aside. In a large saucepan cook white bottoms of green onions, the zucchini, and red sweet pepper in hot butter over medium heat for 5 minutes or until tender, stirring occasionally. Stir in garlic and cook for 30 seconds. Transfer vegetable mixture to a medium bowl and set aside.

2. In the same saucepan combine broth, water, and cornmeal. Bring to boiling, stirring constantly; reduce heat. Simmer, uncovered, for 15 minutes, stirring frequently. Stir in corn. Continue to cook about 10 minutes more or until polenta is thick and tender, stirring frequently. Remove from the heat and stir in zucchini mixture and green onion tops. Spread mixture in an even layer in a greased 2-quart au gratin dish or shallow 2-quart baking dish. Sprinkle with cheese.

3. Preheat oven to 350°F. Bake, uncovered, about 10 minutes or until heated through and cheese is melted. Sprinkle top with tomatoes and basil just before serving.

MAKE-AHEAD DIRECTIONS: Prepare as directed through Step 2. Cover with foil and chill for up to 48 hours. To serve, bake, covered, in a 350°F oven for 20 minutes. Uncover and bake about 10 minutes more or until heated through and cheese is melted. Sprinkle top with tomatoes and basil just before serving.

PER SERVING: 135 cal., 4 g total fat (2 g sat. fat), 8 mg chol., 227 mg sodium, 21 g carb. (2 g fiber, 3 g sugars), 5 g pro. Exchanges: 1.5 starch, 0.5 fat. Carb choices: 1.5.

Caramelized Balsamic Onions

As these onion halves cook, the balsamic mixture becomes syrupy and caramelizes the onions, giving them a bronzed color and a luscious, rich flavor.

SERVINGS 8 (½ onion and 1 tablespoon glaze each)
CARB. PER SERVING 9 g or 7 g

    2   tablespoons butter, melted
    1   tablespoon olive oil
    ⅓   cup balsamic vinegar
    2   tablespoons dry white wine, reduced-sodium chicken broth, or water
    1   tablespoon sugar*
    ¼   teaspoon salt
    ⅛   teaspoon freshly ground black pepper
    4   medium yellow onions (about 1½ pounds total)
        Fresh thyme leaves (optional)

1. Preheat oven to 425°F. In 3-quart rectangular baking dish combine butter and olive oil. Whisk in vinegar, wine, sugar, salt, and pepper. Set aside.

2. Peel off papery outer layers of onions, but do not cut off either end. Cut onions in half from stem through root end. Place onions in dish, cut sides up. Cover loosely with foil and bake for 30 minutes.

3. Remove foil. Using tongs, carefully turn onions over to cut sides down. Bake, uncovered, for 20 to 25 minutes longer or until onions are tender and balsamic mixture is thickened and caramelized. Serve cut sides up. If desired, sprinkle with fresh thyme.

***SUGAR SUBSTITUTES:** Choose from Splenda Granular or Sweet'N Low bulk or packets. Follow package directions to use product amount equivalent to 1 tablespoon sugar.

PER SERVING: 81 cal., 5 g total fat (2 g sat. fat), 8 mg chol., 103 mg sodium, 9 g carb. (1 g fiber, 6 g sugars), 1 g pro. Exchanges: 0.5 carb., 0.5 vegetable, 1 fat. Carb choices: 0.5.
PER SERVING WITH SUBSTITUTE: Same as above, except 76 cal., 7 g carb. (4 g sugars).

Caramelized
Balsamic Onions

Maple-Orange Roasted Carrots and Beets

If you use only yellow beets,
this dish won't turn the ruby red color.

SERVINGS 6 (⅓ cup each)
CARB. PER SERVING 16 g

Nonstick cooking spray
- 6 medium carrots, peeled and cut into 1- to 1½-inch pieces
- 12 ounces small red and/or yellow beets, trimmed, peeled, and quartered
- ¼ teaspoon salt
- ⅛ teaspoon black pepper
- 4 medium shallots, peeled and cut into ¾-inch wedges
- 2 tablespoons light stick butter (not margarine), cut up
- ½ teaspoon finely shredded orange peel
- 2 tablespoons orange juice
- 2 tablespoons light maple-flavored syrup

1. Preheat oven to 425°F. Coat a 3-quart rectangular baking dish with cooking spray. Arrange carrots and beets in a single layer in the prepared dish. Coat the vegetables with cooking spray and sprinkle with the salt and pepper. Toss to coat.

2. Cover with foil and roast for 20 minutes. Carefully uncover and stir in shallots. Replace cover and roast for 15 minutes more. Uncover and roast for 10 to 15 minutes more or until carrots and beets are tender. Add butter, orange peel, orange juice, and maple syrup to the dish. Toss vegetable mixture until butter is melted and vegetables are nicely coated. Serve warm.

PER SERVING: 87 cal., 2 g total fat (1 g sat. fat), 5 mg chol., 227 mg sodium, 16 g carb. (4 g fiber, 10 g sugars), 2 g pro. Exchanges: 1 vegetable, 0.5 carb., 0.5 fat. Carb choices: 1.

Swiss Chard with Peppered Bacon

Grab your extra-large skillet to make this dish.
Eight cups of chard leaves seems like a lot, but the greens
wilt to a manageable amount.

SERVINGS 4 (½ cup each)
CARB. PER SERVING 5 g

- 2 slices thick-sliced peppered bacon or regular bacon
- 1 medium onion, chopped (½ cup)
- 8 cups coarsely chopped fresh Swiss chard leaves
- ½ teaspoon finely shredded lemon peel
- ⅛ teaspoon black pepper

1. In a very large skillet cook bacon over medium heat until crisp. Remove bacon from skillet, reserving drippings in skillet; drain bacon on paper towels. Crumble bacon; set aside.

2. Cook onion in reserved drippings over medium heat about 5 minutes or until tender, stirring occasionally. Add Swiss chard. Cook about 5 minutes or just until tender, tossing occasionally. Stir in bacon and lemon peel. Sprinkle with the pepper.

PER SERVING: 62 cal., 3 g total fat (1 g sat. fat), 8 mg chol., 314 mg sodium, 5 g carb. (2 g fiber, 2 g sugars), 4 g pro. Exchanges: 1 vegetable, 0.5 fat. Carb choices: 0.

Maple-Orange
Roasted Carrots
and Beets

Smashed Parsnips

Smashed Parsnips

*Although using a food processor is better,
you can use a potato masher to make this smash.*
SERVINGS 6 (½ cup each)
CARB. PER SERVING 24 g

2 pounds parsnips, peeled and cut into 2-inch pieces
1 14.5-ounce can reduced-sodium chicken broth
1¼ cups water
¼ cup fat-free milk
1 tablespoon butter
½ teaspoon dried thyme or oregano, crushed
¼ teaspoon black pepper
⅛ teaspoon salt
Ground nutmeg
Fresh thyme sprigs (optional)

1. In a medium saucepan bring parsnips, chicken broth, and the water to boiling; reduce heat. Cover and simmer for 20 to 30 minutes or until parsnips are very tender; drain.
2. Transfer parsnips to a food processor. Add milk, butter, thyme, pepper, and salt; cover and process until almost smooth. Spoon into serving bowls. Sprinkle with nutmeg. If desired, garnish with thyme sprigs.
PER SERVING: 122 cal., 2 g total fat (1 g sat. fat), 5 mg chol., 244 mg sodium, 24 g carb. (6 g fiber, 7 g sugars), 3 g pro. Exchanges: 1.5 starch. Carb choices: 1.5.

Brussels Sprouts with
Crisp Prosciutto

Brussels Sprouts with Crisp Prosciutto

Sizzle prosciutto in a hot skillet and crumble like bacon over just about anything to make it absolutely irresistible.

SERVINGS 12 (¾ cup each)
CARB. PER SERVING 9 g

- 2½ pounds Brussels sprouts
- 1 tablespoon olive oil
- 3 ounces thinly sliced prosciutto
- ½ cup thinly sliced shallots or chopped onion
- 2 tablespoons butter
- ¼ teaspoon salt
- ¼ teaspoon freshly ground black pepper
- 1 tablespoon red wine vinegar

1. Trim stems and remove any wilted outer leaves from Brussels sprouts; wash. Cut any large sprouts in half lengthwise.

2. In a covered large pot cook Brussels sprouts in enough boiling lightly salted water to cover for 6 to 8 minutes or just until tender (centers should still be slightly firm); drain. Spread Brussels sprouts in a shallow baking pan.

3. In a very large skillet heat oil over medium-high heat. Cook prosciutto, half at a time, in the hot oil until crisp. Remove from skillet. Add shallots and butter to skillet. Cook and stir over medium heat about 2 minutes or until shallots start to soften.

4. Add Brussels sprouts, salt, and pepper to skillet. Cook and stir about 6 minutes or until Brussels sprouts are heated through. Drizzle with vinegar; toss gently to coat. Transfer to a serving bowl. Top with prosciutto.

BRUSSELS SPROUTS WITH BACON: Prepare as directed, except substitute 4 slices bacon for the prosciutto and omit the olive oil. Cook bacon until crisp. Remove from skillet, discarding drippings. Drain bacon on paper towels; crumble bacon.

PER SERVING: 91 cal., 5 g total fat (1 g sat. fat), 5 mg chol., 212 mg sodium, 9 g carb. (3 g fiber, 2 g sugars), 5 g pro. Exchanges: 1 vegetable, 1 fat. Carb choices: 0.5.

Farro and Collard Greens

Farro and Collard Greens

Collard greens are typically sold in a bunch. Half a bunch will yield about 8 ounces.

SERVINGS 6 (⅔ cup each)
CARB. PER SERVING 22 g

- 2 cups reduced-sodium chicken broth
- 1 cup semipearled farro or quick-cooking barley
- 8 ounces collard greens, stems removed and greens chopped (5 cups)
- 1 tablespoon olive oil
- ¼ teaspoon black pepper
- ⅛ teaspoon salt
  Lemon or orange peel strips

1. In a large saucepan bring broth to boiling. Stir in farro or barley. Gradually add collard greens. Return to boiling; reduce heat. Simmer, covered, about 20 minutes or until farro is tender. (Cook barley for 12 minutes or until tender.) Remove from heat. Let stand, covered, for 5 minutes.

2. Stir in oil, pepper, and salt. Garnish with citrus peel strips.

PER SERVING: 132 cal., 3 g total fat (0 g sat. fat), 0 mg chol., 247 mg sodium, 22 g carb. (4 g fiber, 2 g sugars), 6 g pro. Exchanges: 1 vegetable, 1 starch, 0.5 fat. Carb choices: 1.5.

Green Beans with Bacon and Walnuts

Set a timer when boiling the beans and pepper strips so they don't overcook. They cook again when stir-fried.
SERVINGS 6 (½ cup each)
CARB. PER SERVING 6 g

Green Beans with Bacon and Walnuts

12 ounces thin fresh green beans, trimmed
1 small red sweet pepper, cut into strips
2 slices bacon
¼ cup chopped walnuts
2 cloves garlic, minced
¼ teaspoon salt
⅛ teaspoon crushed red pepper

1. In a large saucepan cook green beans and sweet pepper in enough boiling water to cover for 3 minutes; drain. Set aside.
2. In a large skillet cook bacon over medium heat until crisp. Using a slotted spoon, remove bacon from skillet, reserving 2 tablespoons of the drippings in skillet (discard the remaining drippings). Drain bacon on paper towels. Crumble bacon; set aside.
3. Add green bean mixture, walnuts, garlic, salt, and crushed red pepper to the reserved drippings in skillet. Cook and stir about 5 minutes or until beans are tender and walnuts are lightly toasted. To serve, sprinkle with crumbled bacon.
PER SERVING: 106 cal., 9 g total fat (2 g sat. fat), 7 mg chol., 156 mg sodium, 6 g carb. (3 g fiber, 1 g sugars), 3 g pro. Exchanges: 1 vegetable, 2 fat. Carb choices: 0.5.

1. For shallot butter, in a small skillet cook shallots in olive oil over medium-low heat about 5 minutes or until shallots are golden, stirring often. Remove from heat; cool. Combine cooled shallot mixture with softened butter.
2. Meanwhile, wash beans; remove ends and strings if necessary. Leave whole or cut into 1-inch pieces. In a large pot cook beans, covered, in a small amount of boiling water for 10 to 15 minutes or until crisp-tender; drain.
3. To serve, transfer hot beans to a serving bowl. Top with shallot butter and, if desired, drizzle with vermouth; toss lightly to coat.
PER SERVING: 44 cal., 2 g total fat (1 g sat. fat), 5 mg chol., 22 mg sodium, 5 g carb. (2 g fiber, 3 g sugars), 1 g pro. Exchanges: 1 vegetable, 0.5 fat. Carb choices: 0.

Green Beans with Shallot Butter

Vermouths are all derived from white wine. They are fortified with a complex blend of botanicals, including herbs, flowers, and seeds. The flavor of dry vermouth quickly dissipates once opened, so be sure to refrigerate it and use within 3 months.
SERVINGS 12 (⅔ cup each)
CARB. PER SERVING 5 g

1 tablespoon finely chopped shallots
1 teaspoon olive oil
2 tablespoons butter, softened
2 pounds fresh green beans
1 tablespoon dry vermouth (optional)

Lemon-Tarragon Peas

This trio of peas also makes a great salad. Just use olive oil instead of butter and chill before serving.
SERVINGS 6 (½ cup each)
CARB. PER SERVING 17 g

½ cup water
3½ cups shelled fresh peas
1½ cups whole sugar snap and/or snow pea pods
1 tablespoon butter, softened
1 tablespoon snipped fresh tarragon
2 teaspoons finely shredded lemon peel
½ teaspoon freshly cracked black pepper
¼ teaspoon salt
Lemon wedges and/or tarragon sprigs (optional)

1. In a medium saucepan bring ½ cup water to boiling. Add shelled sweet peas. Return to boiling; reduce heat and simmer, covered, for 8 minutes. Add the whole sugar snap peas and cook, covered, for 4 minutes more or just until crisp-tender; drain.

2. Add butter, snipped tarragon, lemon peel, pepper, and salt to the peas. Toss gently until butter melts. If desired, garnish with lemon wedges and/or tarragon sprigs. Serve immediately.

PER SERVING: 111 cal., 2 g total fat (1 g sat. fat), 5 mg chol., 125 mg sodium, 17 g carb. (6 g fiber, 5 g sugars), 6 g pro. Exchanges: 1 starch, 0.5 fat. Carb choices: 1.

Light Green Bean Casserole

The green bean casserole gets a new, slim profile with the help of reduced-fat and reduced-sodium cream of mushroom soup. Almonds replace the standard fried onion rings on top.

SERVINGS 6 (1 cup each)

CARB. PER SERVING 14 g

---

1 10.75-ounce can reduced-fat and reduced-sodium cream of mushroom soup

¼ cup bottled roasted red sweet peppers, chopped, or one 2-ounce jar diced pimiento, drained

¼ teaspoon black pepper

⅛ teaspoon salt

3 9-ounce packages frozen French-cut green beans, thawed and drained

½ cup sliced almonds, toasted

1. Preheat oven to 350°F. In a large bowl combine condensed soup, roasted sweet peppers, black pepper, and salt. Stir in green beans. Transfer mixture to an ungreased 2-quart rectangular baking dish. Sprinkle with toasted almonds.

2. Bake, uncovered, for 30 to 35 minutes or until heated through.

PER SERVING: 128 cal., 5 g total fat (1 g sat. fat), 2 mg chol., 217 mg sodium, 14 g carb. (5 g fiber, 4 g sugars), 4 g pro. Exchanges: 1 vegetable, 0.5 starch, 1 fat. Carb choices: 1.

quick tip

To thaw the green beans, place them in a colander and hold it under cold running water. Once thawed, press beans with the back of a spoon to remove excess water.

Light Green Bean Casserole

Peas, Carrots,
and Mushrooms

Broccolini with Cream
Sauce and Pine Nuts

Broccolini with Cream Sauce and Pine Nuts

If Broccolini is not available, substitute broccoli.
Trim off the broccoli stem and discard, then cut the
broccoli into florets and cook as directed.

SERVINGS 6 (1 cup vegetables and 1 tablespoon
sauce each)

CARB. PER SERVING 8 g

1   pound Broccolini
1   medium red sweet pepper, cut into ½-inch-wide strips
1   tablespoon pine nuts
Nonstick cooking spray
1   large clove garlic, minced
4   ounces light semisoft cheese with garlic and fine herbs
    or light tub-style cream cheese
2   tablespoons fat-free milk
⅛   teaspoon salt
⅛   teaspoon black pepper
2   tablespoons snipped fresh oregano

1. In a large skillet cook Broccolini, covered, in a small
amount of boiling water for 4 minutes. Add the sweet
pepper strips. Cover and cook for 2 to 4 minutes more or
until vegetables are just tender. Drain off water and
cover to keep vegetables warm.
2. Meanwhile, in a small nonstick skillet heat pine nuts
over medium heat for 2 to 3 minutes or until lightly
toasted, stirring occasionally. Remove nuts from the
skillet and set aside. Cool skillet about 1 minute.
3. For sauce, coat the cooled skillet with cooking spray
and heat over medium heat. Add garlic; cook and stir for
30 seconds. Reduce heat to low and add cheese. Cook
and stir for 30 to 60 seconds or until cheese is softened
(cheese may separate, but whisking in milk will bring it
back to a smooth consistency). Whisk in the milk, salt,
and black pepper. Cook and stir until well combined and
heated through
4. Transfer Broccolini and pepper strips to a serving
platter. Drizzle with sauce and gently toss. Sprinkle
with pine nuts and oregano.
PER SERVING: 92 cal., 5 g total fat (3 g sat. fat), 14 mg chol.,
191 mg sodium, 8 g carb. (2 g fiber, 3 g sugars), 5 g pro.
Exchanges: 1 vegetable, 0.5 medium-fat meat, 0.5 fat.
Carb choices: 0.5.

Peas, Carrots, and Mushrooms

If you wish, stir together 2 tablespoons snipped
fresh basil, 1 tablespoon finely shredded lemon peel,
and 2 teaspoons minced ginger to create
a gremolata to sprinkle over the top.

SERVINGS 6 (⅔ cup each)

CARB. PER SERVING 9 g

1   medium carrot, sliced (½ cup)
1   10-ounce package frozen peas
2   cups sliced fresh mushrooms
2   green onions, cut into ½-inch pieces
1   tablespoon butter
1   tablespoon snipped fresh basil or ½ teaspoon dried
    basil, crushed
¼   teaspoon salt

1. In a covered medium saucepan cook carrot in a small
amount of boiling salted water for 3 minutes. Add frozen
peas. Return to boiling; reduce heat. Cook about
5 minutes more or until carrot and peas are crisp-
tender. Drain well. Remove carrot and peas from
saucepan; set aside.
2. In the same saucepan cook mushrooms and green
onions in hot butter until tender. Stir in basil, salt, and
dash *black pepper*. Return carrot and peas to saucepan;
heat through, stirring occasionally.
MAKE-AHEAD DIRECTIONS: Prepare as directed through Step 1.
Cool carrot mixture; transfer to a storage container; seal.
Cut up green onions; place in a separate storage
container; seal. Chill carrot mixture and green onions for
24 to 48 hours. To serve, continue as directed in Step 2.
PER SERVING: 69 cal., 3 g total fat (1 g sat. fat), 5 mg chol.,
229 mg sodium, 9 g carb. (3 g fiber, 3 g sugars), 4 g pro.
Exchanges: 0.5 vegetable, 0.5 starch, 0.5 fat. Carb
choices: 0.5.

quick tip

If you have dried cranberries or cherries on hand,
you can use them instead of snipped dried apricots.

Pesto Pasta with Olives and Artichokes

Leftovers? Toss a little shredded cooked chicken or turkey into this creamy Mediterranean-style pasta dish to serve for lunch the next day.

SERVINGS 10 (½ cup each)
CARB. PER SERVING 13 g

½ medium red onion, thinly sliced
2 teaspoons olive oil
1 9-ounce package frozen artichoke hearts, thawed, patted dry, and quartered*
1 red sweet pepper, cut into bite-size strips
2 cloves garlic, minced
4 ounces dried multigrain bow tie or penne pasta
¼ cup purchased basil pesto
1 ounce reduced-fat cream cheese (Neufchâtel) (about 2 tablespoons)
1 medium tomato, chopped
¼ cup assorted pitted olives (such as Kalamata, green, or niçoise), quartered or coarsely chopped
2 tablespoons snipped fresh basil

1. In a large skillet cook onion in hot oil over medium heat for 5 minutes, stirring occasionally. Add quartered artichokes, sweet pepper, and garlic. Cook about 5 minutes more or until vegetables are lightly browned and tender, stirring occasionally.
2. Meanwhile, in a large saucepan cook pasta in enough boiling unsalted water to cover for 8 minutes if using bow tie pasta or 9 minutes if using penne pasta (the pasta will not be fully tender). Just before the cooking time is up, remove ½ cup of the pasta cooking water and set aside. Drain the pasta and add to the onion mixture in the skillet. Add the reserved pasta cooking water, the pesto, and the cream cheese.
3. Cook, uncovered, over medium heat about 2 minutes or until pasta is tender and the cream cheese is melted. Stir in the tomato, olives, and 1 tablespoon of the basil. Transfer pasta mixture to a serving bowl. Sprinkle with remaining basil.
*TEST KITCHEN TIP: Some frozen artichoke hearts have already been quartered.
PER SERVING: 110 cal., 5 g total fat (1 g sat. fat), 4 mg chol., 106 mg sodium, 13 g carb. (4 g fiber, 2 g sugars), 3 g pro. Exchanges: 1 starch, 1 fat. Carb choices: 1.

Loaded Bread Stuffing

Full of veggies—mushrooms, celery, onion, sweet pepper, and carrots—this classic holiday side pairs well with poultry or pork.

SERVINGS 15 (⅔ cup each)
CARB. PER SERVING 13 g

¼ cup butter
1 cup fresh mushrooms, chopped
2 stalks celery, chopped (1 cup)
2 medium onions, chopped (1 cup)
½ cup chopped red sweet pepper
2 cloves garlic, minced
2 tablespoons snipped fresh sage or 2 teaspoons dried sage, crushed
½ teaspoon black pepper
⅛ teaspoon crushed red pepper (optional)
12 cups light whole wheat bread cut into 1-inch pieces and dried*
1 8-ounce can water chestnuts, drained and chopped
2 medium carrots, coarsely shredded (1 cup)
1 14.5-ounce can reduced-sodium chicken broth
½ cup refrigerated or frozen egg product, thawed, or 2 eggs, lightly beaten

1. Preheat oven to 325°F. In a large skillet melt butter over medium heat. Add mushrooms, celery, onions, sweet pepper, and garlic. Cook for 6 to 8 minutes or until vegetables are tender, stirring occasionally. Remove from heat. Stir in sage, black pepper, and, if desired, crushed red pepper.
2. In a very large bowl combine bread cubes, water chestnuts, and carrots. Add mushroom mixture and toss to combine. Add broth and egg, tossing lightly to combine. Transfer bread mixture to a greased 3-quart casserole. Lightly press down and let stand at room temperature for 30 minutes.
3. Bake, covered, for 50 to 55 minutes or until heated through.
*TEST KITCHEN TIP: To make bread cubes, preheat oven to 300°F. Spread bread cubes in a shallow roasting pan. Bake for 10 to 15 minutes or until cubes are dry, stirring twice; cool. (Cubes will continue to dry and crisp as they cool.) Or let bread cubes stand, loosely covered, at room temperature for 8 to 12 hours.
PER SERVING: 108 cal., 4 g total fat (2 g sat. fat), 8 mg chol., 227 mg sodium, 13 g carb. (4 g fiber, 3 g sugars), 6 g pro. Exchanges: 1 starch, 0.5 lean meat, 0.5 fat. Carb choices: 1.

Mediterranean Tabbouleh

Mediterranean Tabbouleh

Use a long sharp knife to cut the radiccchio or romaine into small shreds.

SERVINGS 8 (½ cup each)
CARB. PER SERVING 15 g

- 2 cups boiling water
- ¾ cup bulgur
- ½ teaspoon finely shredded lemon peel
- ¼ cup lemon juice
- 2 tablespoons olive oil
- ½ teaspoon salt
- ½ of a medium cucumber, halved lengthwise and thinly sliced crosswise
- ⅓ cup snipped fresh parsley
- ¼ cup thinly sliced green onions (2)
- ¼ cup snipped dried apricots
- 1 tablespoon snipped fresh mint
- 1 cup radicchio or romaine lettuce, coarsely shredded
- ⅓ cup crumbled reduced-fat feta cheese
- 2 tablespoons toasted pistachio nuts or walnuts, chopped

1. In a medium bowl combine boiling water and bulgur. Cover and let stand for 15 minutes. Meanwhile, in a large bowl whisk together lemon peel, lemon juice, oil, and salt. Drain the bulgur well and add bulgur to the lemon mixture. Add cucumber, parsley, green onions, apricots, and mint. Stir to coat well.

2. Cover and chill for 2 to 24 hours. Stir in radicchio and feta cheese and let stand for 15 minutes. Transfer tabbouleh to a serving bowl and sprinkle with pistachio nuts.

PER SERVING: 116 cal., 5 g total fat (1 g sat. fat), 2 mg chol., 232 mg sodium, 15 g carb. (3 g fiber, 3 g sugars), 4 g pro. Exchanges: 1 starch, 1 fat. Carb choices: 1.

Carrot Ribbon Salad

Use a vegetable peeler to remove the carrot peels and discard. Then, using the peeler, cut long, thin strips from the carrots, being careful not to scrape fingers.

SERVINGS 12 (½ cup each)
CARB. PER SERVING 19 g

- 1 pound large carrots
- 2 cups frozen peas, thawed
- 1 cup thinly sliced green onions (8)
- ½ cup honey
- ¼ cup white wine vinegar
- ½ teaspoon salt
- ¼ teaspoon black pepper

1. Using a vegetable peeler, peel carrots lengthwise into very thin strips.

2. In a large bowl combine carrots, peas, and green onions. For dressing, in a small bowl combine honey, vinegar, salt, and pepper.

3. Pour dressing over vegetables; toss gently to coat. Cover and chill for 2 to 4 hours. Serve with a slotted spoon.

PER SERVING: 81 cal., 0 g total fat, 0 mg chol., 151 mg sodium, 19 g carb. (2 g fiber, 15 g sugars), 2 g pro. Exchanges: 1 vegetable, 1 starch. Carb choices: 1.

Carrot Ribbon Salad

Grapefruit and
Kiwifruit Salad

Pear and
Jicama Salad

Grapefruit and Kiwifruit Salad

When sectioning the grapefruits, hold them over a
bowl to catch the juice. Use some of the juice
to make the vinaigrette.

SERVINGS 4 (1¾ cups each)
CARB. PER SERVING 15 g

- 1 recipe Grapefruit Vinaigrette
- ½ of a head red leaf or green oak lettuce, ribs removed and leaves torn
- 1 cup thinly sliced fennel bulb (about ½ bulb)
- 1 cup ruby red grapefruit sections
- 2 medium kiwifruits, peeled and sliced (1 cup)
- 2 slices bacon, crisp-cooked, drained, and crumbled

1. Prepare Grapefruit Vinaigrette; set aside.
2. In a large bowl toss together lettuce, fennel, and Grapefruit Vinaigrette. Transfer mixture to a large serving platter. Top with grapefruit sections and kiwifruit slices. Garnish with crumbled bacon.
GRAPEFRUIT VINAIGRETTE: In a small bowl whisk together 1 tablespoon grapefruit juice, 1 tablespoon white wine vinegar, 1 teaspoon minced shallot, ½ teaspoon Dijon-style mustard, ½ teaspoon agave nectar or honey, ¼ teaspoon freshly ground black pepper, and ⅛ teaspoon salt. Drizzle in 1 tablespoon olive oil, whisking to combine.
PER SERVING: 116 cal., 5 g total fat (1 g sat. fat), 4 mg chol., 192 mg sodium, 15 g carb. (3 g fiber, 9 g sugars), 3 g pro. Exchanges: 1 vegetable, 0.5 fruit, 1 fat. Carb choices: 1.

Pear and Jicama Salad

Here is a new twist on the classic Waldorf salad.
Made with pears and jicama instead of apples,
this version is coated with a zingy yogurt dressing.

SERVINGS 6 (¾ cup each)
CARB. PER SERVING 15 g

- 1 recipe Lime-Yogurt Dressing
- 1½ cups diced red pears (about 1½ medium)
- 1½ cups peeled jicama julienne sticks (½ large)
- ½ cups seedless grapes, halved
- 1 stalk celery, chopped (½ cup)
- ⅓ cup chopped walnuts, toasted
- 1 tablespoon snipped fresh mint

1. Prepare Lime-Yogurt Dressing; set aside.
2. In a large bowl toss together pears, jicama, grapes, celery, walnuts, and mint. Add Lime-Yogurt Dressing; toss to coat fruit mixture. Serve immediately.
LIME-YOGURT DRESSING: In a small bowl stir together ½ cup plain nonfat Greek yogurt, 2 tablespoons lime juice, 1 teaspoon agave nectar, and ¼ teaspoon black pepper.
PER SERVING: 103 cal., 4 g total fat (0 g sat. fat), 0 mg chol., 16 mg sodium, 15 g carb. (4 g fiber, 8 g sugars), 3 g pro. Exchanges: 1 fruit, 1 fat. Carb choices: 1.

Warm Bacon Salad Dressing

Toss this tasty dressing with fresh spinach and halved grape tomatoes for a classic wilted-style salad.

SERVINGS 4 (2 tablespoons each)
CARB. PER SERVING 4 g or 2 g

- 2 slices bacon
- ½ cup thinly sliced green onions (4)
- 2 cloves garlic, minced
- ¼ cup red wine vinegar
- 2 teaspoons sugar*
- 1 teaspoon coarse-grain mustard
- ¼ teaspoon black pepper

1. In a medium skillet cook bacon over medium heat until crisp. Remove bacon, reserving 2 tablespoons drippings in skillet (discard remaining drippings or add olive oil, if necessary, to measure 2 tablespoons). Drain bacon on paper towels. Crumble bacon; set aside.

2. Add green onions and garlic to the reserved drippings in skillet; cook and stir until onions are tender. Stir in remaining ingredients and crumbled bacon; heat through. Serve warm over desired salad greens.

***SUGAR SUBSTITUTES:** Choose from Splenda Granular, Equal Spoonful or packets, or Sweet'N Low bulk or packets. Follow package directions to use amount equivalent to 2 teaspoons sugar.

PER SERVING: 94 cal., 8 g total fat (3 g sat. fat), 10 mg chol., 116 mg sodium, 4 g carb. (0 g fiber, 2 g sugars), 1 g pro. Exchanges: 1.5 fat. Carb choices: 0.

PER SERVING WITH SUBSTITUTE: Same as above, except 87 cal., 2 g carb.

Warm Bacon
Salad Dressing

Warm Black-Eyed Pea Salad

You can also chill this salad for up to 24 hours and serve it cold.

SERVINGS 6 (½ cup each)
CARB. PER SERVING 18 g or 17 g

- Nonstick cooking spray
- 2 slices turkey bacon, chopped
- 3 green onions
- 1 medium red sweet pepper, chopped (¾ cup)
- 1 small fresh serrano or jalapeño chile pepper, seeded and finely chopped*
- 1 tablespoon canola oil
- 1 15-ounce can no-salt-added black-eyed peas, rinsed and drained
- 1 cup frozen whole kernel corn, thawed
- ¼ cup thinly sliced celery
- 3 tablespoons cider vinegar
- 2 teaspoons sugar**
- ¼ teaspoon dry mustard
- ⅛ teaspoon black pepper

1. Coat an unheated large nonstick skillet with cooking spray; heat over medium heat. Add chopped bacon; cook until bacon is cooked through, stirring occasionally. Remove bacon from skillet and set aside. Thinly slice the green onions, keeping white parts separate from green tops. Add white parts of green onions to the skillet; reserve green tops. Add sweet pepper, serrano pepper, and oil to the skillet. Cook about 5 minutes or until vegetables are just tender, stirring occasionally.

2. Add black-eyed peas, corn, celery, vinegar, sugar, mustard, black pepper, and sliced green onion tops. Cook and stir for 2 to 3 minutes or until well combined and heated through. Transfer to a serving bowl; sprinkle with bacon and serve warm.

***TEST KITCHEN TIP:** Because chile peppers contain volatile oils that can burn your skin and eyes, avoid direct contact with them as much as possible. When working with chile peppers, wear plastic or rubber gloves. If your bare hands do touch the peppers, wash your hands and nails well with soap and warm water.

****SUGAR SUBSTITUTES:** Choose from Splenda Granular or Sweet'N Low bulk or packets. Follow package directions to use product amount equivalent to 2 teaspoons sugar.

PER SERVING: 122 cal., 4 g total fat (1 g sat. fat), 5 mg chol., 80 mg sodium, 18 g carb. (3 g fiber, 3 g sugars), 5 g pro. Exchanges: 1 starch, 0.5 lean meat, 0.5 fat. Carb choices: 1.

PER SERVING WITH SUBSTITUTE: Same as above, except 117 cal., 17 g carb. (2 g sugars).

Cranberry-Pear Gelatin Salads

For sugared cranberries, lightly spritz fresh cranberries with water and then lightly roll in sugar.

SERVINGS 12 (1 individual salad each)
CARB. PER SERVING 18 g or 10 g

- ½ cup sugar*
- 2 envelopes unflavored gelatin
- 2½ cups low-calorie cranberry juice
- 1 cup carbonated water
- 2 pears, peeled, cored, and chopped
- ⅓ cup dried cranberries
- 36 sugared cranberries (optional)

1. In a medium saucepan stir together sugar and gelatin. Stir in ½ cup of the cranberry juice. Cook and stir over medium heat until sugar and gelatin dissolve. Remove saucepan from heat. Stir in the remaining 2 cups cranberry juice and the carbonated water.

2. Transfer gelatin mixture to a large bowl; cover and chill for 1 to 2 hours or until slightly thickened. Stir in pears and dried cranberries. Divide gelatin mixture among twelve 5- to 6-ounce individual molds or custard cups. (Or pour gelatin mixture into a 2-quart baking dish.) Cover and chill for 4 to 24 hours or until firm.

3. Remove gelatin from molds. If desired, garnish each serving with sugared cranberries.

*SUGAR SUBSTITUTES: Choose from Splenda Granular or Sweet'N Low bulk or packets. Follow package directions to use product amount equivalent to ½ cup sugar.

PER SERVING: 71 cal., 0 g total fat, 0 mg chol., 18 mg sodium, 18 g carb. (1 g fiber, 15 g sugars), 1 g pro. Exchanges: 0.5 fruit, 0.5 carb. Carb choices: 1.

PER SERVING WITH SUBSTITUTE: Same as above, except 43 cal., 10 g carb. (8 g sugars), 22 mg sodium. Exchanges: 0 carb. Carb choices: 0.5.

fresh-baked breads

Herbed Boule

*W*hether it's a hand-shaped round, fruit-studded braid, cinnamon-scented roll, or onion-filled scone, fresh-from-the oven breads are holiday-special. The recipes in this collection of loaded-with-goodness treats will make you feel good about adding a serving to your meal.

Herbed Boule

This dough rises faster than many other yeast breads, so watch the rising time carefully.

SERVINGS 24 (1 slice each)
CARB. PER SERVING 23 g

5½ to 6 cups flour
   2 packages active dry yeast
   2 teaspoons salt
   2 cups warm water (120°F to 130°F)
   2 tablespoons snipped fresh thyme, sage, and/or rosemary
     Cornmeal
   1 egg white, lightly beaten
   1 tablespoon water
   2 cups ice cubes

1. In a large bowl combine 2 cups of the flour, the yeast, and salt. Add the 2 cups warm water to the flour mixture. Beat with an electric mixer on low to medium speed for 30 seconds, scraping sides of bowl. Beat on high speed for 3 minutes. Using a wooden spoon, stir in thyme and as much of the remaining flour as you can.
2. Turn dough out onto a lightly floured surface. Knead in enough of the remaining flour to make a stiff dough that is smooth and elastic (8 to 10 minutes total). Shape dough into a ball. Place dough in a lightly greased bowl, turning once. Cover and let rise in a warm place until double in size (about 40 to 45 minutes).
3. Punch dough down. Turn out onto a lightly floured surface. Divide dough in half; cover and let rest for 10 minutes. Meanwhile, lightly grease a baking sheet; sprinkle with cornmeal.
4. Shape each dough portion into a 6-inch round loaf. Transfer the dough rounds to the prepared baking sheet. Cover; let rise in a warm place until nearly double in size (25 to 30 minutes).
5. Adjust one oven rack to the lowest position and another oven rack to the lower-middle position. Set a shallow baking pan on the bottom rack. Preheat the oven to 450°F. Using a sharp knife, make an X in the top of each loaf. In a small bowl combine egg white and the 1 tablespoon water; brush on tops of loaves. Place baking sheet with dough rounds on the lower-middle rack. Place ice cubes in the shallow baking pan (as they melt, they will create steam and help the dough rise and take on a crisp crust). Bake for 22 to 25 minutes or until the loaves sound hollow when tapped. If necessary, cover baking pan with foil after 15 minutes to prevent overbrowning.
PER SERVING: 110 cal., 0 g total fat, 0 mg chol.,198 mg sodium, 23 g carb. (1 g fiber, 0 g sugars), 3 g pro. Exchanges: 1.5 starch. Carb choices: 1.5.

Classic Bread Loaf

Basic enough to toast for breakfast and yummy enough to serve with a holiday meal, this bread is an easy one to master making.

SERVINGS 12 (1 slice each)
CARB. PER SERVING 23 g or 21 g

¾ cup warm water (105°F to 115°F)
1 package active dry yeast
½ cup fat-free milk
2 tablespoons sugar*
2 tablespoons butter
½ teaspoon salt
2½ cups flour
Nonstick cooking spray or olive oil
Cornmeal
1 egg, lightly beaten
2 teaspoons water

1. In a large bowl stir together the ¾ cup water and the yeast. Let stand for 5 minutes. Meanwhile, in a small saucepan heat and stir milk, sugar, butter, and salt just until warm (120°F to 130°F) and butter almost melts. Stir milk mixture into yeast mixture until combined. Stir in flour (dough will be sticky). Lightly coat a medium bowl with cooking spray; transfer dough to the greased bowl. Lightly coat a sheet of plastic wrap with cooking spray; cover bowl with the greased plastic wrap and chill dough overnight.

2. Using a dough scraper or spatula, carefully loosen dough from bowl and turn out onto a floured surface. Cover with the greased plastic wrap and let stand for 30 minutes.

3. Grease a baking sheet; sprinkle lightly with cornmeal. Gently shape dough into an oval loaf (about 6×5 inches). Using a dough scraper or spatula if necessary, transfer loaf to the prepared baking sheet. Cover and let rise in a warm place until nearly double in size (about 1 hour).

4. Preheat oven to 400°F. In a small bowl whisk together egg and the 2 teaspoons water; brush over loaf. Bake about 25 minutes or until an instant-read thermometer inserted in loaf registers at least 200°F and bread sounds hollow when tapped. If necessary, cover with foil during the last 5 minutes of baking to prevent overbrowning.

Remove from baking sheet; cool on a wire rack.

*SUGAR SUBSTITUTES: Choose from Splenda Granular or Sweet'N Low bulk or packets. Follow package directions to use product amount equivalent to 2 tablespoons sugar.

PER SERVING: 134 cal., 3 g total fat (1 g sat. fat), 21 mg chol., 125 mg sodium, 23 g carb. (1 g fiber, 3 g sugars), 4 g pro. Exchanges: 1.5 starch, 0.5 fat. Carb choices: 1.5.

PER SERVING WITH SUBSTITUTE: Same as above, except 127 cal., 21 g carb. (1 g sugars).

Easy Sesame Dinner Rolls

Sesame seeds and cornmeal add a satisfying crunch to these fuss-free rolls.

SERVINGS 16 (1 roll each)
CARB. PER SERVING 15 g

1 16-ounce loaf frozen white or wheat bread dough
¼ cup sesame seeds
2 tablespoons yellow cornmeal
2 tablespoons grated or finely shredded Parmesan cheese
1 teaspoon salt-free lemon-pepper seasoning
3 tablespoons butter, melted

1. Thaw dough according to package directions. Grease a 9×9×2-inch square baking pan; set aside. In a shallow dish combine sesame seeds, cornmeal, Parmesan cheese, and lemon-pepper seasoning. Place butter in a second dish. Cut the bread dough into 16 equal pieces. Shape each piece into a ball by pulling and pinching dough underneath. Roll dough pieces in butter, then in the seasoning mixture to lightly coat. Arrange dough pieces, smooth sides up, in prepared pan.

2. Cover pan with waxed paper and let rise in a warm place until nearly double in size (45 to 60 minutes).

3. Preheat oven to 375°F. Bake, uncovered, about 25 minutes or until golden brown. Remove rolls from pan to a wire rack. Cool slightly before serving.

GARLIC-HERB ROLLS: Prepare as directed, except omit lemon-pepper seasoning and add 1 teaspoon dried Italian seasoning, crushed, and ½ teaspoon garlic powder.

PER SERVING: 109 cal., 4 g total fat (2 g sat. fat), 6 mg chol., 180 mg sodium, 15 g carb. (1 g fiber, 1 g sugars), 2 g pro. Exchanges: 1 starch, 0.5 fat. Carb choices: 1.

quick tip

Use the microwave to melt the
butter in a small bowl, then dip each dough
ball in butter and roll in seasoning
to create the yummy coating on
Easy Sesame Dinner Rolls.

Easy Focaccia Casserole Bread

To loosen the edges from the casserole, run a table knife or straight-sided spreader around side of dish.

SERVINGS 12 (1 slice each)
CARB. PER SERVING 25 g or 24 g

Nonstick cooking spray
- 3 cups flour
- 1 package fast-rising active dry yeast
- 1 cup lukewarm water (120°F to 130°F)
- 1 egg
- 1 tablespoon sugar*
- 2 tablespoons olive oil
- ½ teaspoon salt
- ½ teaspoon dried Italian seasoning, crushed
- 2 tablespoons grated Romano cheese or Parmesan cheese
- 2 tablespoons sliced green onion (1) (optional)
- 2 tablespoons Kalamata olives, quartered lengthwise (optional)

1. Coat a 1½-quart casserole with cooking spray; set aside. In a medium bowl stir together 1½ cups of the flour and the yeast. Add the water, egg, sugar, 1 tablespoon of the olive oil, and the salt. Beat with an electric mixer on low speed for 30 seconds, scraping sides of bowl constantly. Beat on high speed for 3 minutes. Using a wooden spoon, stir in the remaining 1½ cups flour (batter will be stiff).

2. Spoon batter into prepared casserole. Brush with the remaining 1 tablespoon olive oil. Sprinkle with Italian seasoning. Sprinkle with cheese and, if desired, green onion and olives. Cover; let rise in a warm place until nearly double in size (25 to 30 minutes).

3. Preheat oven to 375°F. Bake for 30 to 35 minutes or until bread sounds hollow when lightly tapped. Remove from casserole; cool completely on a wire rack.

*SUGAR SUBSTITUTES: Choose from Splenda Granular or Sweet'N Low bulk or packets. Follow package directions to use product amount equivalent to 1 tablespoon sugar.

PER SERVING: 149 cal., 3 g total fat (1 g sat. fat), 16 mg chol., 117 mg sodium, 25 g carb. (1 g fiber, 1 g sugars), 4 g pro. Exchanges: 1.5 starch, 0.5 fat. Carb choices: 1.5.

PER SERVING WITH SUBSTITUTE: Same as above, except 146 cal., 24 g carb. (0 g sugars).

Spicy Apricot and Sausage Braid

*This spicy-sweet bread could serve as either a hearty
snack or an exciting accompaniment to a holiday meal.*

SERVINGS 16 (1 slice each)

CARB. PER SERVING 23 g

- 4 ounces andouille sausage, finely chopped
- ½ cup finely chopped dried apricots
- ½ to 1 teaspoon crushed red pepper
- ½ cup snipped fresh cilantro
- 2 tablespoons honey
- 3 to 3½ cups all-purpose flour
- 1 package active dry yeast
- ¾ teaspoon salt
- ⅔ cup warm water (105°F to 115°F)
- 2 eggs, lightly beaten
- ¼ cup olive oil
- 1 egg, lightly beaten
- 1 teaspoon water

1. In a large nonstick skillet cook sausage over medium-
high heat until it starts to brown. Stir in apricots and
crushed red pepper. Cook and stir for 1 minute. Stir in
cilantro and honey. Remove from heat; cool.

2. Meanwhile, in a large bowl combine 1 cup of the
flour, the yeast, and salt. Add the ⅔ cup warm water,
the 2 eggs, and the oil. Beat with an electric mixer on
low to medium speed for 30 seconds, scraping sides of
bowl constantly. Beat on high speed for 3 minutes. Stir
in sausage mixture. Using a wooden spoon, stir in as
much of the remaining flour as you can.

3. Turn dough out onto a lightly floured surface. Knead
in enough of the remaining flour to make a soft dough
that is smooth and elastic (3 to 5 minutes total). Shape
dough into a ball. Place dough in a lightly greased bowl,
turning once to grease surface of dough. Cover; let rise
in a warm place until double in size (about 1 hour).

4. Punch dough down. Turn dough out onto a lightly
floured surface; divide dough into three portions. Cover;
let rest for 10 minutes. Meanwhile, line a large baking
sheet with parchment paper.

5. Gently roll each dough portion into a 16-inch-long
rope. Place the ropes 1 inch apart on the prepared
baking sheet; braid.

6. Cover; let rise in a warm place until nearly double in
size (about 40 minutes).

7. Preheat oven to 350°F. In a small bowl combine the
1 egg and the 1 teaspoon water; brush over braid. Bake

Spicy Apricot
and Sausage Braid

for 20 to 25 minutes or until loaf sounds hollow when
lightly tapped. Cool on a wire rack. Store in the
refrigerator.

MAKE-AHEAD DIRECTIONS: Prepare dough as directed through
Step 5. Chill dough for at least 2 hours or up to 24 hours.
Let stand at room temperature for 30 minutes before
baking. Continue as directed in Step 7.

PER SERVING: 158 cal., 5 g total fat (1 g sat. fat), 41 mg chol.,
177 mg sodium, 23 g carb. (1 g fiber, 4 g sugars), 5 g pro.
Exchanges: 1.5 starch, 1 fat. Carb choices: 1.5.

Herbed Braidsticks

Look for semolina flour near the grains in the baking aisle of your supermarket or at an Italian grocery.
SERVINGS 16 (1 braidstick each)
CARB. PER SERVING 15 g or 14 g

- 1 to 1¼ cups all-purpose flour
- 1 package active dry yeast
- 1 tablespoon snipped fresh rosemary, thyme, and/or oregano
- ¼ teaspoon coarsely ground black pepper
- ¾ cup fat-free milk
- 2 tablespoons butter
- 1 tablespoon sugar*
- ½ teaspoon salt
- 1 cup semolina pasta flour or ¾ cup all-purpose flour plus ¼ cup yellow cornmeal
- 1 egg white, lightly beaten
- 1 tablespoon water

1. In a large bowl stir together ¾ cup of the all-purpose flour, the yeast, rosemary, and pepper. In a small saucepan heat the milk, butter, sugar, and salt just until warm (120°F to 130°F) and butter almost melts. Add milk mixture to flour mixture. Beat with an electric mixer on low to medium speed for 30 seconds, scraping sides of bowl constantly. Beat on high speed for 3 minutes. Using a wooden spoon, stir in semolina flour. Let stand for 1 minute. Stir in as much of the remaining all-purpose flour as you can.

2. Turn dough out onto a lightly floured surface. Knead in enough of the remaining all-purpose flour to make a stiff dough that is smooth and elastic (8 to 10 minutes total). Shape into a ball. Place dough in a lightly greased large bowl, turning once to grease surface of dough. Cover; let rise in a warm place until nearly double in size (45 to 60 minutes).

3. Punch dough down. Turn out onto a lightly floured surface. Divide dough in half. Cover and let rest for 10 minutes. Line a baking sheet with foil; grease foil. Roll one dough portion into a 10×9-inch rectangle. Cut lengthwise into 24 strips.

4. For each breadstick, pinch together ends of three strips; braid the dough strips. Pinch the other ends together. Tuck under the thin, pinched ends. Place on the prepared baking sheet. Repeat with remaining dough portion. Cover; let rise in a warm place until nearly double in size (about 30 minutes).

5. Preheat oven to 350°F. In a small bowl beat together egg white and the water. Lightly brush egg white

mixture on breadsticks. Bake for 22 to 25 minutes or until golden. Serve warm.

*SUGAR SUBSTITUTES: Choose from Splenda Granular or Sweet'N Low bulk or packets. Follow package directions to use product amount equivalent to 1 tablespoon sugar.
PER SERVING: 88 cal., 2 g total fat (1 g sat. fat), 4 mg chol., 94 mg sodium, 15 g carb. (1 g fiber, 2 g sugars), 3 g pro. Exchanges: 1 starch. Carb choices: 1.
PER SERVING WITH SUBSTITUTE: Same as above, except 86 cal., 14 g carb. (1 g sugars).

Gruyère Beer Bread

Change the flavor of this stir-together quick loaf by using white cheddar cheese instead of the Gruyère.
SERVINGS 12 (1 slice each)
CARB. PER SERVING 18 g

- 1¼ cups all-purpose flour
- ¾ cup whole wheat pastry flour or whole wheat flour
- 2 teaspoons baking powder
- ¼ teaspoon salt
- 2 tablespoons butter
- 2 tablespoons light stick butter (not margarine)
- 3 ounces Gruyère cheese, shredded (¾ cup)
- ½ cup light beer or nonalcoholic beer
- ¼ cup fat-free milk
- ¼ cup refrigerated or frozen egg product, thawed, or 1 egg, lightly beaten
- 2 tablespoons snipped fresh chives
- 2 tablespoons honey

1. Preheat oven to 350°F. Lightly grease an 8×4×2-inch loaf pan. In a large bowl stir together flours, baking powder, and salt. Using a pastry blender, cut in butter and light butter until mixture resembles coarse crumbs. Stir in cheese. In a medium bowl combine beer, milk, egg, chives, and honey. Add to flour mixture all at once. Stir with a fork just until combined.

2. Spoon into prepared pan and spread evenly. Bake for 40 to 45 minutes or until a wooden toothpick inserted in center comes out clean. Cool in pan on a wire rack for 10 minutes. Remove loaf from the pan and cool completely. Store any leftover bread in an airtight container in the refrigerator.
PER SERVING: 139 cal., 5 g total fat (3 g sat. fat), 15 mg chol., 179 mg sodium, 18 g carb. (1 g fiber, 3 g sugars), 5 g pro. Exchanges: 1 starch, 1 fat. Carb choices: 1.

quick tip

For faster shaping of Herbed Braidsticks, cut the rolled dough into 1-inch-wide strips. Hold each strip at both ends and twist in opposite directions two or three times.

Checkerboard Rolls

Checkerboard Rolls

*To keep the seed topping out of the butter,
make the cheese-topped rolls first and place them in
alternating spaces in the pan. Then coat the remaining
balls with the seed topping and fill the pan.*

SERVINGS 24 (1 roll each)
CARB. PER SERVING 18 g or 17 g

- 3½ to 4 cups flour
- 1 package active dry yeast
- 1 cup fat-free milk
- ¼ cup water
- ¼ cup sugar*
- ¼ cup canola oil
- 1 teaspoon salt
- 1 egg, lightly beaten
- 2 tablespoons sesame seeds
- 2 tablespoons poppy seeds
- 2 teaspoons dried minced onion and/or dried minced garlic
- 2 tablespoons yellow cornmeal
- 2 tablespoons grated Romano cheese or Parmesan cheese
- ¼ cup butter, melted

1. In a large bowl stir together 1½ cups of the flour and the yeast. In a small saucepan heat and stir milk, water, sugar, oil, and salt over medium-low heat just until warm (105°F to 115°F). Add the milk mixture and egg to flour mixture; stir until well combined. Let stand for 5 minutes. Gradually stir in enough of the remaining flour to make a soft dough. Turn dough out onto a lightly floured surface. Knead in enough of the remaining flour to make a moderately soft dough that is smooth and elastic (about 3 minutes total). Shape dough into a ball. Place in a lightly greased bowl, turning once to grease surface of dough. Cover; let rise in warm place until double in size (about 1 hour).

2. Grease a 15×10×1-inch baking pan; set aside. Punch dough down; turn out onto a lightly floured surface. Let dough rest for 10 minutes. Divide dough evenly into 24 pieces. Gently shape into balls. In a shallow dish combine sesame seeds, poppy seeds, and dried minced onion. In another shallow dish combine cornmeal and Romano cheese. Place ¼ cup melted butter in a third dish. Working quickly, roll dough pieces in butter and in one of the seasoning mixtures to lightly coat. Coat half of the rolls with one seasoning mixture and the remaining rolls with the other seasoning mixture. Alternate rolls in prepared pan. Cover rolls with greased plastic wrap and a towel. Let rise in a warm place for 30 minutes.

3. Preheat oven to 400°F. Bake for 12 to 15 minutes or until golden. Remove from pan. Serve warm or at room temperature.

MAKE-AHEAD DIRECTIONS: Prepare as directed through Step 2, except do not cover with a towel. Chill for up to 24 hours. To prepare, let stand at room temperature for 30 minutes. Continue as directed in Step 3. Or bake and cool rolls as directed. Wrap in plastic wrap; place in a resealable plastic freezer bag. Seal, label, and freeze for up to 2 months. Thaw at room temperature. To serve, preheat oven to 375°F. Heat for 5 to 8 minutes.

*SUGAR SUBSTITUTES: Choose from C&H Light Sugar and Stevia Blend, Splenda Sugar Blend for Baking, or Sun Crystals Granulated Blend. Follow package directions to use product amount equivalent to ¼ cup sugar.

PER SERVING: 131 cal., 5 g total fat (2 g sat. fat), 13 mg chol., 127 mg sodium, 18 g carb. (1 g fiber, 3 g sugars), 3 g pro. Exchanges: 1 starch, 1 fat. Carb choices: 1.

PER SERVING WITH SUBSTITUTE: Same as above, except 127 cal., 17 g carb. (2 g sugars).

Multigrain Dinner Rolls

If the rolls are placed on baking sheets, they bake up as golden rounds. For pull-apart rolls, bake them in square baking pans.

SERVINGS 24 (1 roll each)
CARB. PER SERVING 16 g

1¼ cups fat-free milk
⅓ cup quick-cooking rolled oats
2 tablespoons honey
2 tablespoons butter
1 teaspoon salt
1 package active dry yeast
¼ cup warm water (110°F to 115°F)
1 egg, lightly beaten
⅓ cup whole wheat flour
⅓ cup rye flour or brown rice flour
2 tablespoons toasted wheat germ or flaxseed meal
2¾ to 3¼ cups all-purpose flour
2 tablespoons light stick butter, melted

1. In small saucepan stir together milk, oats, honey, 2 tablespoons butter, and salt; heat to lukewarm (110°F to 115°F). In large bowl dissolve yeast in warm water. Add egg and milk mixture to yeast mixture. Stir in whole wheat flour, rye flour, and wheat germ. Gradually stir in enough of the all-purpose flour to make a soft dough.

2. Turn dough out onto lightly floured surface; knead gently for 2 to 3 minutes to make a smooth ball. Knead in just enough remaining flour so dough is no longer sticky. Place dough in greased bowl, turning once to grease surface of dough. Cover; let rise in a warm place until double in size (about 1 hour).

3. Punch dough down. Turn out onto a lightly floured surface. Divide dough in half; cover and let rest for 10 minutes. Lightly grease two large baking sheets; set aside.

4. Divide each dough half into 12 equal portions. Shape the dough portions into balls by pulling dough down and pinching underneath. Place rolls 2 to 3 inches apart on prepared baking sheets. Cover and let rise until nearly double in size (about 30 minutes).

5. Preheat oven to 375°F. Bake rolls for 14 to 16 minutes or until golden brown and rolls sound hollow when lightly tapped. Remove from pan. Brush tops of rolls with melted light butter. Serve warm or cool.

STANDARD DINNER ROLLS: Grease two 9×9×2-inch square baking pans. Divide each dough half into 12 equal portions. Shape the dough portions into balls by pulling dough down and pinching underneath. Arrange balls in prepared pans. Cover; let rise in a warm place until nearly double in size (about 30 minutes). Bake for 15 to 20 minutes or until golden brown and rolls sound hollow when lightly tapped. Immediately remove from pan. Brush tops with melted light butter. Serve warm or cool.

PER SERVING: 95 cal., 2 g total fat (1 g sat. fat), 12 mg chol., 123 mg sodium, 16 g carb. (1 g fiber, 2 g sugars), 3 g pro. Exchanges: 1 starch. Carb choices: 1.

Cheddar-Cornmeal Rolls

A quick whirl in the food processor turns butter, roasted red peppers, and garlic into a creamy spread to serve with these cloverleaf rolls.

SERVINGS 24 (1 roll each)
CARB. PER SERVING 23 g or 22 g

- 4 to 4½ cups flour
- ¾ cup cornmeal
- 2 packages active dry yeast
- 1¼ cups buttermilk or sour milk*
- ¼ cup sugar**
- 3 tablespoons butter or vegetable oil
- 3 tablespoons Dijon-style mustard
- 1 teaspoon salt
- 1 cup shredded reduced-fat sharp cheddar cheese (4 ounces)
- 2 eggs
- 1 recipe Roasted Red Pepper Butter (optional)

1. In a large bowl stir together 1½ cups of the flour, the cornmeal, and yeast; set aside. In a small saucepan heat and stir the buttermilk, sugar, butter, mustard, and salt just until warm (120°F to 130°F) and butter is almost melts. Add buttermilk mixture, cheese, and eggs to flour mixture. Beat with an electric mixer on low to medium speed for 30 seconds, scraping sides of bowl constantly. Beat on high speed for 3 minutes. Using a wooden spoon, stir in as much of the remaining flour as you can.
2. Turn dough out onto a lightly floured surface. Knead in enough of the remaining flour to make a moderately stiff dough that is smooth and elastic (6 to 8 minutes total). Shape into a ball. Place dough in a lightly greased large bowl, turning once to grease surface of dough. Cover; let rise in a warm place until double in size (about 1½ hours).

3. Punch dough down. Turn dough out onto a lightly floured surface. Divide dough in half. Cover and let rest for 10 minutes. Meanwhile, lightly grease twenty-four 2½-inch muffin cups. Set aside.

4. Divide each dough half into 36 portions. Shape each portion into a ball, pulling edges under to make a smooth top. Place three balls, smooth sides up, in each prepared muffin cup. Cover muffin pans. Let rise in a warm place until nearly double in size (about 45 minutes).

5. Preheat oven to 375°F. Bake about 15 minutes or until rolls sound hollow when lightly tapped. Immediately remove from muffin cups; cool slightly on wire racks. Serve warm. If desired, serve with Roasted Red Pepper Butter.

ROASTED RED PEPPER BUTTER: Drain ¼ cup chopped bottled roasted red sweet peppers; pat dry with paper towels. In a food processor combine the chopped peppers; ½ cup butter, cut up and softened; and 1 clove garlic, minced. Cover and process until well mixed.

MAKE-AHEAD DIRECTIONS: Layer cooled baked rolls between waxed paper in an airtight container; seal. Store at room temperature for up to 24 hours. To serve, preheat oven to 350°F. Remove rolls from container; wrap rolls in foil. Bake about 15 minutes or until warm.

*TEST KITCHEN TIP: To make 1¼ cups sour milk, place 4 teaspoons lemon juice or vinegar in a glass measuring cup. Add enough milk to make 1¼ cups total liquid; stir. Let stand for 5 minutes before using.

**SUGAR SUBSTITUTES: Choose from C&H Light Sugar and Stevia Blend, Splenda Sugar Blend for Baking, or Sun Crystals Granulated Blend. Follow package directions to use product amount equivalent to ¼ cup sugar.

PER SERVING: 139 cal., 3 g total fat (2 g sat. fat), 22 mg chol., 250 mg sodium, 23 g carb. (1 g fiber, 3 g sugars), 4 g pro. Exchanges: 1.5 starch, 0.5 fat. Carb choices: 1.5.

PER SERVING WITH SUBSTITUTE: Same as above, except 136 cal., 22 g carb. (2 g sugars).

quick tip

To up the pizza flavor, sprinkle a little snipped fresh rosemary over breadsticks just before baking.

Focaccia Breadsticks

Use a tube of pizza dough to make these tomato- and cheese-filled twists.

SERVINGS 16 (1 breadstick each)

CARB. PER SERVING 12 g

- ¼ cup oil-packed dried tomatoes
- ¼ cup grated Romano cheese
- 2 teaspoons water
- ⅛ teaspoon cracked black pepper
- 1 13.8-ounce package refrigerated pizza dough

1. Preheat oven to 350°F. Lightly grease a baking sheet; set aside. Drain dried tomatoes, reserving 2 teaspoons of the oil; finely snip tomatoes. In a large bowl combine tomatoes, the 2 teaspoons reserved oil, the cheese, water, and pepper. Set aside.

2. Unroll the pizza dough. On a lightly floured surface roll the dough into a 14×8-inch rectangle. Spread the tomato mixture crosswise over half of the dough. Fold plain half of the dough over filled half of the dough (rectangle should now be 7×8 inches); press lightly to seal edges. Cut the folded dough crosswise into sixteen ½-inch-wide strips. Twist each strip two or three times. Place twisted strips 1 inch apart on prepared baking sheet. Bake for 15 to 18 minutes or until golden brown. Transfer to a wire rack; cool slightly. Serve warm or at room temperature.

PER SERVING: 72 cal., 1 g total fat (0 g sat. fat), 1 mg chol., 159 mg sodium, 12 g carb. (0 g fiber, 0 g sugars), 3 g pro. Exchanges: 1 starch. Carb choices: 1.

Rosemary Red Pepper Muffins

You can substitute a lightly beaten egg for each ¼ cup refrigerated or frozen egg product called for in most recipes.

SERVINGS 12 (1 muffin and 2 teaspoons Goat Cheese Butter each)

CARB. PER SERVING 16 g or 14 g

Nonstick cooking spray
- 1 medium red sweet pepper, chopped (¾ cup)
- 2 cloves garlic, minced
- 1 cup all-purpose flour
- ¾ cup whole wheat pastry flour or brown rice flour
- 2 tablespoons sugar*
- 2 teaspoons baking powder
- 2 teaspoons snipped fresh rosemary
- ½ teaspoon salt
- 1 cup fat-free milk

Rosemary Red Pepper Muffins

- ¼ cup refrigerated or frozen egg product, thawed
- ¼ cup light stick butter (not margarine), melted
- 1 recipe Goat Cheese Butter

1. Preheat oven to 375°F. Generously coat twelve 2½-inch muffin cups with cooking spray or line cups with paper bake cups and generously coat paper cups with cooking spray. Coat an unheated large nonstick skillet with cooking spray; heat skillet over medium heat. Add sweet pepper; cook about 5 minutes or just until tender, stirring occasionally. Add garlic; cook and stir for 30 seconds. Remove from heat.

2. In a large bowl stir together flours, sugar, baking powder, rosemary, and salt. In a medium bowl whisk together milk, egg, and ¼ cup melted light butter. Add all at once to flour mixture; stir just until combined. Add sweet pepper mixture; stir just until combined. Spoon batter into prepared muffin cups.

3. Bake for 15 to 18 minutes or until a wooden toothpick inserted in centers comes out clean. Cool in muffin cups on a wire rack for 5 minutes. Remove from muffin cups. Serve Goat Cheese Butter with warm muffins.

GOAT CHEESE BUTTER: In a small bowl stir together 3 ounces soft goat cheese (chèvre), softened; 2 tablespoons light stick butter (not margarine) or tub-style vegetable oil spread, softened; and, if desired, 2 teaspoons snipped fresh chives until well combined.

*SUGAR SUBSTITUTES: Choose from Splenda Granular or Sweet'N Low bulk or packets. Follow package directions to use product amount equivalent to 2 tablespoons sugar

PER SERVING: 122 cal., 5 g total fat (3 g sat. fat), 11 mg chol., 252 mg sodium, 16 g carb. (1 g fiber, 4 g sugars), 4 g pro. Exchanges: 1 starch, 1 fat. Carb choices: 1.

PER SERVING WITH SUBSTITUTE: Same as above, except 115 cal., 14 g carb. (2 g sugars).

Hazelnut-Fig Stollen

Before chopping, toast whole hazelnuts in the oven, then roll them in a clean kitchen towel to remove the skins.

SERVINGS 18 (1 slice each)
CARB. PER SERVING 22 g or 20 g

- ¼ cup golden raisins
- ¼ cup chopped dried Mission figs
- 2 tablespoons brandy or orange juice
- 1¾ to 2¼ cups all-purpose flour
- 1 package active dry yeast
- ¾ cup fat-free milk
- ½ cup butter, cut up
- ¼ cup sugar*
- ¼ teaspoon salt
- ¼ cup chopped, toasted hazelnuts
- 1 teaspoon finely shredded orange peel
- 1 cup whole wheat flour
- 1 recipe Honey-Orange Icing

1. In a small bowl combine raisins, figs, and brandy. Let stand for 15 minutes.

2. In large mixing bowl stir together 1¼ cups of the all-purpose flour and the yeast. In small saucepan heat and stir milk, butter, sugar, and salt just until warm (120°F to 130°F) and butter almost melts. Add to flour mixture. Beat with an electric mixer on low speed for 30 seconds, scraping sides of bowl. Beat on high speed for 3 minutes.

3. Drain raisins and figs, discarding brandy. Add dried fruit to dough with hazelnuts and orange peel. Using a wooden spoon, stir in the whole wheat flour and as much of the remaining all-purpose flour as you can.

4. Turn dough out onto a lightly floured surface. Knead in enough of the remaining all-purpose flour to make a moderately soft dough that is smooth and elastic (3 to 5 minutes total). Shape into a ball. Place dough in a greased bowl; turn once to grease surface. Cover; let rise in a warm place until double in size (1¼ to 1¾ hours).

5. Line a baking sheet with parchment paper; set aside. Punch dough down. Turn out onto a lightly floured surface; cover and let rest for 10 minutes. Roll the dough into a 10×6-inch oval. Without stretching, fold a long side over to within 1 inch of opposite side; press edges to seal. Place on the baking sheet. Cover; let rise in a warm place until nearly double in size (45 to 60 minutes).

6. Preheat oven to 350°F. Bake for 35 to 40 minutes or until golden and bread sounds hollow when lightly tapped. Transfer to a wire rack and cool completely. Spread with Honey-Orange Icing before slicing.

HONEY-ORANGE ICING: In a small bowl whisk 3 tablespoons light tub-style cream cheese until smooth. Add 1½ teaspoons honey and whisk until smooth. Whisk in 1 to 2 teaspoons orange juice to make icing consistency.

***SUGAR SUBSTITUTE:** Choose Splenda Sugar Blend for Baking. Follow package directions to use product amount equivalent to ¼ cup sugar.

PER SERVING: 163 cal., 7 g total fat (4 g sat. fat), 15 mg chol., 96 mg sodium, 22 g carb. (2 g fiber, 7 g sugars), 3 g pro. Exchanges: 1 starch, 0.5 carb., 1 fat. Carb choices: 1.5.

PER SERVING WITH SUBSTITUTE: Same as above, except 159 cal., 20 g carb. (5 g sugars). Exchanges: 0 carb. Carb choices: 1.

Multigrain Mustard Baguette

A few edible embellishments transform frozen bread dough into a tasty delight.

SERVINGS 16 (1 slice each)
CARB. PER SERVING 15 g

- 1 16-ounce loaf frozen wheat bread dough
- ½ cup seeds and/or chopped nuts*
- 1 egg
- 1 tablespoon water
- 1 tablespoon Dijon-style mustard
- 2 tablespoons seeds*

1. Thaw dough according to package directions. Grease a large baking sheet; set aside. On a lightly floured surface roll dough into a 1-inch-thick rectangle. Sprinkle dough with some of the ½ cup seeds and/or nuts. Using a rolling pin, roll seeds and/or nuts into the dough. Fold dough in half crosswise; repeat sprinkling and rolling until seeds and/or nuts are all added and are evenly distributed throughout dough.

2. Using floured hands, gently roll dough rectangle into a spiral and shape into a 16-inch-long baguette. Place shaped dough, seam side down, on prepared baking sheet. Cover loosely and let rise in a warm place until double in size (1 to 1½ hours).

3. Preheat oven to 350°F. In a small bowl whisk together egg and the water. Brush loaf with mustard and then brush with egg mixture. Sprinkle with the 2 tablespoons seeds. Snip small slits diagonally down the top of the loaf. Bake for 25 to 30 minutes or until bread sounds hollow when lightly tapped.

***TEST KITCHEN TIP:** For seeds, try sesame, poppy, or fennel. For nuts, try pecans, walnuts, or pine nuts.

PER SERVING: 111 cal., 4 g total fat (0 g sat. fat), 12 mg chol., 185 mg sodium, 15 g carb. (2 g fiber, 0 g sugars), 5 g pro. Exchanges: 1 starch, 0.5 fat. Carb choices: 1.

Peppery Shallot Scone Bites

A combo of light stick butter and regular butter makes these low-fat scones light and flaky.

SERVINGS 9 (1 scone each)

CARB. PER SERVING 17 g

¾ cup all-purpose flour
¾ cup whole wheat pastry flour or whole wheat flour
2 teaspoons baking powder
¼ teaspoon cream of tartar
¼ teaspoon salt
¼ teaspoon freshly ground black pepper
¼ cup light stick butter (not margarine)
2 tablespoons butter
⅓ cup thinly sliced green onion tops
½ cup fat-free milk
1 to 2 teaspoons fat-free milk (optional)
9 very thin shallot slices
Olive oil nonstick cooking spray
Freshly ground black pepper

1. Preheat oven to 450°F. In a medium bowl stir together all-purpose flour, whole wheat pastry flour, baking powder, cream of tartar, salt, and ¼ teaspoon pepper. Using a pastry blender, cut in light butter and butter until mixture resembles coarse crumbs. Stir in green onion tops. Make a well in the center of the flour mixture. Add ½ cup milk all at once to flour mixture; stir just until dough clings together. If needed, add an additional 1 to 2 teaspoons fat-free milk to reach a soft dough consistency.

2. Turn dough out onto a lightly floured surface. Knead by folding and gently pressing dough for four to six strokes or until nearly smooth. Pat or lightly roll dough into a 7×7-inch square. Cut dough into nine squares. Place 1 shallot slice on top of each square. Coat the tops of the shallot slices with cooking spray and sprinkle with additional pepper. Place squares 1 inch apart on an ungreased baking sheet.

3. Bake for 12 to 14 minutes or until lightly browned. Serve warm.

PER SERVING: 128 cal., 6 g total fat (3 g sat. fat), 14 mg chol., 219 mg sodium, 17 g carb. (2 g fiber, 1 g sugars), 3 g pro. Exchanges: 1 starch, 1 fat. Carb choices: 1.

quick tip

Use a table knife to loosen the muffin edges from the sides of the cups if necessary.

Corn Muffins

Classic corn bread goes with just about any casserole but is outstanding with Mexican-style dishes.

SERVINGS 12 (1 muffin each)
CARB. PER SERVING 19 g or 17 g

Nonstick cooking spray
1 cup flour
¾ cup cornmeal
¼ cup sugar*
2½ teaspoons baking powder
¾ teaspoon salt
2 eggs, beaten
1 cup fat-free milk
¼ cup vegetable oil or melted butter

1. Preheat oven to 400°F. Coat twelve 2½-inch muffin cups with cooking spray. In a medium bowl combine flour, cornmeal, sugar, baking powder, and salt; set aside.

2. In a small bowl combine eggs, milk, and oil. Add egg mixture all at once to flour mixture. Stir just until moistened. Spoon batter into prepared muffin cups, filling each cup two-thirds full. Bake about 15 minutes or until lightly browned and a toothpick inserted near centers comes out clean. Serve warm.

*SUGAR SUBSTITUTES: Choose from C&H Light Sugar and Stevia Blend, Splenda Sugar Blend for Baking, or Sun Crystals Granulated Blend. Follow package directions to use product amount equivalent to ¼ cup sugar.

PER SERVING: 141 cal., 6 g total fat (1 g sat. fat), 31 mg chol., 244 mg sodium, 19 g carb. (1 g fiber, 5 g sugars), 3 g pro. Exchanges: 1 starch, 1 fat. Carb choices: 1.

PER SERVING WITH SUBSTITUTE: Same as above, except 135 cal., 17 g carb. (3 g sugars).

Cinnamon-Spice Butterhorns

A smidge of cayenne pepper gives these warm rolls a slight kick of heat.

SERVINGS 24 (1 roll each)
CARB. PER SERVING 19 g or 18 g

- 1 cup warm water (105°F to 115°F)
- ¼ cup sugar (we do not recommend using a sugar substitute for the dough of this recipe)
- 1 package active dry yeast
- 2 eggs, lightly beaten
- 3 tablespoons butter, melted and cooled, or 3 tablespoons canola oil
- 1¼ teaspoons salt
- 1 cup whole wheat flour
- 2¾ to 3¼ cups all-purpose flour
- Nonstick cooking spray
- ¼ cup sugar*
- ¼ cup toasted wheat germ
- 1 teaspoon ground cinnamon
- ¼ teaspoon ground allspice
- ⅛ teaspoon cayenne pepper
- 1 egg, lightly beaten
- 1 tablespoon water

1. In a large bowl stir together the 1 cup warm water, ¼ cup sugar, and the yeast. Let stand about 10 minutes or until yeast is foamy. Stir in the 2 eggs, melted butter, and salt. Stir in the whole wheat flour. Gradually stir in as much of the all-purpose flour as you can.

2. Turn dough out onto a lightly floured surface. Knead in enough of the remaining all-purpose flour to make a moderately soft dough that is smooth and elastic (3 to 5 minutes total). Shape dough into a ball. Place in a lightly greased bowl, turning once to grease surface of dough. Cover; let rise in a warm place until double in size (1 to 1½ hours).

3. Punch dough down. Turn out onto a lightly floured surface. Divide dough in half. Cover and let rest for 10 minutes. Meanwhile, lightly coat two large baking sheets with cooking spray; set aside.

4. In a small bowl combine ¼ cup sugar, the wheat germ, cinnamon, allspice, and cayenne pepper.

5. On a lightly floured surface roll one ball of dough into a 12-inch circle. Sprinkle dough evenly with half of the cinnamon mixture. Coat cinnamon mixture lightly with cooking spray. Cut circle into 12 wedges.

6. To shape each roll, begin at the wide ends of the wedge and roll dough toward the points. Place, point sides down, 2 to 3 inches apart on one of the prepared baking sheets. Repeat with remaining dough, cinnamon mixture, and cooking spray. Cover and let the rolls rise in a warm place until double in size (about 1 hour).

7. Preheat oven to 400°F. In a small bowl beat together 1 egg and 1 tablespoon water with a fork. Brush lightly over tops of rolls. Bake for 9 to 10 minutes or until golden. Remove and cool slightly; serve warm.

*SUGAR SUBSTITUTES: Choose from Splenda Granular or Sweet'N Low bulk or packets. Follow package directions to use amount equivalent to ¼ cup sugar for spice mix.

PER SERVING: 112 cal., 2 g total fat (1 g sat. fat), 27 mg chol., 144 mg sodium, 19 g carb. (1 g fiber, 4 g sugars), 3 g pro. Exchanges: 1 starch, 0.5 fat. Carb choices: 1.

PER SERVING WITH SUBSTITUTE: Same as above, except 105 cal., 18 g carb. (3 g sugars).

Cinnamon-Spice Butterhorns

homemade food gifts

Chocolate-Ginger Cupcakes

Made-from-scratch foods make the best gifts, especially during the holidays. Use this assortment of festive goodies—from cookies and cupcakes to breads and snack mixes—presented in you-can-do-it packaging ideas to bring smiles and warm hearts.

Chocolate-Ginger Cupcakes

Use a small stencil to create a powdered sugar snowflake on top of each cupcake.

SERVINGS 18 (1 cupcake each)
CARB. PER SERVING 28 g or 22 g

- 2⅓ cups cake flour or 2 cups all-purpose flour*
- ⅔ cup unsweetened cocoa powder
- 1½ teaspoons baking powder
- ½ teaspoon baking soda
- ½ teaspoon ground ginger
- 1¼ cups buttermilk or sour fat-free milk**
- 1 cup granulated sugar***
- ½ cup canola oil or cooking oil
- ½ cup refrigerated or frozen egg product, thawed, or 2 eggs
- 1 tablespoon finely chopped crystallized ginger
- 1 teaspoon vanilla
- 1 teaspoon powdered sugar

1. Preheat oven to 350°F. Line eighteen 2½-inch muffin cups with paper bake cups or coat with *nonstick cooking spray*; set aside. In a large bowl combine flour, cocoa powder, baking powder, baking soda, ground ginger, and ¼ teaspoon *salt*; set aside.

2. In a medium bowl whisk together buttermilk, granulated sugar, oil, eggs, crystallized ginger, and vanilla. Add buttermilk mixture to flour mixture. Beat with a wire whisk just until combined. Fill muffin cups two-thirds full with batter.

3. Bake for 12 to 15 minutes or until a toothpick inserted in centers comes out clean. Cool in cups on a wire rack for 5 minutes. Remove from cups; cool completely. Sift powdered sugar over cupcake tops.

***TEST KITCHEN TIP:** You can substitute whole wheat pastry flour or white whole wheat flour for up to half of the total cake flour or all-purpose flour used.

****TEST KITCHEN TIP:** To make 1¼ cups sour fat-free milk, place 4 teaspoons lemon juice or vinegar in a glass measuring cup. Add enough fat-free milk to measure 1¼ cups total liquid; stir. Let stand for 5 minutes before using.

*****SUGAR SUBSTITUTE:** Choose Splenda Sugar Blend for Baking. Follow package directions to use product amount equivalent to 1 cup sugar.

PER SERVING: 188 cal., 7 g total fat (1 g sat. fat), 1 mg chol., 118 mg sodium, 28 g carb. (0 g fiber, 13 g sugars), 3 g pro. Exchanges: 1 starch, 1 carb., 1 fat. Carb choices: 2.

PER SERVING WITH SUBSTITUTE: Same as above, except 171 cal, 22 g carb. (7 g sugars). Exchanges: 0.5 carb. Carb choices: 1.5.

Vanilla Latte Cupcakes

Fill a pastry bag fitted with a small star tip with frosting to pipe onto each cupcake.

SERVINGS 16 (1 cupcake each)
CARB. PER SERVING 33 g or 28 g

3	egg whites
3	tablespoons butter
1²⁄₃	cups cake flour or 1½ cups all-purpose flour
1½	teaspoons baking powder
¼	teaspoon salt
¼	cup tub-style vegetable oil spread, chilled
¾	cup granulated sugar*
1	teaspoon vanilla
¾	cup fat-free milk
1	recipe Vanilla Latte Frosting
	Chocolate-covered espresso bean (optional)

1. Allow egg whites and butter to stand at room temperature for 30 minutes. Line sixteen 2½-inch muffin cups with paper bake cups; set aside. In a medium bowl stir together flour, baking powder, and salt; set aside.

2. Preheat oven to 375°F. In a large bowl beat vegetable oil spread and butter with an electric mixer on medium to high speed for 30 seconds. Gradually add sugar, about 2 tablespoons at time, beating on medium speed until well mixed, scraping sides of bowl constantly. Beat on medium speed for 2 minutes more. Gradually add egg whites, beating well. Beat in vanilla. Alternately add flour mixture and milk to butter mixture, beating on low speed after each addition just until combined. Fill muffin cups two-thirds full with batter.

3. Bake for 12 to 15 minutes or until a toothpick inserted in centers comes out clean. Cool in cups on a wire rack for 5 minutes. Remove from cups; cool completely on a wire rack. Frost with Vanilla Latte Frosting. If desired, top each with an espresso bean.

VANILLA LATTE FROSTING: In a custard cup combine 2 teaspoons instant espresso coffee powder or instant coffee crystals with 1 teaspoon warm water; stir until dissolved. In a medium bowl beat ¼ cup tub-style vegetable oil spread, chilled, and ½ teaspoon vanilla with an electric mixer on medium speed for 30 seconds. Beat in dissolved espresso powder. Gradually beat in 1½ cups powdered sugar* until very smooth. If needed,

Red Velvet Whoopie Pies

quick tip
Turn a basic box into a beauty—start with a decorated holiday box and add a few glitzy embellishments. Try tulle, ribbons, rhinestones, and more.

add enough fat-free milk, ½ teaspoon at a time, to reach spreading consistency.

*SUGAR SUBSTITUTE: Choose Splenda Sugar Blend for Baking. Follow package directions to use product amount equivalent to ¾ cup granulated sugar. We do not recommend using a sugar substitute for the frosting.

PER SERVING: 198 cal., 7 g total fat (2 g sat. fat), 6 mg chol., 146 mg sodium, 33 g carb. (0 g fiber, 21 g sugars), 2 g pro. Exchanges: 1 starch, 1 carb., 1 fat. Carb choices: 2.

PER SERVING WITH SUBSTITUTE: Same as above, except 184 cal., 28 g carb. (16 g sugars).

Red Velvet Whoopie Pies

A fluffy filling is sandwiched between soft cookies for these hard-to-beat treats.

SERVINGS 30 (1 whoopie pie each)
CARB. PER SERVING 12 g or 10 g

- 2 cups flour
- 2 tablespoons unsweetened cocoa powder
- ½ teaspoon baking soda
- ⅛ teaspoon salt
- ½ cup tub-style vegetable oil spread
- ⅔ cup packed brown sugar*
- ¼ cup refrigerated or frozen egg product, thawed, or 1 egg
- 1 1-ounce bottle red food coloring
- 1 teaspoon vanilla
- ½ cup buttermilk or fat-free sour milk
- 1 cup frozen light whipped dessert topping, thawed
- ¼ cup light sour cream
- 2 teaspoons powdered sugar (optional)

1. Preheat oven to 375°F. Line cookie sheets with parchment paper; set aside. In a medium bowl combine flour, cocoa powder, baking soda, and salt; set aside.
2. In a large bowl combine vegetable oil spread and brown sugar; beat with an electric mixer on medium speed until light and fluffy. Beat in egg, red food coloring, and vanilla. Alternately add flour mixture and buttermilk to egg mixture, beating on low speed after each addition just until combined.
3. Using a rounded measuring teaspoon (about 2 level teaspoons), spoon batter on prepared cookie sheets, leaving 1 inch between rounds. Bake for 5 to 7 minutes or until tops are set. Cool cookies 1 minute on cookie sheets. Transfer cookies to wire racks; cool completely.
4. For filling, in a small bowl stir together ¼ cup of the dessert topping and the sour cream. Fold in the remaining ¾ cup dessert topping.
5. Spread filling on the flat sides of half of the cookies. Top with the remaining cookies, flat sides down. If desired, sprinkle tops with powdered sugar. Serve immediately. Or store cookies and filling separately in airtight containers in the refrigerator for up to 3 days. Fill just before serving.

CHOCOLATE WHOOPIE PIES: Prepare as directed above, except omit red food coloring.

*SUGAR SUBSTITUTE: Choose Splenda Brown Sugar Baking Blend. Follow package directions to use product amount equivalent to ⅔ cup brown sugar. Increase buttermilk to ⅔ cup.

PER SERVING: 82 cal., 3 g total fat (1 g sat. fat), 1 mg chol., 65 mg sodium, 12 g carb. (0 g fiber, 5 g sugars), 1 g pro. Exchanges: 1 carb., 0.5 fat. Carb choices: 1.

PER SERVING WITH SUBSTITUTE: Same as above, except 75 cal., 66 mg sodium, 10 g carb. (3 g sugars). Exchanges: 0.5 carb. Carb choices: 0.5.

Citrus Biscotti

Reach for a Microplane or a small zester to shred the peels from an orange, lemon, and lime.

SERVINGS 28 (1 biscotti each)
CARB. PER SERVING 11 g or 9 g

- ¼ cup butter, softened
- ½ cup sugar*
- 1 teaspoon baking powder
- ¼ teaspoon baking soda
- ⅛ teaspoon salt
- ½ cup refrigerated or frozen egg product, thawed, or 2 eggs
- ½ cup oat bran
- 1 teaspoon finely shredded orange peel
- 1 teaspoon finely shredded lemon peel
- 1 teaspoon finely shredded lime peel
- 1¾ cups flour

1. Preheat oven to 375°F. Line a large cookie sheet with parchment paper; set aside. In a large mixing bowl beat butter with an electric mixer on medium speed for 30 seconds. Add sugar, baking powder, baking soda, and salt, beating until well combined. Beat in eggs. Beat in oat bran, orange peel, lemon peel, and lime peel. Beat in as much of the flour as you can with the mixer. Using a wooden spoon, stir in the remaining flour.

2. Divide dough in half. If necessary, cover and chill dough for 1 hour or until easy to handle. Shape each portion into an 8-inch-long log. Place logs 3 inches apart on prepared cookie sheet; flatten the logs slightly until 2 inches wide. Bake for 18 to 20 minutes or until firm and a toothpick inserted near center of each log comes out clean. Cool on cookie sheet on wire rack for 1 hour.

3. Preheat oven to 325°F. Using a serrated knife, cut each log diagonally into ½-inch-thick slices. Arrange slices, cut sides down, on cookie sheet. Bake for 10 minutes; turn slices over. Bake for 8 to 10 minutes more or until dry and crisp. Transfer to wire racks; cool completely. To store, layer biscotti between waxed paper in an airtight container. Cover and seal. Store at room temperature for up to 3 days or freeze for up to 3 months.

*SUGAR SUBSTITUTE: Choose Splenda Sugar Blend for Baking. Follow package directions to use product amount equivalent to ½ cup sugar.

PER SERVING: 63 cal., 2 g total fat (1 g sat. fat), 4 mg chol., 55 mg sodium, 11 g carb. (0 g fiber, 4 g sugars), 2 g pro. Exchanges: 1 carb., 0.5 fat. Carb choices. 1.

PER SERVING WITH SUBSTITUTE: Same as above, except 58 cal., 9 g carb. (2 g sugars). Exchanges: 0.5 carb. Carb choices: 0.5.

Citrus Biscotti

make it festive

Gather some boxes—Chinese takeout, windowed candy, and hinge-top cigar-style— and bags and turn them into the sweetest presentations ever. Add paper liners, ribbons, holiday shapes, and handcrafted gift tags.

Coconut Cake Balls

The mixture is sticky, so allow enough time to freeze the mounds for 30 minutes before trying to roll them into balls.

SERVINGS 80 (1 cake ball each)
CARB. PER SERVING 10 g

1 package 2-layer-size reduced-sugar or sugar-free yellow cake mix
1 14-ounce can unsweetened light coconut milk
1 8-ounce package reduced-fat cream cheese (Neufchâtel), softened
1 cup shredded coconut
1 pound semisweet or dark chocolate or white baking chocolate
2 tablespoons shortening
⅓ cup shredded coconut, toasted if desired

1. Prepare the cake mix according to package directions, except substitute 1 cup of the coconut milk for 1 cup of the liquid in the cake and decrease the oil by 2 tablespoons. Use any suggested pan size and bake according to package directions. Cool in pan on a wire rack. Line trays or baking pans with waxed paper; set aside.

2. In a very large mixing bowl beat cream cheese with an electric mixer until smooth. Gradually beat in remaining coconut milk until smooth. Stir in the 1 cup coconut. Remove cake from pan and crumble into the cream cheese mixture. Beat until combined. Using a small cookie scoop, drop mixture in 1-inch mounds onto prepared pans; freeze for 30 minutes. Roll mounds into balls. Freeze for 30 to 60 minutes more or until balls are firm.

3. In a medium saucepan heat chocolate and shortening over medium-low heat until melted and smooth, stirring occasionally. Remove from heat. Working in batches, dip balls into melted chocolate; allow excess to drip off and place balls on clean waxed paper-lined trays or baking pans. Immediately sprinkle tops of balls with coconut before chocolate is set. Let stand until chocolate is set. If chocolate in saucepan begins to set up, reheat over low heat. To store, layer cake balls between waxed paper in an airtight container. Cover and seal. Store at room temperature for up to 3 days, in the refrigerator for up to 1 week, or freeze for up to 1 month.

PER SERVING: 81 cal., 5 g total fat (2 g sat. fat), 10 mg chol., 66 mg sodium, 10 g carb. (1 g fiber, 5 g sugars), 1 g pro. Exchanges: 0.5 carb., 1 fat. Carb choices: 0.5.

Pumpkin Bars

Pumpkin Bars

Line the box with a piece of waxed paper or parchment paper before adding the treats.

SERVINGS 25 (1 bar or 1 cookie each)

CARB. PER SERVING 11 g

- ½ cup tub-style vegetable oil spread, softened
- ½ cup packed brown sugar*
- ½ teaspoon baking soda
- ½ teaspoon pumpkin pie spice
- ⅓ cup canned pumpkin
- ¼ cup refrigerated or frozen egg product, thawed, or 1 egg
- 1½ cups all-purpose flour
- ½ of an 8-ounce package reduced-fat cream cheese (Neufchâtel), softened
- 1 cup frozen light whipped dessert topping, thawed
  Freshly grated nutmeg (optional)

1. Preheat oven to 350°F. Grease and lightly flour a 9×9×2-inch baking pan. Set aside.

2. In a large bowl combine vegetable oil spread, brown sugar, baking soda, and pumpkin pie spice; beat with an electric mixer on medium speed until well mixed. Beat in pumpkin and egg. Beat in as much of the flour as you can with the mixer. Using a wooden spoon, stir in any remaining flour.

3. Spread dough into prepared pan. Bake for 12 to 15 minutes or until a toothpick inserted near the center comes out clean. Cool in pan on a wire rack for 10 minutes. Remove from pan; cool completely.

4. For frosting, in a medium bowl beat cream cheese with an electric mixer on medium speed until smooth. Beat in half of the dessert topping. Fold in remaining dessert topping. Spread over cooled pumpkin layer. If desired, sprinkle with nutmeg. Cut into bars.

5. To store bars, arrange frosted bars in a single layer in an airtight container. Cover; seal. Store in the refrigerator for up to 3 days. (Or layer unfrosted bars between waxed paper in an airtight container. Cover; seal. Freeze for up to 1 month. Thaw. Prepare cream cheese mixture and frost as directed.)

PUMPKIN COOKIES WITH CREAM CHEESE FROSTING: Prepare batter and cream cheese mixture as directed. Preheat oven to 350°F. Drop batter by rounded teaspoonfuls 1 inch apart on ungreased cookie sheets. Bake for 8 to 10 minutes or until tops are set. Transfer to wire racks; cool completely. Frost cooled cookies with cream cheese mixture. If desired, sprinkle with freshly grated nutmeg. Makes about 25 cookies.

*SUGAR SUBSTITUTE: We do not recommend using a sugar substitute for this recipe.

PER SERVING: 90 cal., 4 g total fat (2 g sat. fat), 3 mg chol., 75 mg sodium, 11 g carb. (0 g fiber, 5 g sugars), 1 g pro. Exchanges: 1 carb., 0.5 fat. Carb choices: 1.

1. Preheat oven to 350°F. Grease the bottom and ½ inch up the sides of two 5¾×3×1¾-inch loaf pans or one 8×4×2-inch loaf pan; set aside. In a large bowl stir together flours, baking powder, cinnamon, allspice, salt, and nutmeg. Make a well in the center of the flour mixture; set aside.

2. In a medium bowl combine shredded pear, sugar, oil, egg, and syrup. Add pear mixture all at once to flour mixture; stir just until moistened (batter will be lumpy). Fold in chopped pear. Spoon batter into prepared pan(s).

3. Bake for 35 to 40 minutes for 5¾×3×1¾-inch pans or 40 to 45 minutes for the 8×4×2-inch pan or until a toothpick inserted near center(s) comes out clean. Cool in pan(s) on a wire rack for 10 minutes. Remove from pan(s). Cool completely on wire rack. Wrap and store overnight before slicing.

*SUGAR SUBSTITUTE: Choose Splenda Sugar Blend for Baking. Follow package directions to use product amount equivalent to ⅓ cup sugar.

PER SERVING: 139 cal., 6 g total fat (0 g sat. fat), 0 mg chol., 88 mg sodium, 20 g carb. (1 g fiber, 9 g sugars), 2 g pro. Exchanges: 1 starch, 1 fat. Carb choices: 1.

PER SERVING WITH SUBSTITUTE: Same as above, except 130 cal., 17 g carb. (6 g sugars).

Pear-Maple Spice Bread

A custom-made gift tag gives a printed cellophane bag a wow factor.

SERVINGS 12 (1 slice each)
CARB. PER SERVING 20 g or 17 g

- ⅔ cup all-purpose flour
- ⅔ cup whole wheat pastry flour or whole wheat flour
- 1½ teaspoons baking powder
- 1 teaspoon ground cinnamon
- ¼ teaspoon ground allspice
- ⅛ teaspoon salt
- ⅛ teaspoon ground nutmeg
- ¾ cup coarsely shredded, cored, unpeeled pear
- ⅓ cup sugar*
- ⅓ cup canola oil
- ¼ cup refrigerated or frozen egg product, thawed, or 2 egg whites, lightly beaten
- ¼ cup light maple-flavor syrup or sugar-free maple-flavor syrup
- ½ cup chopped, cored, unpeeled pear

Pear-Maple Spice Bread

quick tip

Look for a patterned box that best fits the food you are giving. If you can't find a box you like, make one by wrapping a plain box with colorful wrapping paper.

Apricot-Cranberry Panettone

Paper baking molds are available in specialty or kitchenware stores or from kingarthurflour.com.

SERVINGS 16 (1 slice each)
CARB. PER SERVING 27 g or 24 g

⅓ cup snipped dried apricots
⅓ cup dried cranberries or dried tart cherries, coarsely chopped
2 teaspoons apricot brandy, orange liqueur, or orange juice
¾ cup fat-free milk
1 teaspoon package active dry yeast
2¼ to 2¾ cups bread flour
½ cup refrigerated or frozen egg product, thawed, or 2 eggs
¼ cup granulated sugar*
¼ cup butter, softened
½ teaspoon salt
½ cup yellow cornmeal
⅓ cup chopped almonds, toasted
2 tablespoons flaxseeds
Nonstick cooking spray
1 teaspoon water
Powdered sugar (optional)

1. In a small bowl combine apricots, cranberries, and brandy; cover and let stand for 15 minutes, stirring occasionally. In a small saucepan heat milk just until warm (105°F to 115°F). Pour into a large mixing bowl. Sprinkle yeast over milk and let stand for 5 minutes or until the yeast dissolves. Add 1½ cups of the flour, ¼ cup of the egg product or 1 of the eggs, the granulated sugar, butter, and salt. Beat with an electric mixer on low to medium speed for 30 seconds, scraping sides of bowl constantly. Beat on high speed for 3 minutes more. Using a wooden spoon, stir in cornmeal, almonds, flaxseeds, undrained apricot mixture, and as much of the remaining flour as you can. Dough should be just stiff enough to knead.
2. Turn dough out onto a floured surface. Knead in enough of the remaining flour to make a moderately soft dough that is smooth and elastic (3 to 5 minutes total). Shape into a ball. Place dough in a large greased bowl, turning once to grease surface of dough. Cover; let rise in a warm place until double in size (1¼ to 1½ hours).
3. Coat a 7-cup panettone mold or 8-inch springform pan with cooking spray; set aside. Or place a 6×4½-inch round panettone paper baking mold on a baking sheet; set aside.

4. Punch dough down; shape into a ball. Transfer dough to the prepared mold or pan and flatten slightly to fit shape of mold or pan. Cover and let rise until nearly double in size (1 to 1¼ hours).
5. Preheat oven to 350°F. In a small bowl combine the remaining ¼ cup egg product or 1 egg and the water; beat together with a fork. Brush over top of loaf. Bake about 50 minutes for panettone mold, 45 minutes for springform pan, or until bread sounds hollow when tapped and internal temperature of the bread reaches 195°F to 200°F on an instant-read thermometer. If necessary, cover top of bread loosely with foil the last 15 to 20 minutes of baking to prevent overbrowning. Cool for 10 minutes in pan on a wire rack. Remove from pan. Cool bread completely. If desired, sprinkle top of bread with powdered sugar.

*SUGAR SUBSTITUTES: Choose from Splenda Granular or Sweet'N Low bulk or packets. Follow package directions to use product amount equivalent to ¼ cup sugar.

PER SERVING: 169 cal., 5 g total fat (2 g sat. fat), 8 mg chol., 114 mg sodium, 27 g carb. (2 g fiber, 8 g sugars), 5 g pro. Exchanges: 1 starch, 1 carb., 1 fat. Carb choices: 2.
PER SERVING WITH SUBSTITUTE: Same as above, except 159 cal., 24 g carb. Exchanges: 0.5 carb. (5 g sugars). Carb choices: 1.5.

make it festive

With the addition of a paper flower, a patterned box can be converted into a basketlike carrier for a wrapped loaf of bread, a bag of cookies, or a container of snack mix. To make the poinsettia, cut out one leaf shape, approximately 1x3 inches, from textured wallpaper or scrapbooking paper. Use the cutout as a template to trace other leaves; you will need 18 total.

To make the flower, attach one leaf to another with crafts glue, overlapping slightly. Repeat as you attach them all in circles. Glue three mini ball ornaments in the center of the flower. Attach the flower to the box using crafts glue.

Sweet Party Mix

For an extra punch of protein and fiber, replace 1 cup of the corn or rice cereal with bite-size wheat square cereal.

SERVINGS 36 (⅓ cup each)
CARB. PER SERVING 13 g or 10 g

Nonstick cooking spray
4 cups bite-size corn square cereal
3 cups bite-size rice square cereal
2 cups pretzel knots
⅔ cup sliced almonds
½ cup packed brown sugar*
¼ cup butter
2 tablespoons light-color corn syrup
⅛ teaspoon baking soda
¾ cup dried cranberries, blueberries, or cherries

1. Lightly coat a large piece of foil with cooking spray; set aside. In a large roasting pan toss together corn cereal, rice cereal, pretzels, and almonds; set aside.
2. In a medium saucepan combine brown sugar, butter, and corn syrup. Cook and stir over medium heat until mixture just begins to bubble. Continue cooking at a moderate, steady rate, without stirring, for 5 minutes more. Remove saucepan from heat; stir in baking soda. Pour over cereal mixture; stir gently to coat.
3. Bake in a 300°F oven for 15 minutes; stir cereal mixture and bake 5 minutes more. Remove from oven; stir in dried fruit. Spread on prepared foil to cool. Store in an airtight container.
SUGAR SUBSTITUTES: Choose from Sweet'N Low Brown or Sugar Twin Granulated Brown. Follow package directions to use product amount equivalent to ½ cup brown sugar. Butter mixture may appear separated when cooking.
PER SERVING: 74 cal., 2 g total fat (1 g sat. fat), 3 mg chol., 106 mg sodium, 13 g carb. (1 g fiber, 5 g sugars), 1 g pro. Exchanges: 1 starch. Carb choices: 1.
PER SERVING WITH SUBSTITUTE: Same as above, except 63 cal., 10 g carb. (2 g sugars). Exchanges: 0.5 starch. Carb choices: 0.5.

Honey-Mustard Snack Mix

Crunchy and spicy, this snack mix has it all. Customize the mix by substituting your favorite type of nut for the almonds and peanuts specified in the recipe.

SERVINGS 15 (½ cup each)
CARB. PER SERVING 8 g

1½ cups crispy corn-and-rice cereal
1 cup bite-size shredded wheat biscuits
¾ cup unblanched whole almonds
¼ cup peanuts
2 tablespoons butter
3 tablespoons honey mustard
1 teaspoon Worcestershire sauce
¼ teaspoon garlic powder
⅛ teaspoon cayenne pepper
4 cups plain popped popcorn

1. Preheat oven to 300°F. Line a 13×9×2-inch baking pan with foil, extending the foil over edges of pan. In the prepared pan toss together crispy cereal, wheat biscuits, almonds, and peanuts; set aside.
2. In a small saucepan heat butter over medium heat until melted. Remove from heat. Stir in mustard, Worcestershire sauce, garlic powder, and cayenne pepper. Drizzle mustard mixture over cereal mixture; toss gently to coat.
3. Bake for 20 minutes, stirring gently after 10 minutes. Stir in popcorn. Using the edges of the foil, lift popcorn mixture out of pan; cool. Store in an airtight container at room temperature for up to 3 days.
PER SERVING: 103 cal., 7 g total fat (1 g sat. fat), 4 mg chol., 59 mg sodium, 8 g carb. (2 g fiber, 1 g sugars), 3 g pro. Exchanges: 0.5 starch, 1.5 fat. Carb choices: 0.5.

quick tip

Fill a set of nested mixing bowls with different snacks for different people. Spoon some of the snack mix into a clear plastic bag and place the bag in a bowl. Gather the bag at the top and tie closed with tulle and ribbon bows.

Caramel Popcorn

Use a wooden spoon or a heat-resistant rubber spatula to stir the caramel mixture while it cooks.

SERVINGS 11 (1 cup each)
CARB. PER SERVING 19 g or 9 g

- ½ cup packed brown sugar*
- ¼ cup granulated sugar*
- ¼ cup tub-style vegetable oil spread
- ¼ teaspoon salt
- 1½ teaspoons vanilla
- 12 cups popped light popcorn

1. Preheat oven to 300°F. In a 4-quart Dutch oven heat and stir the brown sugar, granulated sugar, vegetable oil spread, and salt over medium heat until just boiling and sugar is dissolved. Remove from heat. Stir in vanilla. Add popcorn and toss until coated.

2. Place coated popcorn in a shallow roasting pan. Bake, uncovered, for 15 minutes, stirring once. Transfer to a large piece of foil to cool. Store in an airtight container.

*SUGAR SUBSTITUTES: Choose from Sweet'N Low Brown or Sugar Twin Granulated Brown to substitute for the brown sugar. Follow package directions to use product amount equivalent to ½ cup brown sugar. We do not recommend using a sugar substitute for the granulated sugar.

PER SERVING: 105 cal., 4 g total fat (1 g sat. fat), 0 mg chol., 139 mg sodium, 19 g carb. (1 g fiber, 14 g sugars), 1 g pro. Exchanges: 1 carb., 0.5 fat. Carb choices: 1.

PER SERVING WITH SUBSTITUTE: Same as above, except 67 cal., 9 g carb. (5 g sugars). Exchanges: 0.5 carb. Carb choices: 0.5.

Italian Soup Mix

A wide mouth on the jar makes adding each ingredient in layers easier. A canning funnel can help with this process, too.

SERVINGS 12 (1½ cups each; 2 jars [enough to make 2 batches of Italian Meatball Soup])

CARB. PER SERVING 11 g

- 2 tablespoons reduced-sodium instant chicken bouillon granules or 6 reduced-sodium chicken bouillon cubes
- ½ teaspoon dried thyme, crushed
- ½ teaspoon dried oregano, crushed
- ½ teaspoon dried rosemary, crushed
- ½ teaspoon black pepper
- ¼ teaspoon garlic powder
- 2 cups dried multigrain farfalle pasta (3 ounces)
- ⅓ cup dried chopped onion
- ½ cup chopped dried tomatoes (not oil-packed)
- ¼ cup dried green sweet pepper
- ¾ cup dried porcini mushrooms

1. In a small bowl stir together chicken bouillon granules, thyme, oregano, rosemary, black pepper, and garlic powder. Spoon evenly into two 1-pint glass jars. Top evenly with layers of pasta, onion, tomatoes, sweet pepper, and mushrooms. Tap jars gently on the counter to settle each layer before adding the next one. Seal; attach directions for making Italian Meatball Soup. Store in a cool, dry place for up to 6 months.

TO PREPARE ITALIAN MEATBALL SOUP (USING 1 JAR OF MIX): Remove the mushrooms from the top of the jar and place in a small bowl. Add enough boiling water to cover; let stand for 20 minutes. Remove mushrooms from water with a slotted spoon; discard water. Rinse mushrooms and chop. Empty the remaining contents into a Dutch oven. Stir in 8 cups water and the chopped mushrooms. Bring to boiling; reduce heat. Cover and simmer for 8 minutes. Add one 12-ounce package (12 meatballs) frozen cooked Italian-flavor turkey meatballs, thawed, and 3 cups coarsely chopped fresh kale. Return to boiling; reduce heat. Simmer, uncovered, for 2 to 3 minutes or until pasta is tender and meatballs are heated through.

PER SERVING: 162 cal., 8 g total fat (2 g sat. fat), 61 mg chol., 597 mg sodium, 11 g carb. (1 g fiber, 2 g sugars), 13 g pro. Exchanges: 1 starch, 2 lean meat, 1 fat. Carb choices: 1.

make it festive

Anything in a jar—from dry mixes to finished soups, sauces, jellies, and more—makes great gifts to give. Jars with hinged lids, screw-top lids, and screw-band-and-disk lids can be used, but be sure to choose a jar size that best fits the quantity of the recipe. Decorate the jar with holiday adornments such as ornaments, stickers, and ribbons, then carefully fill it using a canning funnel. Make sure to include directions for preparing or heating the contents.

Turkey and Rice Soup

Serve crispy breadsticks with this homey meal in a bowl.

SERVINGS 6 (1½ cups each)

CARB. PER SERVING 16 g

- 2 14.5-ounce cans reduced-sodium chicken broth
- 1½ cups water
- 1 teaspoon snipped fresh rosemary or ¼ teaspoon dried rosemary, crushed
- ¼ teaspoon black pepper
- 1 medium carrot, thinly sliced (½ cup)
- 1 stalk celery, thinly sliced (½ cup)
- ⅓ cup thinly sliced onion
- 1 cup instant brown rice
- 1 cup frozen cut green beans
- 2 cups chopped cooked turkey or chicken breast (10 ounces)
- 1 14.5-ounce can no-added-salt diced tomatoes, undrained

1. In a large saucepan or Dutch oven combine broth, the water, fresh or dried rosemary, and pepper. Add carrot, celery, and onion. Bring to boiling.

2. Stir in uncooked rice and frozen green beans. Return to boiling; reduce heat. Cover and simmer for 10 to 12 minutes or until vegetables are tender.

3. Stir in turkey and tomatoes; heat through.*

*FOR GIFT-GIVING: For gift-giving (and if the soup won't be eaten immediately), prepare soup through Step 2. Stir in the cooked turkey and tomatoes. Thoroughly chill the mixture. Ladle into two storage jars or airtight containers. Keep soup refrigerated for up to 3 days. Be sure to include instructions for the recipient to reheat the soup quickly up to 165°F before serving.

PER SERVING: 143 cal., 1 g total fat (0 g sat. fat), 39 mg chol., 384 mg sodium, 16 g carb. (3 g fiber, 4 g sugars), 18 g pro. Exchanges: 1 vegetable, 0.5 starch, 2 lean meat. Carb choices: 1.

festive endings

Mocha Shortcakes with White Chocolate Peppermint Mousse

Holiday meals wouldn't be the same without a stunning dessert or two to crown the menu. So this season, pull out one of these lightened-up showstopper recipes to please all sweet-craving palates. Guests will savor every bite!

Mocha Shortcakes with White Chocolate Peppermint Mousse

Grab your pastry blender or two knives to cut the butter into the flour mixture.

SERVINGS 10 (1 shortcake and ¼ cup mousse each)

CARB. PER SERVING 32 g or 28 g

- 1 cup all-purpose flour
- ⅓ cup whole wheat pastry flour or brown rice flour
- ¼ cup unsweetened cocoa powder
- 3 tablespoons packed brown sugar*
- 2 teaspoons baking powder
- 2 teaspoons instant espresso coffee powder
- ⅛ teaspoon salt
- 2 tablespoons butter
- 2 tablespoons light stick butter (not margarine)
- ½ cup fat-free half-and-half
- ¼ cup refrigerated or frozen egg product, thawed, or 1 egg, lightly beaten
- 2 tablespoons reduced-calorie or sugar-free chocolate-flavor syrup
- 2½ cups frozen light whipped dessert topping, thawed
- ½ teaspoon peppermint extract
- 2 ounces white baking chocolate, grated
- 4 sugar-free or regular striped round peppermint candies, coarsely crushed

1. Preheat oven to 375°F. Grease a large baking sheet; set aside. In large bowl combine flours, cocoa powder, brown sugar, baking powder, espresso powder, and salt. Cut in butters until mixture resembles coarse crumbs. In a bowl combine half-and-half, egg, and chocolate syrup. Add to flour mixture. Stir just until combined.

2. Using a scant ¼ cup, drop dough into 10 mounds 2 inches apart on prepared baking sheet. Bake for 10 to 12 minutes or until tops are set and edges are firm. Transfer cakes to a wire rack; cool.

4. For mousse, in a bowl combine dessert topping and peppermint extract, folding gently to combine.

5. To serve, split shortcakes in half horizontally. Place shortcake bottoms on 10 plates. Top with half of the mousse and half of the white chocolate. Add shortcake tops and top each with remaining mousse. Sprinkle with remaining white chocolate and the crushed mints.

*****SUGAR SUBSTITUTES:** Choose from Sweet'N Low Brown or Sugar Twin Granulated Brown. Follow package directions to use amount equivalent to 3 tablespoons brown sugar.

PER SERVING: 207 cal., 8 g total fat (6 g sat. fat), 12 mg chol., 177 mg sodium, 32 g carb. (2 g fiber, 8 g sugars), 3 g pro. Exchanges: 1 starch, 1 carb., 1.5 fat. Carb choices: 2.

PER SERVING WITH SUBSTITUTE: Same as above, except 191 cal., 28 g carb. (4 g sugars), 4 g pro.

Cashew Truffles

Lightly dampen your hands to shape each chocolaty portion into a ball.

SERVINGS 20 (2 truffles each)

CARB. PER SERVING 9 g

- 8 ounces bittersweet chocolate, chopped
- ½ cup fat-free half-and-half
- 1 tablespoon pure maple syrup
- ¾ cup whole cashews
- ¼ teaspoon coarse salt

1. Place chocolate in a medium bowl; set aside. In a small saucepan bring half-and-half just to boiling; pour over chocolate. Stir until chocolate is melted. Stir in maple syrup. Cover; freeze about 2 hours or until firm.

2. Meanwhile, preheat oven to 350°F. Place cashews on a shallow baking pan. Bake for 8 to 10 minutes or until golden, stirring once. Set aside 40 whole cashews. In a food processor combine the remaining cashews and the salt. Cover and process with several on/off turns until nuts are finely chopped. Transfer finely chopped nuts to a small bowl; set aside.

3. Divide chocolate mixture into 40 portions. Place a whole cashew in the center of one of the portions; shape into a ball. Roll ball in the chopped cashew mixture. Place on a baking sheet. Repeat to make 40 truffles total. Cover and chill until serving time. Let stand at room temperature for 30 minutes before serving. If desired, serve in small paper candy cups.

PER SERVING: 93 cal., 7 g total fat (3 g sat. fat), 1 mg chol., 62 mg sodium, 9 g carb. (1 g fiber, 5 g sugars), 2 g pro. Exchanges: 0.5 carb., 1.5 fat. Carb choices: 0.5.

Cashew Truffles

Pecan-Cornmeal Biscotti

Slip a few cookies into a clear cellophane bag and tie it closed with a decorative ribbon for a simple food gift.

SERVINGS 32 (1 biscotti each)

CARB. PER SERVING 19 g or 15 g

- 1½ cups yellow cornmeal
- 1½ cups all-purpose flour
- ½ cup whole wheat flour
- 1½ teaspoons baking powder
- ½ teaspoon salt
- 1 cup packed brown sugar*
- 3 eggs
- 3 tablespoons canola oil
- ½ cup chopped pecans, toasted
- 1 ounce white chocolate (with cocoa butter), chopped
- ⅛ teaspoon shortening

1. Preheat oven to 325°F. Line a large cookie sheet with parchment paper; set aside. In a large bowl combine cornmeal, flours, baking powder, and salt; set aside. In another large bowl combine brown sugar, eggs, and oil; beat with an electric mixer on medium to high speed until well mixed. Beat in as much of the flour mixture as you can with the mixer. Stir in any remaining flour mixture. Stir in pecans. If necessary, use your hands to knead the dough until it comes together.

2. Divide dough in half. On a lightly floured surface shape dough into two 12-inch-long logs. Flatten each log to a 2-inch width. Place logs on prepared cookie sheet.

3. Bake about 25 minutes or until a toothpick inserted near center of each log comes out clean. Cool on cookie sheet on wire rack for 40 minutes.

4. Using a serrated knife, cut each log diagonally into ¾-inch-thick slices. Arrange slices, cut sides down, on cookie sheet. Bake for 10 minutes; turn slices over. Bake for 10 minutes more. Transfer to wire racks; cool completely.

5. In a very small saucepan combine white chocolate and shortening; heat over low heat until melted, stirring constantly. Drizzle over cookie slices.

*****SUGAR SUBSTITUTE:** Choose Splenda Brown Sugar Blend. Follow package directions to use product amount equivalent to 1 cup brown sugar.

PER SERVING: 113 cal., 3 g total fat (1 g sat. fat), 20 mg chol., 63 mg sodium, 19 g carb. (1 g fiber, 7 g sugars), 2 g pro. Exchanges: 1 carb., 1 fat. Carb choices: 1.

PER SERVING WITH SUBSTITUTE: Same as above, except 102 cal., 15 g carb. (4 g sugars).

Store these crisp dippin' cookies in an airtight container at room temperature for up to 3 days or in the freezer for up to 3 months.

Pecan-Cornmeal Biscotti

Coconut Raspberry Thumbprints

Stock your freezer—when company arrives, pull out the number you need, fill, and eat.

SERVINGS 36 (1 cookie each)
CARB. PER SERVING 8 g or 7 g

- ¼ cup butter, softened
- ½ cup sugar*
- 1 teaspoon baking powder
- ⅛ teaspoon salt
- 2 egg whites
- ½ teaspoon vanilla
- ¼ teaspoon coconut extract
- 1 cup all-purpose flour
- ½ cup whole wheat pastry flour
- 1 cup shredded or flaked coconut
- ¼ cup low-sugar red raspberry preserves
  Small fresh raspberries (optional)

1. In a large bowl beat butter with an electric mixer on medium to high speed for 30 seconds. Add sugar, baking powder, and salt. Beat until well combined, scraping sides of bowl. Beat in egg whites, vanilla, and coconut extract until combined. Beat in flours. Wrap dough in plastic wrap. Chill dough 2 hours or until easy to handle.

2. Preheat oven to 375°F. Lightly grease two large cookie sheets. Shape dough into ¾-inch balls. Roll balls in the coconut to coat. Place on prepared cookie sheets. Using your thumb or the back of a small measuring spoon, make an indentation in the center of each cookie.

3. Bake for 7 to 9 minutes or until edges are lightly browned. If indentations puff during baking, gently press the back of a small measuring spoon into indentations when cookies are removed from oven. Cool cookies on cookie sheet for 1 minute. Transfer to a wire rack; cool completely.

4. Spoon a rounded ¼ teaspoon of preserves evenly into the indentations in cookies. If desired, top each cookie with a fresh raspberry. Store unfilled cookies layered between sheets of waxed paper in an airtight container at room temperature for up to 3 days or freeze for up to 1 month. Add raspberry preserves before serving.

*SUGAR SUBSTITUTES: Choose from Splenda Sugar Blend for Baking or Sun Crystals Sugar Blend. Follow package directions to use amount equivalent to ½ cup sugar.

PER SERVING: 59 cal., 2 g total fat (2 g sat. fat), 3 mg chol., 41 mg sodium, 8 g carb. (0 g fiber, 5 g sugars), 1 g pro. Exchanges: 0.5 carb., 0.5 fat. Carb choices: 0.5.

PER SERVING WITH SUBSTITUTE: Same as above, except 54 cal., 7 g carb. (3 g sugars).

Chocolate-Orange Pistachio Bars

You will need one to two oranges to yield enough peel and juice for these oat-crusted treats.

SERVINGS 35 (2 bars each)
CARB. PER SERVING 21 g or 20 g

- Nonstick cooking spray
- 3 cups regular rolled oats
- ¾ cup pistachio nuts, finely chopped
- ½ cup honey
- ⅓ cup whole wheat flour
- 1 tablespoon finely shredded orange peel
- ⅓ cup orange juice
- ¼ cup packed brown sugar*
- ¼ cup unsalted butter, melted
- 1 teaspoon vanilla
- ½ teaspoon baking soda
- 1⅔ cups semisweet chocolate pieces

1. Preheat oven to 325°F. Line a 15×10×1-inch baking pan with foil, extending the foil over the edges of the pan. Lightly coat the foil with cooking spray; set aside.

2. In a large bowl stir together oats, ½ cup of the pistachio nuts, the honey, flour, orange peel, orange juice, brown sugar, butter, vanilla, and baking soda; mix well. Press mixture into prepared pan.

Chocolate-Orange Pistachio Bars

3. Bake about 20 minutes or until set in center and lightly browned. Cool completely in pan on a wire rack.

4. In a small microwave-safe bowl heat chocolate pieces on 50 percent power (medium) for 2 to 2½ minutes or until melted and smooth, stirring twice. Spread melted chocolate over cooled bars in pan. Sprinkle with the remaining ¼ cup pistachio nuts. Let stand until set. Use a sharp knife to cut into 70 (2×1-inch) bars.

*SUGAR SUBSTITUTES: Choose from Sweet'N Low Brown or Sugar Twin Granulated Brown. Follow package directions to use product amount equivalent to ¼ cup brown sugar.

PER SERVING: 145 cal., 6 g total fat (3 g sat. fat), 3 mg chol., 31 mg sodium, 21 g carb. (2 g fiber, 11 g sugars), 3 g pro. Exchanges: 0.5 starch, 1 carb., 1 fat. Carb choices: 1.5.

PER SERVING WITH SUBSTITUTE: Same as above, except 139 cal., 20 g carb. (9 g sugars). Exchanges: 0.5 carb. Carb choices: 1.

Carrot Cake Cookies

Carrot Cake Cookies

A food processor is a quick way to shred the carrots. If you don't have one, use the fine shred of a box grater.

SERVINGS 18 (2 cookies each)

CARB. PER SERVING 30 g or 27 g

Nonstick cooking spray
½ cup honey
¼ cup packed brown sugar*
1 tablespoon unsalted butter, softened
¼ cup canola oil
1 egg
1 egg white
3 cups shredded carrots (6 medium)
2 cups all-purpose flour
½ cup whole wheat flour
1½ teaspoons pumpkin pie spice
½ teaspoon baking powder
½ teaspoon baking soda
¼ teaspoon salt
¾ cup chopped walnuts or pecans
2 ounces reduced-fat cream cheese (Neufchâtel), softened
½ cup powdered sugar
2 to 3 teaspoons fat-free milk
¼ cup chopped walnuts or pecans (optional)

1. Preheat oven to 350°F. Coat two large cookie sheets with cooking spray or line with parchment paper; set aside. In a large bowl combine honey, brown sugar, and butter; beat with an electric mixer on medium speed until well mixed. Beat in oil, egg, and egg white. Stir in carrots.

2. In a medium bowl stir together flours, pumpkin pie spice, baking powder, baking soda, and salt. Add flour mixture to carrot mixture, half at a time, stirring until moistened after each addition. Stir in the ¾ cup nuts.

3. Using a tablespoon measuring spoon, drop 36 mounds of dough 2 inches apart onto prepared cookie sheets. If desired, press with moistened fingers to flatten each mound slightly. Bake for 10 to 12 minutes or until lightly browned. Transfer to wire racks; cool completely.

4. For drizzle, in a small bowl combine cream cheese and powdered sugar; beat with an electric mixer on medium speed until well mixed. Beat in enough of the milk to make drizzling consistency. Drizzle over cooled cookies. If desired, sprinkle with the ¼ cup nuts.

*SUGAR SUBSTITUTES: Choose from Sweet'N Low Brown or Sugar Twin Granulated Brown. Follow package directions to use product amount equivalent to ¼ cup brown sugar.

PER SERVING: 200 cal., 8 g total fat (1 g sat. fat), 14 mg chol., 110 mg sodium, 30 g carb. (2 g fiber, 15 g sugars), 4 g pro. Exchanges: 1 starch, 1 carb., 1.5 fat. Carb choices: 2.

PER SERVING WITH SUBSTITUTE: Same as above, except 189 calories, 27 g carb. (12 g sugars).

Crunchy Chocolate
and Peanut Clusters

Gingerbread Cupcakes with Marshmallow Cream Cheese Frosting

For a little spice that's extra nice, give each cake a sprinkle of pumpkin pie spice just before serving.
SERVINGS 15 (1 cupcake each)
CARB. PER SERVING 26 g or 24 g

Nonstick cooking spray for baking
¼ cup butter, softened
2 tablespoons light stick butter (not margarine), softened
¼ cup sugar*
2 teaspoons pumpkin pie spice
1½ teaspoons baking powder
¼ teaspoon baking soda
½ cup refrigerated or frozen egg product, thawed, or 2 eggs
1 cup water
½ cup mild-flavor molasses
1¾ cups flour
3 ounces reduced-fat cream cheese (Neufchâtel), softened
2 tablespoons butter, softened
½ cup marshmallow creme

1. Preheat oven to 350°F. Line fifteen 2½-inch muffin cups with paper bake cups. Spray paper bake cups with cooking spray; set aside.
2. In a mixing bowl beat butter and light butter together on medium speed for 30 seconds. Add sugar, pumpkin pie spice, baking powder, and baking soda. Beat until combined, scraping sides of bowl. Beat in eggs.
3. In a medium bowl whisk together water and molasses. Alternately add flour and molasses mixture to the butter mixture, beating on low speed after each addition just until combined. Spoon batter evenly into prepared muffin cups, filling each about two-thirds full.
4. Bake for 15 to 20 minutes or until a toothpick comes out clean. Cool on a wire rack for 5 minutes. Carefully remove cupcakes from pans; cool on a wire rack.
5. In a bowl beat cream cheese and 2 tablespoons butter until well combined and smooth. Stir in marshmallow creme. Spread or pipe on top of cooled cupcakes. Store frosted cupcakes in the refrigerator.
*SUGAR SUBSTITUTE: Use Splenda Sugar Blend for Baking. Follow package directions to use product amount equivalent to ¼ cup sugar.
PER SERVING: 174 cal., 7 g total fat (4 g sat. fat), 18 mg chol., 150 mg sodium, 26 g carb. (0 g fiber, 12 g sugars), 3 g pro. Exchanges: 1 starch, 1 carb., 1 fat. Carb choices: 2.
PER SERVING WITH SUBSTITUTE: Same as above, except 169 cal., 24 g carb. (10 g sugars). Exchanges: 0.5 carb. Carb choices: 1.5.

Crunchy Chocolate and Peanut Clusters

Puffed corn cereal in addition to the peanuts helps lighten these classic candies.
SERVINGS 48 (1 cluster each)
CARB. PER SERVING 11 g

1 12-ounce package semisweet chocolate pieces
12 ounces vanilla-flavored candy coating, chopped
¼ cup creamy peanut butter
3 cups puffed corn cereal
1 cup lightly salted dry-roasted peanuts

1. Line two trays or large baking sheets with waxed paper; set aside. In a large heavy saucepan heat and stir the semisweet chocolate pieces, candy coating, and peanut butter over medium-low heat until melted and smooth. Stir in cereal and peanuts until well coated.
2. Drop from slightly rounded teaspoons onto prepared trays. Chill about 15 minutes or until set. Store in an airtight container in the refrigerator for up to 1 week or freeze for up to 3 months.
PER SERVING: 105 cal., 7 g total fat (4 g sat. fat), 0 mg chol., 22 mg sodium, 11 g carb. (1 g fiber, 9 g sugars), 1 g pro. Exchanges: 1 carb., 1.5 fat. Carb choices: 1.

Gingerbread Cupcakes with
Marshmallow Cream Cheese Frosting

Vanilla Tres Leches Cake

Use the scraped-out vanilla bean to make vanilla sugar. Place the scraped-out bean in an airtight container with granulated sugar. Cover and shake a few times. Let stand for at least 1 week or up to 6 months.

SERVINGS 16 (1 slice each)
CARB. PER SERVING 28 g or 23 g

- ¾ cup refrigerated or frozen egg product, thawed, or 3 eggs
- 1 cup evaporated fat-free milk
- ½ cup butter, softened
- Nonstick cooking spray for baking
- 1½ cups all-purpose flour
- ¾ cup brown rice flour or all-purpose flour
- 1 teaspoon baking powder
- ¼ teaspoon salt
- ¾ cup granulated sugar*
- ½ of a vanilla bean
- 1 tablespoon pure vanilla
- 2 tablespoons fat-free sweetened condensed milk
- 2 tablespoons whipping cream or fat-free milk
- 2 teaspoons powdered sugar
- Fresh berries (optional)

1. Allow eggs, milk, and butter to stand at room temperature for 30 minutes. Preheat oven to 325°F. Coat a 10-inch fluted tube pan with cooking spray for baking; set aside. In a medium bowl stir together flours, baking powder, and salt; set aside.

2. In a large mixing bowl beat butter with an electric mixer on medium speed for 30 seconds. Add granulated sugar and beat on medium speed about 5 minutes or until very light and fluffy. Using a small sharp knife, split the vanilla bean half in half lengthwise and use the knife to scrape the seeds into the butter mixture. Add 1½ teaspoons of the vanilla. Add eggs, ¼ cup or 1 egg at a time, beating well after each addition.

3. Alternately add flour mixture and ¾ cup of the evaporated milk to butter mixture, beating on low speed after each addition just until combined. Pour batter into prepared pan, spreading top evenly. Bake for 30 to 35 minutes or until a wooden skewer inserted in the center comes out clean. (Cake will appear shallow in the

Chocolate-Mascarpone-Filled Meringues

pan.) Cool in the pan on a wire rack for 15 minutes. Invert cake onto a wire rack.

4. Meanwhile, in a bowl combine remaining ¼ cup evaporated milk, the sweetened condensed milk, whipping cream, and remaining 1½ teaspoons vanilla. Using a long skewer, poke holes all over top of hot cake. Using small spoonfuls, spoon the condensed milk mixture over the hot cake, allowing it to soak into cake before adding more. Cool cake. Store in the refrigerator. To serve, sift the powdered sugar over the top before slicing the cake. If desired, garnish with fresh berries.

*SUGAR SUBSTITUTES: Choose from Splenda Sugar Blend for Baking or Sun Crystals Sugar Blend. Follow package directions to use amount equivalent to ¾ cup sugar.

PER SERVING: 192 cal., 7 g total fat (4 g sat. fat), 18 mg chol., 155 mg sodium, 28 g carb. (1 g fiber, 13 g sugars), 4 g pro. Exchanges: 1 starch, 1 carb., 1 fat. Carb choices: 2.

PER SERVING WITH SUBSTITUTE: Same as above, except 178 cal., 23 g carb. (8 g sugars). Exchanges: 0.5 carb. Carb choices: 1.5.

Chocolate-Mascarpone-Filled Meringues

Assemble only as many sandwiches as you need to serve. Store the remaining cookies in an airtight container and place the piping bag of filling in another airtight container and chill for up to 1 week. To assemble additional cookies, remove the filling from the refrigerator and let it stand at room temperature for 15 minute to soften before piping.

SERVINGS 20 (1 meringue sandwich each)

CARB. PER SERVING 7 g

---

 2 egg whites
 ¼ teaspoon cream of tartar
 ⅛ teaspoon salt
 ⅓ cup sugar*
 1 tablespoon cornstarch
 2 tablespoons honey
 2 tablespoons sesame seeds, lightly toasted
 1 ounce semisweet chocolate, finely grated
 1 tablespoon fat-free milk
 ½ of an 8-ounce carton mascarpone cheese or ½ of an 8-ounce tub light cream cheese, softened

1. In a medium bowl allow egg whites to stand at room temperature for 30 minutes. Preheat oven to 300°F. Line two large cookie sheets with parchment paper; set aside.

2. Add cream of tartar and salt to egg whites. Beat on medium to high speed until soft peaks form (tips curl). In a bowl combine sugar and cornstarch. Gradually add the sugar mixture to the egg white mixture, about 1 tablespoon at a time, beating on high speed until mixture nearly holds stiff peaks. Add 1 tablespoon of the honey and beat on high speed until stiff peaks form (tips stand straight). Fold in sesame seeds.

3. Transfer egg white mixture to a disposable piping bag fitted with a large round tip. Pipe 1½-inch circles that are between ¼ and ½ inch thick on the prepared cookie sheets, leaving 1 inch between circles.

4. Place cookie sheets on separate oven racks; bake for 12 minutes. Turn off oven; let cookies dry in oven with door closed for 1 hour. Carefully lift cookies off parchment paper. Transfer to wire racks; let stand just until cookies are cool. (The cookies can quickly become tacky, especially if the weather is humid. To prevent this, store unfilled cookies in an airtight container at room temperature for up to 3 days.)

5. For filling, in a microwave-safe bowl combine the chocolate, remaining 1 tablespoon honey, and milk. Microwave on 100 percent power (high) about 15 seconds or until chocolate melts. Stir until smooth. Set aside to cool. Fold in the mascarpone cheese, stirring until well combined.

6. Just before serving, place the filling in a piping bag fitted with a large round tip. Pipe a generous teaspoon of filling onto the flat sides of half of the cooled cookies. Top with remaining cookies, flat sides together, to make sandwiches. Serve cookies immediately after filling.

*SUGAR SUBSTITUTES: We do not recommend using a sugar substitute for this recipe.

PER SERVING: 59 cal., 3 g total fat (2 g sat. fat), 7 mg chol., 24 mg sodium, 7 g carb. (0 g fiber, 6 g sugars), 2 g pro. Exchanges: 0.5 carb., 0.5 fat. Carb choices: 0.5.

quick tip

Before you cut the
dough logs into
slices, reshape them
as necessary to
make them round.

Cranberry-Almond
Slice-and-Bake Cookies

Cranberry-Almond Slice-and-Bake Cookies

*Another time, try dried cherries instead of the dried
cranberries and toasted pecans in place of the almonds.*

SERVINGS 48 (1 cookie each)

CARB. PER SERVING 8 g

⅔ cup butter, softened
1 8-ounce can almond paste
¼ cup sugar*
1 teaspoon baking powder
¼ teaspoon salt
¼ cup refrigerated or frozen egg product, thawed, or 1 egg
2 teaspoons finely shredded orange peel (optional)
2 cups all-purpose flour
⅓ cup dried cranberries, finely chopped
¼ cup toasted almonds, very finely chopped
1 recipe Orange Glaze (optional)

1. In a large bowl beat butter with an electric mixer on
medium speed for 30 seconds. Add almond paste, sugar,
baking powder, and salt; beat until well combined. Beat
in egg and, if desired, the 2 teaspoons orange peel. Beat
in as much of the flour as you can. Stir in any remaining
flour, the cranberries, and the almonds.
2. Divide dough in half. Shape each dough portion into
an 8-inch-long log. Wrap logs in plastic wrap. Chill about
2 hours or until firm enough to slice.
3. Preheat oven to 350°F. Cut logs crosswise into
¼-inch-thick slices. Place slices 1 inch apart onto
ungreased cookie sheets.
4. Bake for 8 to 10 minutes or until edges are firm and
centers are set. Transfer cookies to a wire rack and let
cool. If desired, drizzle with Orange Glaze. Store
unglazed cookies layered between sheets of waxed
paper in an airtight container at room temperature for
up to 3 days or freeze for up to 3 months. If desired,
drizzle with glaze before serving.

ORANGE GLAZE: In a small bowl combine ½ cup powdered
sugar and ¼ teaspoon finely shredded orange peel.
Using 2 to 3 teaspoons orange juice or fat-free milk, stir
in enough to make drizzling consistency.

*SUGAR SUBSTITUTES: Choose from C&H Light Sugar and
Stevia Blend, Splenda Sugar Blend for Baking, or Sun
Crystals Granulated Blend. Follow package directions to
use product amount equivalent to ¼ cup sugar.

PER SERVING: 73 cal., 4 g total fat (2 g sat. fat), 7 mg chol.,
45 mg sodium, 8 g carb. (0 g fiber, 3 g sugars), 1 g pro.
Exchanges: 0.5 starch, 0.5 fat. Carb choices: 0.5.

PER SERVING WITH SUBSTITUTE: Same as above, except 72 cal.

Pumpkin
Cheesecake

Pumpkin Cheesecake

*Make each serving more indulgent by topping
with light whipped dessert topping, chopped toasted
hazelnuts, and chocolate shavings.*

SERVINGS 12 (1 wedge each)
CARB. PER SERVING 28 g or 16 g

Nonstick cooking spray
1　cup finely crushed chocolate graham crackers
2　tablespoons sugar*
2　tablespoons butter, melted
2　8-ounce packages reduced-fat cream cheese
　　(Neufchâtel), softened
1　12.3-ounce package firm silken-style tofu (fresh bean
　　curd), well drained
1　6-ounce carton plain fat-free Greek yogurt
¾　cup sugar*
1　tablespoon cornstarch
2　egg whites
2　tablespoons vanilla
1　15-ounce can pumpkin
2　teaspoons ground cinnamon
½　teaspoon ground ginger
½　ounce semisweet chocolate, melted, or 2 tablespoons
　　chocolate-flavor syrup

1. Preheat oven to 350°F. Coat a 9-inch springform pan
with cooking spray. For crust, in a small bowl combine
crushed graham crackers, the 2 tablespoons sugar, and
the butter. Press crumb mixture onto the bottom of the
prepared pan. Bake for 10 minutes. Cool completely in
pan on a wire rack. Reduce oven temperature to 325°F.

2. In a large bowl combine cream cheese, tofu, yogurt,
the ¾ cup sugar, and the cornstarch. Beat with an
electric mixer on medium speed just until combined
and mixture is nearly smooth. Add egg whites and
vanilla, beating just until combined. Set aside 2 cups of
the cream cheese mixture. Stir pumpkin, cinnamon,
and ginger into the remaining cream cheese mixture.
Spread the pumpkin mixture over the cooled crust.
Carefully spoon the reserved 2 cups cream cheese
mixture over the pumpkin mixture; spread evenly over
the pumpkin mixture.

3. Bake in the 325°F oven for 50 to 60 minutes or until a
2½-inch area around the outside edge appears set when
gently shaken.

4. Cool in pan on a wire rack for 15 minutes. Using a
thin metal spatula, loosen the cheesecake from the side
of the pan. Cool for 30 minutes more. Remove side of the
springform pan. Cool completely. Cover and chill for 4 to
24 hours before serving.

5. To serve, cut into wedges. Drizzle each wedge with
melted chocolate or chocolate syrup.

***SUGAR SUBSTITUTES:** Choose from Splenda Granular or
Sweet'N Low bulk or packets. Follow package directions
to use product amounts equivalent to 2 tablespoons and
¾ cup sugar.

PER SERVING: 259 cal., 13 g total fat (7 g sat. fat), 33 mg chol.,
216 mg sodium, 28 g carb. (2 g fiber, 21 g sugars), 8 g pro.
Exchanges: 2 carb., 1 lean meat, 2.5 fat. Carb choices: 2.
PER SERVING WITH SUBSTITUTE: Same as above, except 209 cal.,
16 g carb. (8 g sugars). Exchanges: 1 carb. Carb choices: 1.

Cinnamon-Orange
Pumpkin Bread Pudding

Cinnamon-Orange Pumpkin Bread Pudding

Arrange the bread cubes in an even layer in the baking dish so all of them soak in the custardy pumpkin mixture.

SERVINGS 8 (⅔ cup each)
CARB. PER SERVING 23 g or 21 g

 5 cups ½-inch cubes light oatmeal bread or light whole wheat bread (about 7 slices)
 Nonstick cooking spray
 2 cups fat-free milk
 1 cup canned pumpkin
 ¾ cup refrigerated or frozen egg product, thawed, or 3 eggs, lightly beaten
 3 tablespoons granulated sugar*
 1 teaspoon finely shredded orange peel
 1 teaspoon ground cinnamon
 ⅓ cup light tub-style cream cheese, softened
 1 tablespoon light stick butter (not margarine), softened
 3 tablespoons powdered sugar
 2 to 3 teaspoons orange juice

1. Preheat oven to 300°F. Arrange bread cubes in a single layer on a shallow baking pan. Bake for 10 to 15 minutes or until dry, stirring once or twice. Let cool (cubes will continue to dry as they cool).
2. Increase oven temperature to 350°F. Coat a 2-quart oval or rectangular baking dish with cooking spray. Arrange dry bread cubes in dish; set aside.
3. In a large bowl combine milk, pumpkin, eggs, granulated sugar, orange peel, and cinnamon. Slowly pour pumpkin mixture over bread mixture in baking dish. Gently press bread mixture down into liquid to moisten. Let stand for 15 minutes.
4. Bake, uncovered, for 40 to 45 minutes or until a knife inserted in center comes out clean. Cool slightly on a rack.
5. Meanwhile, in a small bowl beat cream cheese and butter on medium speed until smooth. Gradually beat in powdered sugar and enough of the orange juice until smooth and drizzling consistency. Drizzle evenly over warm bread pudding and serve immediately.

*SUGAR SUBSTITUTES: Choose from Splenda Sugar Blend for Baking or Sweet'N Low bulk or packets. Follow package directions to use product amount equivalent to 3 tablespoons granulated sugar.

PER SERVING: 142 cal., 3 g total fat (2 g sat. fat), 8 mg chol., 211 mg sodium, 23 g carb. (1 g fiber, 13 g sugars), 7 g pro. Exchanges: 1 starch, 0.5 carb., 0.5 lean meat, 0.5 fat. Carb choices: 1.5.

PER SERVING WITH SUBSTITUTE: Same as above, except 135 cal., 21 g carb. (10 g sugars).

White Chocolate Cream Pie with Raspberries

For easy cleanup, place the graham cracker squares in a heavy resealable plastic bag and use a rolling pin to finely crush them.

SERVINGS 12 (1 wedge each)
CARB. PER SERVING 22 g or 20 g

 Nonstick cooking spray
 ¼ cup butter, melted
 2 tablespoons sugar*
 ⅛ teaspoon ground cinnamon
 1¼ cups graham crackers, finely crushed (about 18 squares)
 2 4-serving-size packages fat-free sugar-free reduced-calorie white chocolate instant pudding mix
 2¼ cups fat-free milk
 ¾ cup fresh raspberries
 ⅓ cup low-sugar raspberry preserves
 1 teaspoon water
 ⅛ teaspoon almond extract (optional)
 2 tablespoons sliced almonds, toasted (optional)
 Fresh mint leaves (optional)

1. For crust, preheat oven to 375°F. Lightly coat a 9-inch pie plate with cooking spray; set aside. In a medium bowl combine melted butter, sugar, and cinnamon. Add crushed crackers; toss to mix well. Spread in the prepared pie plate, pressing evenly onto bottom and sides. Bake for 5 minutes or until edges are light brown. Cool completely on a wire rack.
2. For filling, in a large bowl whisk together pudding mixes and milk for 2 minutes until smooth. Pour into the crust-lined pie plate. Cover and chill for 2 to 3 hours or until set.
3. To serve, sprinkle top of pie with raspberries. In a small microwave-safe bowl combine raspberry preserves and water. Cover loosely with plastic wrap and microwave on 50 percent power (medium) for 30 seconds or until preserves are melted. If desired, stir in almond extract. Drizzle over raspberries on pie. If desired, garnish with sliced almonds and mint leaves.

*SUGAR SUBSTITUTES: Choose from Splenda Granular or Sweet'N Low bulk or packets. Follow package directions to use product amount equivalent to 2 tablespoons sugar

PER SERVING: 148 cal., 6 g total fat (3 g sat. fat), 11 mg chol., 333 mg sodium, 22 g carb. (1 g fiber, 11 g sugars), 3 g pro. Exchanges: 0.5 starch, 1 carb., 1 fat. Carb choices: 1.5.

PER SERVING WITH SUBSTITUTE: Same as above, except 141 cal., 20 g carb. (9 g sugars). Exchanges: 0 starch. Carb choices: 1.

Chocolate-Hazelnut Whoopie Pies

*Give these pudding-filled cookies a light sifting
of snowy powdered sugar before serving.*

SERVINGS 25 (1 whoopie pie each)

CARB. PER SERVING 10 g or 7 g

½	**cup flour**
1	**tablespoon baking powder**
1¼	**cups refrigerated or frozen egg product, thawed,** **or 5 eggs**
⅔	**cup sugar***
2¼	**cups hazelnuts, toasted****
½	**cup light tub-style cream cheese, softened**
4	**teaspoons fat-free, sugar-free instant chocolate** **pudding mix**
½	**cup fat-free milk**

1. Preheat oven to 350°F. Line two large cookie sheets
with parchment paper; set aside. In a large bowl
combine flour and baking powder; set aside.
2. In a blender or food processor combine eggs and
sugar; cover and blend until combined. Add nuts. Cover
and blend until nearly smooth, scraping sides. Add egg
mixture to flour mixture; stir until combined.
3. Working quickly, drop dough by level measuring

tablespoons 2 inches apart onto prepared cookie sheets,
keeping the mounds as round as possible. Bake for 8 to
10 minutes or until the edges are firm and centers are
set. Cool on cookie sheets for 2 minutes. Transfer
cookies to a wire rack; cool completely. Store unfilled
cookies between sheets of waxed paper in an airtight
container at room temperature for up to 3 days or in the
refrigerator for up to 1 week.
4. For filling, in a medium bowl beat cream cheese on
medium speed until smooth; set aside. In a separate
bowl gradually whisk pudding mix into milk, whisking
until thickened. Beat pudding mixture into beaten
cream cheese until combined. Adjust consistency as
needed with additional fat-free milk. Chill until needed.
5. Just before serving, spread flat sides of half the cookies
with about 2 teaspoons filling each. Top with remaining
cookies, flat sides down.
***SUGAR SUBSTITUTES:** Choose from Splenda Blend for Baking
or Sun Crystals Sugar Blend for Baking. Follow package

directions to use amount equivalent to ⅔ cup sugar.

**TEST KITCHEN TIP: To toast nuts, place nuts in a shallow baking pan. Bake in a 350°F oven about 10 minutes or until toasted. Place warm nuts on a clean kitchen towel. Rub nuts with towel to remove loose skins

PER SERVING: 92 cal., 5 g total fat (1 g sat. fat), 2 mg chol., 109 mg sodium, 10 g carb. (1 g fiber, 6 g sugars), 3 g pro. Exchanges: 0.5 starch, 1 fat. Carb choices: 0.5.

PER SERVING WITH SUBSTITUTE: Same as above, except 84 cal., 7 g carb. (4 g sugars).

Apple-Cherry Crisp Mini Pies

If you wish, add a spoonful of light whipped dessert topping and a sprinkling of ground cinnamon to the top of each warm pie.

SERVINGS 12 (1 mini pie each)
CARB. PER SERVING 25 g or 21 g

Butter-flavor nonstick cooking spray
6 sheets frozen phyllo dough (14×9-inch rectangles), thawed
3½ cups chopped, unpeeled red-skin cooking apples, such as Rome, Cortland, or Jonathan
½ cup dried cherries, coarsely chopped
¼ cup packed brown sugar*
2 tablespoons water
½ teaspoon ground cinnamon
¼ teaspoon ground cardamom (optional)
½ cup rolled oats
⅓ cup chopped pistachio nuts
2 tablespoons whole wheat pastry flour
2 tablespoons packed brown sugar*
¼ cup tub-style vegetable oil spread

1. Preheat oven to 350°F. Lightly coat twelve 2½-inch muffin cups with cooking spray; set aside. Unroll phyllo. Lay 1 sheet of phyllo on a flat, clean work surface. Cover the remaining sheets with plastic wrap to keep them from drying out. Lightly coat the sheet of phyllo with cooking spray. Top with a second phyllo sheet and lightly coat top with cooking spray. Top with a third phyllo sheet and lightly coat top with cooking spray.
2. Using a pizza cutter or knife, cut the phyllo stack lengthwise in half and crosswise into thirds, making six roughly 4½-inch squares. Press each square into one of the prepared muffin cups, pleating phyllo as needed to fit the cup. Repeat with the remaining sheets of phyllo to fill all the muffin cups.

3. For filling, in a large bowl combine apples, cherries, ¼ cup brown sugar, water, the ½ teaspoon cinnamon, and, if using, the cardamom. Spoon evenly into the phyllo-lined muffin cups.
4. For streusel topper, in a small bowl combine oats, nuts, flour, and 2 tablespoons brown sugar. Cut in vegetable oil spread until mixture resembles coarse crumbs. Spoon over apple filling in cups.
5. Bake for 20 to 24 minutes or until phyllo is lightly browned and apples are tender. Cool pies in pan on a wire rack for 5 minutes. Carefully remove pies from cups and serve warm.

*SUGAR SUBSTITUTES: Choose from Sweet'N Low Brown or Sugar Twin Granulated Brown. Follow package directions to use product amounts equivalent to ¼ cup and 2 tablespoons brown sugar.

PER SERVING: 153 cal., 6 g total fat (1 g sat. fat), 0 mg chol., 74 mg sodium, 25 g carb. (2 g fiber, 14 g sugars), 2 g pro. Exchanges: 0.5 fruit, 1 carb., 1 fat. Carb choices: 1.5.

PER SERVING WITH SUBSTITUTE: Same as above, except 135 cal., 21 g carb. (10 g sugars).

Apple-Cherry Crisp Mini Pies

quick tip

To arrange the pears, start with one slice and position it with the top, or pointed end, of the slice toward the edge of the crust. Add pear slices, slightly overlapping each.

Pear-Pecan Tart

Pear-Pecan Tart

Use one pear of each color for a touch of red and green. Alternately arrange them over the cream cheese layer.

SERVINGS 10 (1 wedge each)
CARB. PER SERVING 23 g or 17 g

- 1 cup flour
- 3 tablespoons finely chopped toasted pecans
- 3 tablespoons packed brown sugar*
- ⅛ teaspoon salt
- ⅓ cup cold butter, cut up
- 1 egg yolk
- 1 tablespoon ice water
- Nonstick cooking spray
- 3 ounces reduced-fat cream cheese (Neufchâtel), softened
- 2 tablespoons light or sugar-free maple-flavor syrup
- 2 ripe red or green-skinned pears, cored, quartered, and very thinly sliced
- 2 tablespoons granulated sugar*
- ¼ teaspoon ground ginger
- ⅛ teaspoon ground nutmeg

1. In a medium bowl stir together flour, pecans, brown sugar, and salt. Using a pastry blender, cut in cold butter until pieces are pea size. In a small bowl combine egg yolk and ice water. Gradually stir egg mixture into flour mixture. Using your fingers, gently knead dough just until a ball forms. Wrap and chill for 30 to 60 minutes or until dough is easy to handle.

2. Preheat oven to 375°F. Coat a 9-inch tart pan with a removable bottom with cooking spray. Pat dough evenly on the bottom and up the sides of the tart pan. Line pastry with a double thickness of foil that has been coated with cooking spray. Bake for 4 minutes. Remove foil. Bake for 3 minutes more. Cool.

3. In small bowl combine cream cheese and maple-flavor syrup. Spread over the crust. Arrange pear slices over the cream cheese filling, overlapping slices as needed. In a small bowl combine granulated sugar, ginger, and nutmeg. Sprinkle evenly over pear slices. Cover top of tart loosely with foil.

4. Bake for 30 minutes. Uncover and bake for 10 to 15 minutes more or until crust is golden brown and pear slices are just tender. Cool for 20 to 30 minutes on a wire rack. To serve, remove tart from pan; cut into wedges.

*SUGAR SUBSTITUTES: Choose from Sweet'N Low Brown or Sugar Twin Granulated Brown to substitute for the brown sugar. Choose from Splenda Granular or Sweet'N Low bulk or packets to substitute for the granulated sugar.

Follow package directions to use product amounts equivalent to 3 tablespoons brown sugar and 2 tablespoons granulated sugar.

PER SERVING: 191 cal., 10 g total fat (5 g sat. fat), 41 mg chol., 124 mg sodium, 23 g carb. (2 g fiber, 11 g sugars), 3 g pro. Exchanges: 1 starch, 1 carb., 2 fat. Carb choices: 1.5.
PER SERVING WITH SUBSTITUTES: Same as above, except 167 cal., 17 g carb. (5 g sugars). Exchanges: 0 carb. Carb choices: 1.

Malted Chocolate Panna Cotta

If the dessert seems stuck, hold the ramekin upside down and slip the knife down one side to gently lift dessert from the bottom and it should pop out.

SERVINGS 4 (½ cup each)
CARB. PER SERVING 29 g or 24 g

- 1 envelope unflavored gelatin
- 2 cups fat-free half-and-half
- 2 ounces semisweet or milk chocolate, finely chopped
- 2 tablespoons sugar*
- 1 tablespoon malted milk powder
- 1 teaspoon vanilla
- Dark and/or white chocolate curls (optional)

1. In a small saucepan combine unflavored gelatin and half-and-half; let stand for 5 minutes. Add chocolate, sugar (if using), and malted milk powder.

2. Cook over medium heat, whisking constantly until gelatin is dissolved and chocolate is melted. Remove from heat; stir in vanilla and sugar substitute (if using). Place saucepan in a large bowl half-filled with ice water. Stir the chocolate mixture for 2 minutes to cool quickly. Pour mixture evenly into four 6-ounce ramekins or custard cups. Cover and chill for at least 6 hours or overnight.

3. To serve, dip ramekins into a bowl of hot water for about 30 seconds. Run a thin sharp knife around the edge of each panna cotta. Invert each panna cotta onto a dessert plate. If desired, garnish with chocolate curls.

*SUGAR SUBSTITUTES: Choose from Splenda Granular or Sweet'N Low bulk or packets. Follow package directions to use product amount equivalent to 2 tablespoons sugar

PER SERVING: 216 cal., 7 g total fat (4 g sat. fat), 7 mg chol., 156 mg sodium, 29 g carb. (1 g fiber, 21 g sugars), 11 g pro. Exchanges: 2 carb., 1.5 lean meat, 1 fat. Carb choices: 2.
PER SERVING WITH SUBSTITUTE: Same as above, except: 194 cal., 24 g carb. (16 g sugars). Exchanges: 1.5 carb. Carb choices: 1.5.

Mini Raspberry-
Chocolate Tarts

¾ cup sugar*
2 teaspoons finely shredded lemon peel
1 tablespoon lemon juice
1 tablespoon honey
1 5- to 6-ounce carton plain fat-free Greek yogurt
1 cup frozen light whipped dessert topping, thawed
¼ cup pomegranate seeds

1. Allow eggs to stand at room temperature for 30 minutes. Meanwhile, grease and lightly flour two 8-inch round cake pans; set pans aside. In a medium bowl stir together flour, poppy seeds, baking powder, and salt; set aside.
2. Preheat oven to 350°F. In a small saucepan bring milk just to boiling; remove from heat. Add tea bags. Cover and let steep for 4 minutes. Remove and discard tea bags, pressing out any liquid from the bags. Add butter, 2 tablespoons honey, 1 tablespoon lemon peel, and the vanilla to the hot milk mixture and stir until well combined. Set aside.
3. In a large mixing bowl beat eggs with an electric mixer on high speed about 4 minutes or until thick. Gradually add sugar, beating on medium speed for 4 to 5 minutes or until light and fluffy. Add the flour mixture; beat on low to medium speed just until combined. Add milk mixture and beat until combined. Pour batter evenly into the prepared pans.
4. Bake for 18 to 22 minutes or until a toothpick inserted near centers comes out clean. Cool cakes in pans on wire racks for 10 minutes. Remove cakes from pans and cool completely on wire racks.
5. For filling, in a medium bowl combine 2 teaspoons lemon peel, the lemon juice, and 1 tablespoon honey. Stir in yogurt until smooth. Fold in dessert topping until combined. Cover and chill until ready to use.
6. To assemble cake, place one of the cooled cake layers on a cake plate. Spread top evenly with half of the filling. Top with second cake layer and spread top with remaining filling. Sprinkle with pomegranate seeds.
*SUGAR SUBSTITUTES: Choose from Splenda Blend for Baking or Sun Crystals Sugar Blend for Baking. Follow package directions to use product amount equivalent to ¾ cup sugar.
PER SERVING: 201 cal., 6 g total fat (3 g sat. fat), 54 mg chol., 149 mg sodium, 33 g carb. (1 g fiber, 19 g sugars), 5 g pro. Exchanges: 1 starch, 1 carb., 1 fat. Carb choices: 2.
PER SERVING WITH SUBSTITUTE: Same as above, except 182 cal., 27 g carb. (13 g sugars).

Mini Raspberry-Chocolate Tarts

Perfect sweets to add to an appetizer buffet, these little treats will disappear before you know it.
SERVINGS 5 (3 tarts each)
CARB. PER SERVING 19 g

1 1.9-ounce package baked miniature phyllo dough shells (15 shells)
3 ounces milk chocolate or dark chocolate, melted
15 fresh raspberries
2 tablespoons slivered almonds, toasted if desired

1. Place phyllo dough shells on a serving platter. Spoon melted chocolate into shells. Top chocolate in each shell with a raspberry and some of the almonds.
PER SERVING: 175 cal., 9 g total fat (4 g sat. fat), 4 mg chol., 43 mg sodium, 19 g carb. (2 g fiber, 9 g sugars), 3 g pro. Exchanges: 1 carb., 2 fat. Carb choices: 1.

Lemon Poppy Seed Tea Cake

Use a long serrated knife to carefully cut this stacked cake into wedges. Between cuts, wipe the knife clean with a damp paper towel.
SERVINGS 12 (1 wedge each)
CARB. PER SERVING 33 g or 27 g

3 eggs
1½ cups flour
2 tablespoons poppy seeds
1½ teaspoons baking powder
¼ teaspoon salt
¾ cup fat-free milk
2 bags green tea
3 tablespoons butter, cut up
2 tablespoons honey
1 tablespoon finely shredded lemon peel
1 teaspoon vanilla

Lemon
Poppy Seed
Tea Cake

Using Our Nutrition Information

At the end of every one of our recipes, you'll see the nutrition information listed for each serving. You'll find the amount of calories (cal.), total fat, saturated fat (sat. fat), cholesterol (chol.), sodium, total carbohydrate (carb.) (fiber, sugars), and protein (pro.). In addition, you'll find the number of diabetic exchanges for each serving and the number of carbohydrate choices, in case you prefer those methods to keep track of what you're eating.

Interpreting the Numbers
Use our nutrition analyses to keep track of the nutritional values of the foods you eat, following the meal plan you and your dietitian have decided is right for you. Refer to that plan to see how a recipe fits the number of diabetic exchanges or carbohydrate choices you're allotted for each day. When you try a recipe, jot down our nutrition numbers to keep a running tally of what you're eating, remembering your daily allowances. At the end of each day, see how your numbers compare with your plan.

Diabetic Exchanges
The exchange system allows you to choose from a variety of items within several food groupings. Those groupings include starch, fruit, fat-free milk, carbohydrate, nonstarchy vegetables, meat and meat substitutes, fat, and free foods. To use the diabetic exchange system with our recipes, follow your plan's recommendations on the number of servings you should select from each exchange group in a day.

Carbohydrate Counting
Our recipes help you keep track of carbohydrates in two ways—tallying grams of carbohydrate and the number of carbohydrate choices. For counting grams, add the amounts of total carbohydrate to your running total for the day. For carbohydrate choices, one choice equals 15 grams of carbohydrate. For example, a sandwich made with two slices of bread is 2 carbohydrate choices. The benefit of this system is that you're keeping track of small numbers.

Calculating Method
To calculate our nutrition information and offer flexibility in our recipes, we've made some decisions about what's included in our analyses and what's not. We follow these guidelines when we analyze recipes that list ingredient options or serving suggestions:

Inside Our Recipes
• Precise serving sizes (listed below the recipe title) help you manage portions.
• Ingredients listed as optional are not included in the per-serving analysis.
• Tub-style vegetable oil spread refers to 60% to 70% vegetable oil product.
• Lean ground beef refers to 95% or leaner ground beef.
• Nutrition facts per serving, diabetic exchanges, and carb choices are noted with each recipe.
• Test Kitchen tips and sugar substitutes are listed after the recipe directions.
• When ingredient choices appear, we use the first one to calculate the nutrition analysis.

metric information

The charts on this page provide a guide for converting measurements from the U.S. customary system, which is used throughout this book, to the metric system.

Product Differences

Most of the ingredients called for in the recipes in this book are available in most countries. However, some are known by different names. Here are some common American ingredients and their possible counterparts:

* All-purpose flour is enriched, bleached or unbleached white household flour. When self-rising flour is used in place of all-purpose flour in a recipe that calls for leavening, omit the leavening agent (baking soda or baking powder) and salt.
* Baking soda is bicarbonate of soda.
* Cornstarch is cornflour.
* Golden raisins are sultanas.
* Light-colored corn syrup is golden syrup.
* Powdered sugar is icing sugar.
* Sugar (white) is granulated, fine granulated, or castor sugar.
* Vanilla or vanilla extract is vanilla essence.

Volume and Weight

The United States traditionally uses cup measures for liquid and solid ingredients. The chart below shows the approximate imperial and metric equivalents. If you are accustomed to weighing solid ingredients, the following approximate equivalents will be helpful.

* 1 cup butter, castor sugar, or rice = 8 ounces = 1/2 pound = 250 grams
* 1 cup flour = 4 ounces = 1/4 pound = 125 grams
* 1 cup icing sugar = 5 ounces = 150 grams

Canadian and U.S. volume for a cup measure is 8 fluid ounces (237 ml), but the standard metric equivalent is 250 ml.

1 British imperial cup is 10 fluid ounces.

In Australia, 1 tablespoon equals 20 ml, and there are 4 teaspoons in the Australian tablespoon.

Spoon measures are used for smaller amounts of ingredients. Although the size of the tablespoon varies slightly in different countries, for practical purposes and for recipes in this book, a straight substitution is all that's necessary. Measurements made using cups or spoons always should be level unless stated otherwise.

Common Weight Range Replacements

Imperial/U.S.	Metric
1/2 ounce	15 g
1 ounce	25 g or 30 g
4 ounces (1/4 pound)	115 g or 125 g
8 ounces (1/2 pound)	225 g or 250 g
16 ounces (1 pound)	450 g or 500 g
1 1/4 pounds	625 g
1 1/2 pounds	750 g
2 pounds or 2 1/4 pounds	1,000 g or 1 Kg

Oven Temperature Equivalents

Fahrenheit Setting	Celsius Setting*	Gas Setting
300°F	150°C	Gas Mark 2 (very low)
325°F	160°C	Gas Mark 3 (low)
350°F	180°C	Gas Mark 4 (moderate)
375°F	190°C	Gas Mark 5 (moderate)
400°F	200°C	Gas Mark 6 (hot)
425°F	220°C	Gas Mark 7 (hot)
450°F	230°C	Gas Mark 8 (very hot)
475°F	240°C	Gas Mark 9 (very hot)
500°F	260°C	Gas Mark 10 (extremely hot)
Broil	Broil	Grill

*Electric and gas ovens may be calibrated using celsius. However, for an electric oven, increase celsius setting 10 to 20 degrees when cooking above 160°C. For convection or forced air ovens (gas or electric), lower the temperature setting 25°F/10°C when cooking at all heat levels.

Baking Pan Sizes

Imperial/U.S.	Metric
9×1 1/2-inch round cake pan	22- or 23×4-cm (1.5 L)
9×1 1/2-inch pie plate	22- or 23×4-cm (1 L)
8×8×2-inch square cake pan	20×5-cm (2 L)
9×9×2-inch square cake pan	22- or 23×4.5-cm (2.5 L)
11×7×1 1/2-inch baking pan	28×17×4-cm (2 L)
2-quart rectangular baking pan	30×19×4.5-cm (3 L)
13×9×2-inch baking pan	34×22×4.5-cm (3.5 L)
15×10×1-inch jelly roll pan	40×25×2-cm
9×5×3-inch loaf pan	23×13×8-cm (2 L)
2-quart casserole	2 L

U.S. / Standard Metric Equivalents

1/8 teaspoon = 0.5 ml	
1/4 teaspoon = 1 ml	
1/2 teaspoon = 2 ml	
1 teaspoon = 5 ml	
1 tablespoon = 15 ml	
2 tablespoons = 25 ml	
1/4 cup = 2 fluid ounces = 50 ml	
1/3 cup = 3 fluid ounces = 75 ml	
1/2 cup = 4 fluid ounces = 125 ml	
2/3 cup = 5 fluid ounces = 150 ml	
3/4 cup = 6 fluid ounces = 175 ml	
1 cup = 8 fluid ounces = 250 ml	
2 cups = 1 pint = 500 ml	
1 quart = 1 litre